Acknowledgements

Additional text: Art Gompper, Wayne Van Dien, Chris Halla

Design: Frank Seiy

Production: Bellwether Communications

Printing: Wirth Press

Separations: Prestige Graphics

First published in 1991 by Harley Davidson, Inc., P. O. Box 653, 3700 West Juneau Avenue, Milwaukee, Wisconsin 53201 U.S.A.

© Harley-Davidson, Inc., 1991

Printed and bound in the United States of America.

The information in this book is true and complete to the best of our knowledge. All recommendations are made without any guarantee on the part of the author or publisher, who also disclaim any liability incurred in connection with the use of this data or specific details.

Library of Congress Cataloging-in Publication Data
Bolfert, Thomas C.
    The Big Book of Harley-Davidson: official publication/ by Harley-Davidson, Inc.; Thomas C. Bolfert. — New, rev. ed.
        p.   cm.
    Includes index.
    ISBN 0-9624113-1-0: $39.95
    1. Harley-Davidson motorcycle—History. 2. Harley-Davidson motorcycle—Catalogs. I. Harley-Davidson Motor Company. II. Title.
TL448.H3B65 1991
338.7'629227'50973—dc20
91-19475
CIP

Sole book trade distribution by:
Motorbooks International Publishers & Wholesalers, Inc.
P. O. Box 2
729 Prospect Avenue
Osceola, Wisconsin 54020 U.S.A.

THE BIG BOOK
OF HARLEY-DAVIDSON®

Official Publication by Harley-Davidson, Inc.

—————— **New, Revised Edition** ——————

THE BIG BOOK OF

HARLEY-DAVIDSON®

— New, Revised Edition —

Official Publication by
Harley-Davidson, Inc.

Thomas C. Bolfert

TABLE OF CONTENTS

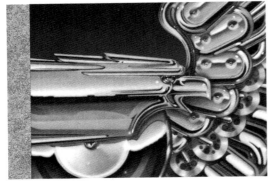

TABLE OF CONTENTS

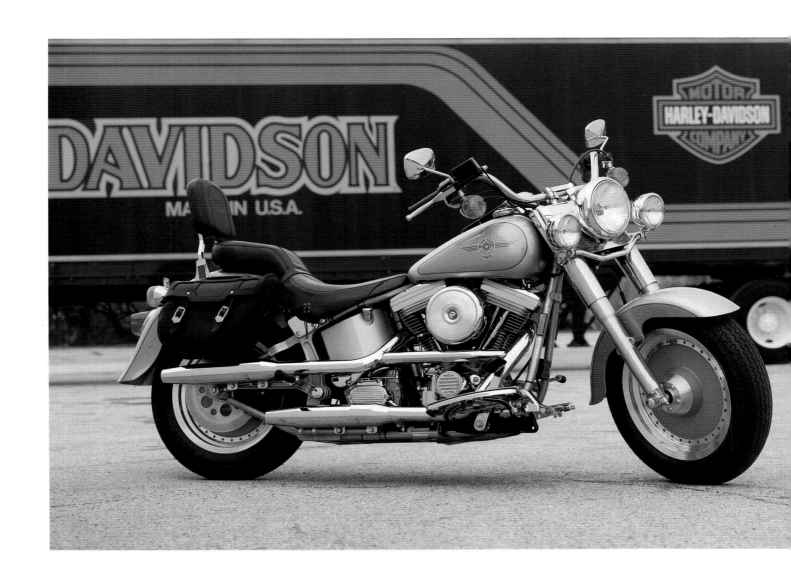

INTRODUCTION

The building looms behind a tiny shopping center, a towering monument to the great manufacturing might of Milwaukee. Rising six stories high, this massive red brick structure, surrounded by a residential area, is the main headquarters of an internationally known success story called Harley-Davidson, Inc.

While many of the area's great corporate names of the past have either closed their doors or moved to gentler climates, Harley-Davidson has stayed in this industrial center of the Midwest and not only weathered the ravages of Wisconsin winters and economic downturns, but has emerged stronger and healthier than ever before.

At first glance, the building—in fact, the entire complex—looks old; and it is. Harley-Davidson has been headquartered at this Juneau Avenue site since 1906, only a block away from its 1903 birthplace. Having gone through numerous expansion programs, the main building attained its current configuration in 1914. An adjacent building, which houses the company's parts and accessories operations, was erected in 1918.

The image the building portrays, like that of the company itself, is deceptive. Instead of being a decaying symbol of America's declining industrial strength, it is rock solid, the end result of years of updating and modernizing. No dingy, grime-encrusted bricks here. The walls of Harley-Davidson are deep red with gleaming white mortar joints. Brand new, steel-sash windows have replaced the earlier wooden-framed windows with blacked-out glass dating back to World War II.

The main lobby also denies the age of the building. Replaced are the institutional metal walls and tile floors of years past. The lobby of Harley-Davidson exudes warmth and welcome. A black slate floor and gray carpet leads to the reception area, where visitors are greeted by both the past and present of America's sole remaining domestic motorcycle manufacturer. Under muted lighting and raised on pedestals are a current production-year motorcycle, and an impeccably restored original from the very first years of the company's existence. Adorning the walls are tastefully-framed portraits of the four founders, one Harley and a trio of Davidsons, plus early photos of the plant.

Inside, the offices of Harley-Davidson are simple and functional. Even those of the corporate officers are small and comfortable, decorated with personal momentos and keepsakes, rather than sprawling penthouses decorated with power trophies. Everywhere throughout the company, employees' offices and work areas are liberally decorated with articles closest to their hearts, or funnybones. Each area has its own personality, reflecting the interests and humor of each employee.

And, of course, Harley-Davidson memorabilia is everywhere. Mountains of it. Employees wear shirts, jackets, belts, buckles, sunglasses and sweaters with Harley-Davidson logos to work every day. Walls, doors and file cabinets

are virtually papered with posters, calendars, pictures and photographs of Harley-Davidson motorcycles and related products. Harley coffee cups, mugs, coasters and pens are on almost every desk. Motorcycle models, sculptures and toys line the shelves and seem to fill every available nook. And if there's a place where a sticker might fit, there's probably one there. There's absolutely no doubt that this is Harley-Davidson.

There is a strong devotion toward Harley-Davidson, not only on the part of the employees, but also on the part of the dealers, riders and even suppliers who service the company. Almost everyone owns a Harley, rides one or rides on one. Many of the people working for Harley-Davidson are second and even third generation employees. It's not uncommon, even in this time of heightened job hopping, for an employee to have 20, 30 or even 40 years of service with the company. One gentleman, who worked in the engineering area, began his very first job at Harley-Davidson as a secretary in 1918 and finally retired in 1982, 64 years later.

There are dealerships all over the country, from New Jersey to Texas, which have sold and serviced Harley-Davidson motorcycles since the 1920s. The nation's oldest family-owned Harley-Davidson dealership first joined the fold in 1914 and has operated continuously in the San Francisco Bay area since. Even older is the Portland, Oregon dealership which began operating in 1912, and the dealership in Columbus, Ohio which dates back to 1913.

It is the riders, however, who are the staunchest Harley-Davidson enthusiasts. Their devotion, at times, borders on outright fanaticism. What other motor vehicle manufacturer—or any other product, for that matter—can claim customers who get married sitting on their vehicles, store them in their living rooms for the winter, tattoo the product name on their bodies, and even name their children after it? These people, men and women alike, are loyalists in the truest sense of the word, absolutely refusing to acknowledge that any brand of motorcycle other than Harley even exists. To suggest that one of the offshore Harley look-alikes might be a viable alternative to the genuine article would be as incomprehensible to them as claiming that Ronald Reagan was a Marxist.

What is it about this company, these products, that inspires such a loyal following among a group of enthusiasts which transcends social, economic and age barriers? How does it happen that this Milwaukee manufacturer and the vehicles it produces can capture the minds and hearts of people the world over, to the point that Harley-Davidson permeates a large portion of their lifestyle and, in fact, creates a lifestyle of its own?

The fact that Harley-Davidson is the sole remaining American motorcycle manufacturer is part of the overall Harley mystique, of course, but a small part. Much of it is the product itself. Harley-Davidson motorcycles are basic. They are updated throwbacks to the early years of the sport, when the rider used his motorcycle for everyday transportation, maintained it himself and developed a bond of interdependence between himself and his mount. By necessity, he and his motorcycle became one.

Today's Harleys are much the same. They are easy to work on, and feature a wide range of parts that are interchangeable with older models. Styling changes have been gradual and subtle over the years and, by design, many of today's models bear a marked resemblance to their counterparts of forty years ago. And for good reason. Harley-Davidson riders are, by and large, traditionalists with fixed values and preconceptions on how a real motorcycle should look and feel.

It is the understanding of that rider which is perhaps the real strength behind Harley-Davidson. Over the years, the company has stressed the importance of involvement both in the sport and in the people who enjoy it so much. Employees from the chairman on down enjoy riding the product to motorcycling events all over the country, meeting with the riders to learn their likes and dislikes and to fully understand every aspect of the sport. They encourage motorcyclists to take a demostration ride on a Harley. Whether they own a Harley or some other brand, the comments of these riders are welcome.

When the rider speaks, Harley-Davidson listens.

Harley-Davidson is more than just a company. It is more than just a collection of people who like motorcycles. Harley-Davidson is a way of life, a slice of Americana that typifies the basic values of the country, and takes the rider back to a simpler time. Its road has been a long one—nearly nine decades—and often not an easy one, but it has always been an interesting trip.

To put the entire story of Harley-Davidson into one book is an impossible task. Parts of it are obscured by the sands of time. Sidebars, personal glimpses and historical vignettes make it difficult to follow a straight-line narrative and, indeed, maybe it's best not to attempt one. Oftentimes, a straight historical record presents only the dry facts as they exist and fails to project the character of the times, just as an interstate is a quick trip across a state but gives little feel for the character of the surrounding area. Sometimes a meander down the side roads, with an occasional look at the map for reference, will give the traveler a more enjoyable and understanding journey.

PREFACE

The history of Harley-Davidson is a long one, spanning nearly nine decades. To present a totally-accurate, all-inclusive account of the people, products and events that shaped it is all but impossible. At times, records were sketchy or incomplete. People with knowledge of certain events eventually pass away, and memories dim with time. Occasionally, errors in reporting were made and later accepted as fact. Separating truth from near-truth is difficult, if not impossible.

The chronicle of Harley-Davidson as told in this book was compiled solely from information taken from the company's extensive archives. All models and historical dates are from documented sources, even though they may differ from previously published accounts. Attitudes and company policies were gleaned from letters, speeches, published articles and newsletters, and quite often were arrived at by interpreting what was said or done in terms of the political or economic climate of the times.

What this book intends to do is give the reader an overview of America's sole remaining motorcycle manufacturer, and the historical framework in which it prevailed. If an incident of relative importance has been omitted, as some astute reader will no doubt discover, or some favorite motorcycle was not mentioned, I offer my apologies. While I tried to give a true and accurate account, I didn't feel that every fact, figure and model change was necessary to tell the story.

Compiling this historical record required months of research, pouring through musty, 85-year-old magazines, hundreds of files, and thousands of photographs and documents. It was, at times, tedious and backbreaking, interesting and informative, dusty and oppressive, thrilling and exciting, overwhelming and intimidating. But above all that, it was one more thing.

It was fun.

For the Harleys and the Davidsons who built the company, for Vaughn Beals, Charlie Thompson, Rich Teerlink and Willie G. who made it so great, for the thousands of loyal dealers and employees who kept it alive, and especially for the uncounted enthusiasts over the years and decades who loved and enjoyed its products, this book is for you.

Thomas C. Bolfert

THE 1900'S

An Idea Becomes Reality.

THE 1900'S

While the motorcycle is generally regarded as a product of the Twentieth Century, its origins actually go back all the way to the late 1700s, when the steam engine was being developed as a source of power. As early as 1785, William Murdock—a pupil of James Watt, inventor of the steam engine—built what was called a steam tricycle. In 1868, an early pioneering effort called the Austin velocipede marked the mating of a steam engine to a two-wheeled vehicle. This was also attempted later in 1884 by two Californians, L.D. and W.E. Copeland. Like Murdock's tricycle, these proved unsuccessful. Over the decades, many other inventors experimented with steam-powered vehicles with little success.

By the late 1800s, when the gasoline engine was going through the same formative period as the steam engine did a century earlier, a Frenchman by the name of Delamare-Deboutteville produced what is generally regarded as the first motor-driven tricycle, utilizing a carburetor which he patented in 1884. While it marked the first successful mating of a gasoline engine to a tricycle chassis, the contraption apparently was never produced on any scale and slipped into obscurity.

Carl Benz of Mannheim, Germany, later of Mercedes-Benz fame, developed a gasoline tricycle about the same time and actually patented it in 1885. His invention was not a commercial success, either.

Gottlieb Daimler, a German contemporary of Deboutteville and Benz, was also developing a gasoline-powered machine at this time, but his was two-wheeled. Propelled by a half-horsepower motor, Daimler's wooden-wheeled invention was successfully ridden for the first time on November 10, 1885 and marked the inauspicious beginning of the true motor bicycle or motorcycle, as it was later called.

Whether unable to see the practical application of his remarkable invention, despite earning a U. S. patent for it in 1885, or perhaps occupied with other interests, Gottlieb Daimler produced that one and only machine. He died in 1899, unaware of the future of the sport he had pioneered.

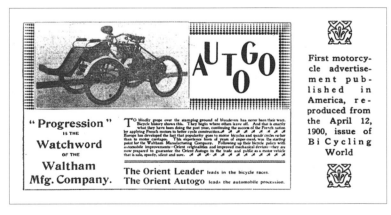

First motorcycle advertisement published in America, reproduced from the April 12, 1900, issue of Bi Cycling World

THE FIRST MOTORCYCLE

Gottlieb Daimler, of Wurtemberg, Germany, is generally regarded as the inventor of the first gasoline powered motorcycle, taking his inaugural ride on November 10, 1885. From that humble beginning over a century ago, a sport and industry sprang into being. Hundreds of makers worldwide began producing well over a thousand different models of motorcycles, capturing the minds, hearts and imagination of tens of millions of devotees and enthusiasts.

Daimler's invention bore little resemblance to the motorcycles of today, other than it was a two-wheeled vehicle and even that was subject to interpretation. Evidently harboring some doubts regarding the stability of his creation, Daimler outfitted it with rather large outrigger or trundle wheels to keep it from falling sideways.

This grandfather of motorcycles sported a springless wooden frame with a vertical fork and iron-tired wooden wheels, topped by a padded saddle. The motor was a half-horsepower, single-cylinder affair with a thin metal jacket surrounding the cylinder. Air was forced around the cylinder by a fan on the crankshaft to provide cooling for the tiny powerplant. Final drive was achieved by means of a flat leather belt, tensioned by an idler pulley.

Gottlieb Daimler's motorized velocipede was crude by today's standards, and few, if any, of his concepts are still in use in their original form. However, many of his ideas formed the basics of early motorcycles and were used throughout the first decades of motorcycle building. Of course, from those humble beginnings grew the motorcycles we're all familiar with today.

Popular music and advertising provided evidence of the interest in motorized transportation

Interestingly, there was little advancement in the development of the motorcycle prior to 1900, despite the efforts of Daimler and the others. Instead, it was paced bicycle racing that was the rage in the closing years of the Nineteenth Century. As speed records for human-powered bicycles inched higher and higher, it was felt that men simply could not go much faster under their own power. Gradually, bicycle builders began thinking again of combining the rapidly developing gasoline engine with the bicycle frame to reduce effort and increase speed. Toward that end, by 1900 about a dozen companies were building motor bicycles in the United States, and the sport was born.

While motorcycling was still in its infancy, another sport was too: major league baseball

England's Queen Victoria was featured on cigar bands, along with other notables of the time.

City Hall, Milwaukee, as seen from East Water Street and what is now Wisconsin Avenue.

WILLIAM S. HARLEY

WALTER DAVIDSON, SR.

Enter 21-year-old William S. Harley and his next door neighbor and friend since boyhood, 20-year-old Arthur Davidson. The two young men worked at the same Milwaukee manufacturing company, Harley as an apprentice draftsman and Davidson as a pattern maker. Like many of their contemporaries—the great automotive pioneers—they were hobby designers, ever tinkering to put their designs to practical use, while people around them just shrugged their shoulders. One idea they had was to produce a motor-driven bicycle for their own personal use, since a motor obviously removed much of the work from cycling. Fortunately, a German draftsman who knew something of early European motorcycles and the DeDion gasoline engine also worked at the same firm.

Using the German draftsman's special knowledge, Harley's earlier experience in building bicycles and Davidson's patterns for a small, air-cooled gasoline engine, they spent their evenings experimenting in a basement workshop. Finances were modest, and the tools they worked with were unsophisticated. And yet, the project progressed. That is, progressed as far as it could without the help of a skilled mechanic.

FPG

Arthur Davidson's brother, Walter, was just such a skilled mechanic, then working as a railroad machinist in Parsons, Kansas and soon due in Milwaukee for the wedding of a third Davidson brother, William. So Arthur Davidson wrote to Walter, offering him a ride on their new motorcycle when he arrived and painting a glorious picture of how great the event would be.

As Walter later said, "Imagine my chagrin to find that the motor bicycle in question had reached the stage of blue-prints, and before I could have the promised ride, I had to help finish the machine." Infected by their enthusiasm, Walter stayed in Milwaukee to help.

An early motor bicycle shortly after the turn of the century.

It wasn't long before William Davidson also joined in the project, lending his skills as an experienced toolmaker. Every spare minute that Bill Harley and the Davidson brothers could find was devoted to putting their idea in motion. Assistance in overcoming various mechanical problems came from the German draftsman. Another friend and neighbor lent them the use of his small shop, lathe and drill press for completing the machine, in return for a complete set of the engine castings they were building. Evenings and weekends ran together as parts were machined by hand, and the first Harley-Davidson motorcycle began taking shape.

To truly appreciate the kinds of problems the young men from Milwaukee encountered, we have to put ourselves in a turn-of-the-century state of mind. Problems that would seem simple to solve today were major roadblocks during the early years of the 20th Century. There were few books or engineering manuals on the subject and no ready-made parts. All parts had to be fabricated from limited existing materials with plenty of good old American ingenuity. And you didn't go to the local filling station for five gallons of gas. You bought it at the corner drugstore, a pint at a time.

The first Harley-Davidson carburetor was allegedly made from a tomato can. "The first spark plugs were as big as doorknobs," Bill Harley remarked later, "and they cost us $3 each."

The first completed engine was an extremely primitive affair, with a 2-1/8 x 2-7/8 inch bore and stroke for a 25 cubic inch displacement. With its tiny five-inch diameter flywheel, the engine was designed to fit into a bicycle frame. Realizing it would be too underpowered to take all of the work out of cycling, they went back and redesigned a larger engine using the same proportions.

The next task for the young inventors was developing a new frame to hold the more powerful motor. The diamond-shaped bicycle frame used on motor bicycles of that time would simply not be strong enough. Eventually, they settled on a loop frame design. It proved to be so ideal, it was used for decades to follow.

ARTHUR DAVIDSON, SR. **WILLIAM A. DAVIDSON**

Finally, in 1902, Harley and the Davidson brothers completed the first true Harley-Davidson engine. Bore and stroke on the new engine was increased to 3 x 3-1/2 inches to produce three horsepower. The flywheel more than doubled in size, growing to 11-1/2 inches. It also had side pocket valves, and featured one-inch radiating fins to dissipate heat. With help from Ole Evinrude, who was later to make his mark in the outboard motor field, several months were spent finding a satisfactory carburetor design. At last, Bill Harley and the Davidson brothers were ready to put their idea into production.

The year was 1903, and Teddy Roosevelt was running for his first full term, having become president following McKinley's assassination. In Milwaukee, the first production Harley-Davidson motorcycle— a single-cylinder, belt-driven machine painted gloss black with pinstriping —was ready to take its place alongside the 15 or so other makes which served an eager, growing group of enthusiasts. However, motorcycle production meant the need for more space; a friend's shop was no longer suitable. With the help of the Davidsons' cabinetmaker father, William C., a 10- x 15-foot "factory" was erected in the family's backyard, just a block away from the current site of Harley-Davidson's main offices. They painted *Harley-Davidson Motor Co.* on the door, and a legend was born.

The fact that there were three Davidsons and only one Harley suggests the name should have been "Davidson-Harley Motor Co." However, the brothers felt Bill Harley's name should take key billing because he had engineered the first cycle. It's interesting to speculate whether, had the names been reversed, we would now abbreviate the name by refering to it as a "Davidson" rather than a "Harley."

During 1903, Harley-Davidson Motor Company turned out a grand total of three motorcycles, all bought and paid for before completion. A fellow named Meyer took delivery of the first production cycle and rode it for 6,000 miles before selling it to George Lyon, who put another 15,000 miles on it. It was then owned by a Dr. Webster, Louis Fluke and Stephen Sparrow, in that order, who collectively accumulated another 62,000 miles of dependable travel. In 1913, Harley-Davidson advertised that their first motorcycle had covered over 100,000 miles, was still in operation with its original bearings and had no major components replaced. Durability was the byword, right from the start.

In 1900, Americans enjoyed life under President McKinley enough to re-elect him, with "Rough Rider" Teddy Roosevelt as Vice President. The next year, McKinley would be assassinated.

1904 saw the size of the original Harley-Davidson factory, in the backyard of the Davidson family's Milwaukee home double to 10 x 30 feet.

1904
Vacuum electron tube for
radio telephony invented
by Fleming in England.

Christian Hulsmeyer of
Germany introduces radar
with one-mile range.

1905:
John McGraw's Giants
beat Connie Mack's
Athletics in World Series.

Gyrocompass invented
by Elmer A. Sperry.

General strike in Russia;
first workers' soviet is
set up.

First Rotary Club founded
in Chicago.

1906:
San Francisco earthquake
and three-day fire kills
over 500.

Norwegian explorer
Amundsen fixes magnetic
North Pole.

Pure Food and Drug Act
and Meat Inspection Act
are passed.

1907:
Financial panic and
economic depression
in U.S.

First world cruise of U.S.
Navy's "Great White Fleet."

Second Hague Peace
Conference.

Spangler introduces
electric vacuum
cleaner in U.S.

The original Harley; the first
production model, of which, three
were built in 1903 and three
more in 1904.

Early Harley-Davidsons soon earned the nickname of "Silent Gray Fellow," for several reasons. "Silent" came from the company's campaign to keep motorcycling a quiet activity by installing large, quiet mufflers and by condemning the practice of opening muffler cutouts to increase exhaust noise. "Gray" became the standard color following the first few years' basic black machines, although black was still available as an option. And, Harley-Davidson's efforts to promote their motorcycle as a companion on the lonesome road gave it human traits, which led to the "Fellow."

Three more machines were built in 1904, and the next year the size of the original factory doubled, delivering seven machines. In 1905, the company also hired its first employee outside of the small group of founders. By year-end, the company was selling not only motorcycles, but motorcycle motors, marine motors, reversible propellers and float feed carburetors. A sales brochure of the time stated: "In making our motorcycle, we have not endeavored to see how cheap we could make it, but how good." The price was $200.

Harley-Davidson Motor Company was definitely heading in the right direction on the road to success. When the calendar turned to 1906, the first building on Harley-Davidson's current Juneau Avenue site was erected, although then it was called Chestnut Street. It was a whopping 28- x 80-foot structure, financed by a loan from the Davidsons' uncle, James McLay in Madison, Wisconsin. Since Uncle James was a beekeeper, this first loan was always referred to as coming from the "honey uncle."

The first Harley-Davidson plant was built a block away from the original, at 38th and Chestnut (now Juneau Avenue).

Following the incorporation of Harley-Davidson Motor Company in 1907, the proud founders and their employees lined up outside the 2,380-square-foot factory. On the far right is Arthur Davidson, while William Davidson—sporting the mustache he wore at the time— is fifth from the right. Seventh from the right is Walter Davidson, wearing a light-colored jacket and black cap. William Harley had just graduated from the University of Wisconsin and was not present for this photograph.

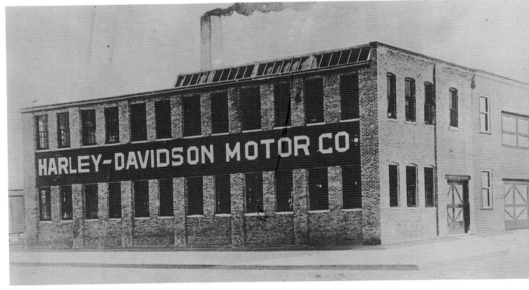

"After we had the framework up," Walter Davidson later recalled, "the railroad surveyors notified us that we were encroaching on the right-of-way of the adjacent railroad. So we got about eight or ten fellows, picked up the entire shop and moved it back about a foot and a half, so that we were safe."

1906 saw Harley-Davidson production leap to 50 motorcycles, and five extra workers were hired to meet the demand. The bikes got their first spring front end, as constant improvement became a design philosophy from the very beginning. By then, Bill Harley and Arthur, Walter and William Davidson had given up their regular jobs to devote their full time and energies to the new, rapidly growing company.

As Walter Davidson recalled those early days, "We worked every day, Sunday included, until at least 10 o'clock at night. I remember it was an event when we quit work on Christmas night at 8 o'clock to attend a family reunion."

It was now becoming obvious that Harley and the Davidsons had a going—and growing—business venture. They could foresee nothing that might hinder the production of their machines but their own limitations as technicians. So while the Davidsons stayed in Milwaukee to tend the store, Bill Harley packed his bags and headed for the University of Wisconsin at Madison. At UW, he majored in engineering, specializing in internal combustion engines, and worked his way through school by waiting on tables at a fraternity house.

AN AGE OF INVENTION

Perhaps through a coincidence of factors, 1903 stands out as a hallmark year in transportation history. American enterprise and creativity in adapting the internal combustion engine for a variety of uses was gaining momentum. In Dearborn, Michigan, a couple of hundred miles east of the site where the Davidsons and Harley were putting their motorized bicycle into production, an automotive pioneer named Henry Ford revolutionized the automobile industry by mass producing his Model A car.

Meanwhile, another motorized marvel of transportation was born at Kitty Hawk, North Carolina, when the Wright brothers soared over a sandy beach in man's first powered flight.

Both events were part of an era of inventive genius in American history. Within a few years, Albert Einstein would announce his General Theory of Relativity. Thomas Edison, whose inventions included incandescent lighting, the phonograph, the concept behind motion pictures and countless others (his patents totalled 1,033), was currently developing the storage battery. Perhaps not as well known is that Edison's invention of the carbon transmitter was a major factor in bringing Alexander Graham Bell's telephone into practical use. Such inventions would play dramatic roles in America's transition from an agrarian to an industrial society.

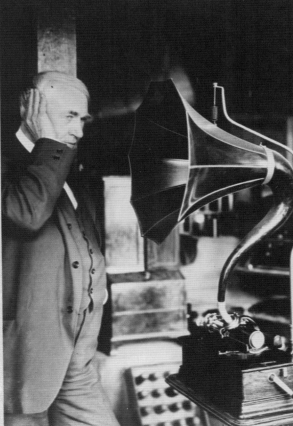

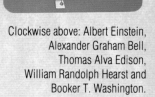

Clockwise above: Albert Einstein,
Alexander Graham Bell,
Thomas Alva Edison,
William Randolph Hearst and
Booker T. Washington.

Orville and Wilber Wright and their sister Kathereen.

WILL HE RISK IT?

Everyman's Car
The Brush Runabout

Henry Ford

Although America was experiencing a stock market fall and national depression, Harley-Davidson Motor Company was incorporated in 1907, and shares were purchased by the company's 17 employees. Money from the stock sale went to finance yet another new building, needed to keep up with constantly increasing orders for new machines. The first president was Walter Davidson; William Harley was chief engineer and treasurer; Arthur Davidson became secretary and general sales manager; and William Davidson was works manager. Yet titles were of little importance. Whatever had to be done was handled by whoever was available with the know-how and the time. William Davidson's desk was said to be a laboratory covered with semifinished hubs, shafts, bearings and pistons. When rapid expansion demanded new manufacturing methods, Walter Davidson learned the heat-treating process and then taught employees. He and Walter Davidson went to Chicago to learn oxygen-acetylene welding, and then instructed others when they returned to Milwaukee.

With Harley and the Davidson brothers devoting their total efforts to the company, production tripled in 1907 to 150 machines. This year, too, the first Harley-Davidsons were sold specifically for police duty.

In 1908, Bill Harley graduated and returned to Milwaukee, immediately beginning design of a more powerful engine. The demand was high, and Harley-Davidson wasn't about to ignore it. The only limits were the number of hours in a day and the factory space—so a 40- x 60-foot brick addition was erected and production soared to 410 motorcycles.

MINERVA
THE SPEED KING
5 H.P. and 8 H.P.
Bosch Magneto   Spring Forks
Speed 55 to 65 miles an hour
Double Grip Control Price, 5 H.P. complete, $325.00
" 8 " " 350.00
CONTINENTAL NON-SKID TIRES
Geo. V. Lyons Motor Co.
Broadway and 87th Street, New York

Tenor Enrico Caruso was an early gramophone recording star.

FPG

Hello, Mr. Torpedo!

How is it, or who is it that makes you so popular?

The Torpedo always speaks for itself.

Thank you! Enough said.

Did you see me at the Chicago Show? I was the one best bet. The colors of my suits are vermilion and French gray. If you did not meet me at the Show, write me at once and I will be pleased to send you one of my photographs.

My home is at Geneseo, Illinois.

Torpedo Model F. Twin Cylinder

THE MIDGET BI-CAR

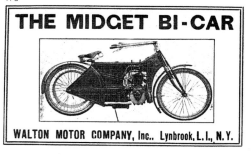

WALTON MOTOR COMPANY, Inc., Lynbrook, L.I., N.Y.

In late July of 1908, the Chicago Motorcycle Club sponsored a motorcycle hill climb in Algonquin, Illinois in which top honors went to Harvey Bernard aboard a Harley-Davidson, powered by a V-twin engine. Competing in the 61 cubic inch class, Harvey and his Harley made the ascent in the fastest time of the day, marking an impressive first-time performance for this new engine from Milwaukee.

There is a mystery surrounding this midsummer appearance in 1908 since, by all accounts, the Harley-Davidson V-twin did not officially appear until February of the next year. The picture of Harvey Bernard clearly shows him astride a Harley-Davidson with a V-twin engine; yet, the gas tank is definitely pre-1909, when all the gas tanks underwent a radical design change.

The classic 1909 Harley V-twin,
subject of historical controversy.

The single cylinder Harley-Davidson engine was a proven quantity in 1908, dependable in performance and popular with riders. Since its introduction, it had increased by 10 cubic inches to 35 cubic inches, delivering four horsepower and a top speed of about 45 miles per hour.

Attesting to the reliability of the Harley-Davidson motorcycle, *The Bicycling World and Motorcycle Review*, a leading publication of the time, had this to say in an April 25, 1908 issue concerning 1908 models: "Of the latter-day motorcycles, none so quickly earned a reputation as the Harley-Davidson. It is a machine the very appearance of which suggests substantiability and power, and its performance has borne out its appearance. It has proven so satisfactory that nothing but the refinement of trivial details was found necessary."

Curiously, the article went on to describe a six-horsepower, twin-cylinder model of 53 cubic inch displacement, which contradicts the generally accepted belief that the Harley-Davidson V-twin debuted as a 1909 61-cubic-inch model. Additionally, an August issue of the same magazine carried a story and photo of a Mr. Harvey Bernard who took first place at a hillclimb aboard a Harley-Davidson 61 cubic inch V-twin, noting it was the first competitive appearance for this engine. The photo shows a V-twin engine in a Harley-Davidson frame with a 1908 style gas tank. However, it wasn't until the 1909 literature that the V-twin was officially mentioned by the company, stating it would be available to ship on February 15, 1909. It rated the engine at seven horsepower. The V-twin engine, with its cylinders canted at 45 degrees, would subsequently become not only the classic configuration of the American motorcycle engine, but the very symbol of Harley-Davidson in future years.

Astride 1909 single-cylinder Harley-Davidson motorcycles are, from left: William Harley, foreman Frank Ollerman and Walter Davidson. These four-horsepower models, with magneto ignitions, sold for $250.

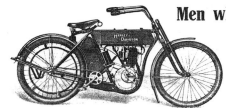

A DIAMOND FOR DAVIDSON

At precisely six a.m. on June 29, 1908, the first motorcycle rider left the starting line, heralding the beginning of the seventh annual Federation of American Motorcyclist (FAM) endurance and reliability contest held in the scenic Catskill Mountains of New York. Of the 65 entrants in the gruelling two-day, 365-mile event, only 61 actually started that morning. Five were mounted on Harley-Davidson motorcycles. One of the five, riding a stock single-cylinder machine, was the president of Harley-Davidson Motor Company, Walter Davidson. In all, 17 brands of motorcycles were represented.

Following a complaint that previous events had been too easy, the 1908 contest was the most rugged to date. The first day's course, 175 miles long, followed a meandering route over gravel and dirt roads, up mountains and down through valleys, from Catskill, south to New York City. Following an inspection by FAM officials, each machine was sealed, numbered and dispatched in the order of their numbering, at four minute intervals. Walter Davidson was number 35.

According to the FAM, the purpose of the contest was "to test the endurance, skill and judgment of the competitors, and the capability, endurance and reliability of the motorcycles they use, and the consistent performance of both."

The event certainly lived up to its credo as competitors braved primitive roads, demanding mountain passes, punctured tires, collisions with livestock, heat, dust and mechanical break-downs. They raced against the clock from checkpoint to checkpoint, ever mindful of the man who might jump out of the bushes waving a green flag, the signal for an emergency braking test. To attain the coveted perfect score of 1,000 points—or even to simply finish the event—a rider had to possess both the skill to traverse the rugged course and the confidence in his mount.

Walter Davidson knew his company built a reliable motorcycle. "So strong was my confidence," he later said, "that I carried with me no additional parts or repairs, which was quite in contrast with many of the manufacturers' riders who had automobiles with complete duplicate parts following them." Indeed, he finished the first day's ride without a mishap, passing through every checkpoint perfectly.

At the next morning's start of the second phase of the event, only 43 competitors were able to leave the starting line. It was obvious that the previous day's demanding route had levied a heavy toll on motorcycle and rider alike. Fortunately for both, the 190-mile route circumnavigating Long Island was comparatively mild. Just the same, accumulated wear and tear, as well as wandering cows, plagued the entrants. Davidson's only incident was a punctured tire, as he and his motor-cycle again performed flawlessly the entire way.

When the results were tallied, Walter Davidson had earned the perfect score of 1,000 points, plus an additional five points and the diamond medal—the only one awarded for consistency of both rider and machine.

The FAM declared, "Davidson's title to the medal is beyond question. During the two days of the contest, he varied by eight minutes from the exact schedule, which places him so far in advance of all others as to leave his qualification for the award beyond dispute."

Willian Harley, left, and Walter Davidson giving a 1909 model a little assistance over a rocky stretch of shoreline.

The year 1910 started in a big way for Harley-Davidson, with the completion of the company's first reinforced concrete building. Production space was boosted to 9,520 square feet and the number of employees to 149. But the new decade also saw a major disappointment for the company.

The new V-twin engine, announced at the end of the previous decade, was developed to compete with the many foreign and domestic twins and multi-cylinder motorcycles on the market. The Harley-Davidson twin employed an automatic intake valve—a system that worked well in single-cylinder engines, but not in the V-twin configuration. The engine was a failure.

Only a few dozen twins were produced by Harley-Davidson in 1909, and none of the 3,200 motorcycles built in 1910 were twin-cylinder models. Only single-cylinder models were advertised and sold, as Harley-Davidson engineers went back to the drawing boards to redesign the engine.

This plant illustration appeared in the 1910 brochure.

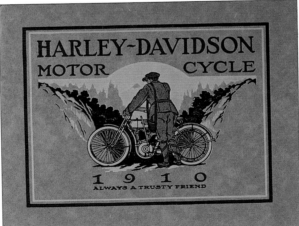

Have You Been Watching the Remarkably Consistent Winning of the 1910 Single Cylinder

HARLEY-DAVIDSON?

New York Quarterly Trials, April 3—One Entry—Perfect Score.
Linden Endurance Contest, April 17—One Entry—Perfect Score.
Minneapolis Hill Climb, May 22—One Entry—Finished First.
South Bend Endurance Contest, May 15—Five Entries—Five Perfect Scores.
Oklahoma City Racemeet, April 22—Won First, Second and Third in Every Event.
Los Angeles Annual Endurance Contest—Two Perfect Scores.
Denver Stock Machine Race, Tuilleries Track—Won First.
Denver-Greeley Road Race—Won First and Second, Defeating the Time of the Fastest Double Cylinder Entry by Nearly Ten Minutes.

The Harley-Davidson Makes Good Because It Is Made Good

HARLEY-DAVIDSON MOTOR CO., Milwaukee, Wis.

In 1911, Harley-Davidson reintroduced the V-twin model, this time with a new frame which substantially lowered the seat position without sacrificing any ground clearance. Vanadium, chrome and nickel steels and, in some places, high-carbon steel were used to produce a motorcycle renowned for its endurance and reliability. Best of all, perhaps, was the introduction of mechanical inlet valves which solved the earlier problem and made the twin-cylinder Harley-Davidson the equal of its peers.

A leading theatrical star of the time was actress Sarah Bernhardt.

Samuel Clemens, better known as Mark Twain, died in 1910.

nnovation was key in the year 1912. On a national scale, voters elected Woodrow Wilson, the first Democratic president since 1896. At Harley-Davidson, the twin-cylinder X8E featured the first commercially successful motorcycle clutch, a "free wheeling" rear wheel mechanism designed by Bill Harley. This made it possible to use a roller chain to power the motorcycle instead of the commonly used leather belt, which was prone to slip when wet. Up to that point, the company had used a left-hand-controlled belt tensioner, which made it possible to disengage power to the rear wheel when stopping. However, the chain showed great promise of being more efficient. "Separate and independent chain adjustments are provided for all three chains," said the product literature. Pedals were still connected by chain to the rear wheel to start the motorcycle. Another Bill Harley innovation that year was the introduction of the center post saddle suspension, or "Full-Floating Seat."

All the while, Harley-Davidson machines were entering and winning races with independent owners in the saddle. The company's policy, at that time, was to build no special racing machines, and there were no "factory riders." A Harley-Davidson ad, which appeared September 21, 1911 in *Motorcycle Illustrated*, proclaimed: "No, we don't believe in racing and we don't make a practice of it, but when Harley-Davidson owners win races with their own stock machines hundreds of miles from the factory, we can't help crowing about it."

Early Harley-Davidson employees on Highland Avenue in Milwaukee, circa 1912. Note the Davidson house in the center of the picture, with the old wooden factory building still standing in the backyard.

The 1912 presidential election was a three-way battle, with Wilson winning over Republican William Howard Taft and Progressive Teddy Roosevelt.

1910:
Panama Canal opens.

Boy Scouts of America founded.

1911:
First transcontinental airplane flight takes 82 hours, 4 minutes — plus stops.

1912:
Teddy Roosevelt gives 80-minute speech in Milwaukee, despite a recent wound from assassination attempt.

Titanic sinks, drowning over 1,500.

1913:
First movie version of *Quo Vadis* opens in New York.

1914:
Ford raises basic wage rates from $2.40 for nine-hour day, to $5 for eight-hour day.

1915:
Alexander Graham Bell makes first transcontinental phone call—New York to San Francisco.

D. W. Griffith makes *Birth of a Nation.*

British ship, Lusitania, sunk by German submarine.

Einstein publishes *General Theory of Relativity.*

In 1912, stone stock eight-horsepower twins ridden by private owners won the Bakersfield and San Jose Road Races. At San Jose, the winning rider finished *17 miles* ahead of the number two machine. During 1913, Harley-Davidsons took the first three places in a 225 mile race from Harrisburg to Philadelphia and back.

Later that year, in what was intended to be a challenge race between Indian and Excelsior motorcycles, a dealer entered a Harley-Davidson with Curley Fredericks riding. Floyd Clymer, who became a dealer/rider for Harley-Davidson, was riding the Excelsior. He later recalled the exciting race in his Motor Scrapbook: "I got away first and Boyd on his Indian gradually drew near me. We were about nip and tuck at the end of the first mile. Then I heard a quiet hum. Not even making much noise, Fredericks went by so fast that we could not even get in his draft. He was carrying a very high gear ratio, and at the finish he must have been a quarter mile ahead of both of us."

A new single-cylinder model was added to the Harley-Davidson line for 1913. Designated as the 5-35 model, the numbers signified the engine specifications of five horsepower and 35 cubic inches. The choice of a chain or belt drive to accompany the new single was given to the customer. A two-speed rear hub was also introduced that year.

Before then, the motorcycle had been started in one of two ways: either pedaling in bicycle fashion or running alongside until the engine started. Harley-Davidson introduced a step starter in 1914, eliminating the need to put the machine on its rear stand for starting. The internal expanding rear brake and carburetor choke were offered as well, followed a year later by the revolutionary three-speed sliding gear transmission and engine clutch.

FPG

Irish immigrants at Ellis Island.

While motorcycling was generally looked upon as a purely masculine sport, a surprising number of women were also early enthusiasts. The June 18, 1910 issue of *The Bicycling World and Motorcycle Review* has this report on one of these feminine iconoclasts, Leda Leslie, who is shown in the photograph below:

"Just now, Akron, Ohio has more than tires and rubber to interest it and to test the elasticity of its inhabitants' necks. A young woman who rides a motor bicycle is the new cause for interest and neck-stretching.

"She is Miss Leda Leslie, who, astride her Harley-Davidson, is the subject of the accompanying illustration. Miss Leslie is reputed a skillful rider, even if she did 'get herself into print' by plunging through a plate glass show window."

In Miss Leslie's defense, the article continued: "That was an accident that might have happened to even a masculine rider and 'doesn't count' anyway."

One of the best-loved and most popular figures of the time was humorist Will Rogers.

Ed Wynn was one of America's favorite funny men.

By 1914, the Harley-Davidson motorcycle had earned such a solid reputation that nine departments of the federal government employed its service. The U.S. Postal Service alone used over 4,800 Harleys for rural deliveries.

In 1915, a new delivery side-van was introduced for commercial use. Essentially, it was a large wooden box with a hinged top for loading. Mounted on the standard sidecar chassis, it had the added benefit of being interchangeable with the sidecar body, so the owner could use the equipped motorcycle for both business and pleasure. The side-van bodies could be ordered from the factory with their company name and information painted on it for ten cents per letter. The sidecar could be ordered with a folding top and side curtains, offering all-weather protection for its occupant. Comfort had come to motorcycling.

Just four of the 4,800 Harley-Davidson motorcycles employed by the U. S. Postal Service in 1914.

Author,
Carl Sandburg.

The side-van
proved very poplaur
and useful for
companies seeking
a speedy and
economical way to
deliver their goods.

From the very beginning, there has been a deep feeling of comraderie among the employees of Harley-Davidson. This family-like atmosphere prompted a group of employees to help out a fellow employee who lived in a tarpaper shanty with his wife and two children. Using materials supplied by William Davidson, well-known for his kindness and generosity, the employees built their fellow worker's family a fine two-story home.

WHAT HAPPENED TO MR. MOORMAN

"Happenings" Began in Moorsville and the Young Man is Glad He's Alive—His Motorcycle "Fatally Injured."

If only a moving picture man had been present to see it all on April 17, at Moorsville, Ind., he would have had a film that would have taken rank with the "six best renters," for what happened to Bert Moormann, an amateur motorcycle rider, and his new motorcycle on that day in that town was little short of a miracle. The whirl started with a puncture. Moormann laughed. 'Twas nothing!

A boy threw a rock at him. Moormann spoke to the boy's father, who chased Moormann with a knife.

"B-r-r-r-r" from the new motorcycle, and Moormann was out of reach. He laughed. Then things really began to happen.

Moormann bumped a traction car. Later he was forced to jump from his machine to avoid death under a C. H. & D. train. The motorcycle was struck. Moormann was bruised, but he just laughed.

Moormann then continued on his explosive way, until he hit Prosecutor Dennis O'Neil. Both hit the street. Moormann did not dare laugh, because O'Neil did not see the humor in the situation.

"Me for the country and the open road," said Moormann.

The new motorcycle sputtered gayly forth and was "going good," much to Moormann's exhilaration, when it struck an automobile. The collision was mutual, with the motorcycle underneath. Moormann was thrown many feet, but escaped with only a bruise or two. The new motorcycle was damaged beyond using and Moormann's headlong career was ended for the day.

While the popularity of motorcycling grew as a sport, there were probably few who found more excitement in it than Bert Moormann, whose one-day adventure was humorously described in this April 22, 1911 story from *The Bicycling World And Motorcycle Review.*

Unable to ignore the racing success of independent Harley-Davidson riders, Bill Harley established the company's official Racing Department in 1914. Before the year was out, Harley-Davidson had captured the win at the One Hour National Championships under FAM Sanction at Birmingham, Alabama. The following year, Harley-Davidson motorcycles raced to a total of 26 major firsts.

1916 saw more of the same. There were 15 victories in all—on board tracks, flat tracks and in the FAM Nationals—and more than a couple were complete sweeps. Racing had become such an important part of the motorcycling scene that Harley-Davidson began selling stripped stock models for competition. A brochure of that year offered 11-horsepower, twin-cylinder racers that were capable of 70 to 75 miles per hour, direct from the factory. Optional equipment included different oiling systems, seats, tires and even the wheelbase. In addition, a choice of gas tanks was offered, which included the new, sleeker rounded tank introduced that year. Price was $250 F.O.B Milwaukee.

FPG

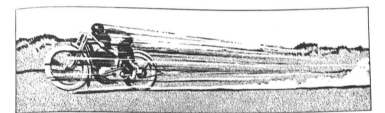

Harley-Davidson
1915 Long Distance Champion

IN the three big races of the year the 1915 stock Harley-Davidson has won both first and second.

It has taken remarkable reliability, and sustained speed previously unheard of in a stock machine, to make these unparalleled performances possible.

Venice International Grand Prize
300 Miles. Average 68½ Miles an Hour

Oklahoma City Road Race
150 Miles. Average 64³⁄₁₀ Miles an Hour

Phoenix 200-Mile Race
Average 64.07 Miles an Hour

Ride A Winner

Harley-Davidson Motor Co., Milwaukee Wis., U.S.A.

The advertiser wants to know. Therefore mention MOTOR CYCLE ILLUSTRATED.

Leslie "Red" Parkhurst establishes new motorcycle 24-hour record at Sheepshead Bay, N.Y., of 1,452 miles.

An early example of motorcycle clothing was this suit supplied by a Chicago firm, made of English whipcord.

Otto Walker, with passenger Carl Lutgens, establishes new motorcycle-sidecar record of 1,158 miles.

Suffragist Susan B. Anthony did not live to see the proposal of the 19th Amendment, granting women the right to vote, in 1919.

1916:
Auto/truck production passes million mark for first time; average car price is $600.

Margaret Sanger opens first birth control clinic.

U. S. establishes military government in Dominican Republic.

1917:
U. S. enters WWI, sends first combat troops to France.

Congress approves Prohibition Amendment.

Balfour Declaration promises Jewish homeland in Palestine.

1918:
Over a million American troops in Europe before WWI ends.

First airmail service with regular flights between New York and Washington.

1919:
First transatlantic non-stop flight by U. S. Navy seaplane.

White Sox loss in World Series to Reds later becomes "Black Sox" scandal.

WAR INTERRUPTS AMERICANS' TOUR OF SWEDEN

A 1915 article in *The Bicycling World and Motorcycle Review* indicates the coming war in Europe. According to the story, Carl A. Peterson of Natick, Mass., shown in the photo with his wife, had his motorcycle vacation trip through Sweden "rudely interrupted by the European war. The tourists did considerable traveling in Sweden, mostly over excellent roads, before they decided to curtail their outing.

"Swedish riders were deeply impressed by the power of Peterson's Harley-Davidson," the article continued, "and by the ease with which he whisked Mrs. Peterson about the country on the tandem seat.

"The Petersons had planned to ride through Germany before sailing on the return trip, but when war broke out, there was confusion on all sides, and it was considered advisable to get out of Europe with all possible speed. Accordingly, the motorcycle was recrated, and after much difficulty and unraveling a great deal of official red tape, the machine was taken on board the ship.

"In some respects the outing did not come up to our expectations," says Peterson, "but the machine performed perfectly, and the riding we managed to do while in Sweden amply repaid us."

DELLA'S FAMOUS ADVENTURE

In the first few decades of the Twentieth Century, the roads made motorcycle touring a rugged sport. Before concrete interstates and blacktop secondary roads crisscrossed America, most roads were dirt or gravel trails. Venturing far outside the city required a flair for adventure, a lot of stamina and a rugged machine. The fact that American men ventured forth under those conditions was unquestioned, but for women to do the same caused a great deal of attention, because of their presumably more passive role.

Even among these exceptional female motorcycle pioneers, some stood out. . .like a Waco, Texas woman named Della Crewe. On June 24, 1915, she set out to see America by motorcycle, after rejecting both train and steamship as being not only too expensive, but also uninteresting. With only 10 days of riding experience on her 1914 Harley-Davidson V-twin, she filled her sidecar with 125 pounds of baggage, including her dog, appropriately named "Trouble," and began her tour. Despite warnings from friends that she would get held up by hobos or kill herself in an accident, she wanted the freedom and mobility offered only by a motorcycle.

Her first destination was the June 3 motorcycle races in Dodge City, Kansas. With today's modern roads, it would be a one or two day trip, but things were different in 1915. An extremely wet winter and spring had made roads across Texas and Oklahoma badly rutted mires of mud and sand. And if that weren't enough, there was the added danger of hidden stumps, logs and rocks in the so-called roads. All those miles of sand beds and rugged hills took their toll on both the rider and the motorcycle.

Despite a collision with a stump which knocked her sidecar out of line, Della made it to the paved streets of Oklahoma City without a major mishap. The 75 miles of macadam in the city were a welcome relief to the lady motorcyclist, but upon entering Kansas, heavy rains made the road such a quagmire she had to install tire chains. Finally, even chains couldn't provide enough traction and with Trouble in the sidecar, Della struck out through four miles of Kansas wheat fields before finding a usable road. She made it to Dodge City in time for the race, one of the premier motorcycle events of the time.

Deciding to head to New York and see the country along the way, the pair headed north through the beautiful scenery of Missouri. With good weather and fine roads, they made good time as they raced up one hill and down another. After a 15¢ ferry ride across the Mississippi River, they were into Illinois and more hills. The trip to Chicago and then to the Harley-Davidson factory in Milwaukee was comparatively quick and uneventful.

After leaving Milwaukee, they headed south again, through Chicago and into Indiana, where authorities stopped her twice because of the dog. There was a quarantine in Indiana because of hoof and mouth disease, and Della had to promise that her dog wouldn't leave the sidecar before they could proceed. Nevertheless, upon arriving in Goshen, Indiana, they were invited to participate in a local parade, which gave them an excellent opportunity to see the city. Traveling at a mile and a half per hour in a parade was taxing for a relatively new rider like Della, and she was glad when it was over. Resuming her journey shortly thereafter, Della and her dog encountered a considerable number of road repairs, causing numerous detours.

Having spent the summer and fall months heading north and then east, the travelers inevitably ran into cold November weather in Ohio, an indication of what was ahead for the rest of the trip. Bitter cold forced a three-day layover in Toledo, and the ride around the southern edge of Lake Erie turned into a snowy one as they approached Cleveland. Traveling northeast up the coast toward Painesville, Ohio, the drifting snow sent the motorcycle into the ditches several times, and eventually they were forced to seek shelter at a farmhouse. The farmer refused her request at first, with the illogical excuse that she didn't belong on the road in that kind of severe weather. Fortunately, the farmer's wife was the boss of that house, and Della soon found herself drying her clothes before a warm fire.

On Thanksgiving Day, Della and her canine partner were back on the road again. Thawing snow had made the roads so bad it took them two hours to travel 2-1/2 miles to the nearest town. Several times she needed the aid of local farm boys to free the motorcycle and get it rolling again. The Texans were forced to pick their way through eighteen miles of obstacles such as rutted roads, slippery conditions, and stuck or sliding cars, riding most of the way in low gear. While a number of motorcyclists on solo machines were forced to lay over and wait for better conditions, Della was thankful that the stability of a sidecar allowed her to continue.

Crossing the corner of Pennsylvania, the pair entered New York State. Approaching Buffalo, they had to struggle through nine miles of sticky clay which clung to everything and clogged the wheels. Physically spent, Della had to hire a farmer and his horse to pull them the last mile.

Thankfully, the ride across the state was easy. However, bitter cold and heavy snow returned to haunt them as they left Albany, making the trip to their long-sought destination of New York City a rugged two-day journey.

From Waco to Milwaukee to New York City with numerous side trips, Della and Trouble logged a total of 5,378 miles as their motorcycle performed flawlessly. As Della stated after completing the journey, "I had a glorious trip. I am in perfect health, and my desire is stronger than ever to keep going."

A few days later, Della Crewe, Trouble and their 1914 Harley-Davidson twin with sidecar sailed for Jacksonville, Florida with plans to tour the South, Cuba and South America.

While racing symbolized the ultimate in exciting motorcycle challenge, international events were forcing attention on a more serious side. Much as it might protest, the United States was being brought into the international conflicts that raged around the globe.

In 1916, Harley-Davidson motorcycles saw their first military duty in border skirmishes with Pancho Villa. The Mexican revolutionary was angered at President Wilson's support of his opponents and retaliated by raiding U. S. territory along the border. General "Black Jack" Pershing was sent with his troops to quiet things down. In order to track down this elusive bandit, the use of motorcycles with mounted machine guns, which had been in the War Department's service for many years, was increased dramatically to combat the rugged southeastern terrain.

On March 16, 1916, the War Department telegraphed Harley-Davidson requesting a dozen motorcycles to be shipped immediately. They arrived at the border two days later, ready for service. A second order was received March 27, and those machines arrived 33 hours later. The motorcycles were equipped with a sidecar gun carriage, developed by William Harley, to serve as a platform for mounting a Colt machine gun.

Uncle Sam's Choice
Harley-Davidsons

Nine o'clock Thursday morning, March 16, the Harley-Davidson Motor Co. received a telegraphic order from Fort Sam Houston for 12 Harley-Davidson Motorcycles. All 12 machines were shipped on the afternoon of the same day. Monday morning, March 27th, at 10 o'clock a telegraphic order was received for 6 more machines. These 6 were shipped on the same afternoon. Uncle Sam now has 34 Harley-Davidsons in Mexican frontier service.

Harley-Davidson machine
gun squad scouting on
U.S.-Mexican border.

In the meantime, the black clouds of war stormed over Europe. The "war to end all wars" had started in 1914, and Harley-Davidson was ready to do its part when America was forced into the conflict.

On April 6, 1917, the United States formally declared war, and the motorcycle industry immediately swung its efforts over to military production. At an August sales meeting in Milwaukee, Arthur Davidson pointed out the need for everyone associated with Harley-Davidson to ally himself with the spirit of Americanism. He said: "The time is coming when no man can be in the middle of the road. He must be either for America or against America, and the sooner we get together on this question, the better able we will be to win the war."

And Harley-Davidson responded. During the first year of the U.S. involvement in the war, approximately half of Harley-Davidson's production went to the military. By the time the war ended, *all* new Harley-Davidson motorcycles were made for the government. All of the motorcycle manufacturers halted racing until the victory in Europe was won.

FPG

Actress Mary Pickford was known as "America's Sweetheart."

Just as World War I altered the lives of individuals around the world, it also made a major impact on the young Harley-Davidson Motor Co. During the period just prior to the United States' entry into the war, suspension of British civilian cycle production had forced the world's nonmilitary riders to look Stateside for new mounts. Harley-Davidson drew a good share of this business, and its reputation overseas grew accordingly.

Prior to the war, copies of Harley-Davidson service bulletins emphasized the value of civilian preparation and organization for military action. When the war came, those who knew the ins and outs of motorcycles would be ready to perform a valuable service for their country. In total, some 20,000 cycles would see dispatch and scout duty before the war ended, and most of those would come from Milwaukee.

Harley-Davidson's "now and then" publication (meaning it was published every now and then), *The Enthusiast*, was launched in 1916. It, too, stood firmly behind the war effort, keeping riders on both sides of the Atlantic informed on military motorcycle matters. *The Enthusiast* is still published today, making it America's longest continuously published motorcycle magazine.

The War was responsible for another Harley-Davidson tradition that has continued into modern times. As the Army continued to build its fleet of motorcycles, it soon became apparent that it had no program to maintain them. To meet that need, the first Harley-Davidson Service School was established in 1917 to help train military personnel to repair and maintain all of those hard working cycles abroad. Also, Harley-Davidson began sending an expert serviceman to accompany each shipment of machines to its assigned army camp. Once the motorcycles were properly set up by a designated squad of men, the serviceman would have the job of selecting and training the riders. Eventually, he would set up and train a staff for the on-camp service area.

For more comprehensive training, Harley-Davidson created a service school at its Milwaukee plant where mechanics could learn about proper repair procedures and tools in an intensive three-week course. The very first class, in July of 1917, consisted of nine corporals from Fort Sam Houston, Texas. Eventually, three classes were conducted at a time, with 45 men per class.

By the end of the war, Harley-Davidson was preparing to train 1,000 riders and mechanics per month in a special Milwaukee area service school. After the war, the regular school was continued to provide qualified mechanics for civilian motorcycles.

Public service was a way of life at Harley-Davidson from the early days. Shown in this photo is Margaret Davidson, six year old daughter of Arthur Davidson and youngest member of Milwaukee's Washington Park Division of the Red Cross.

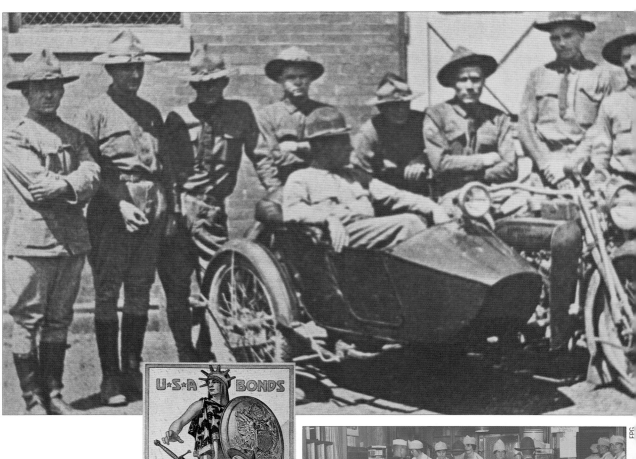

Harley-Davidson
motorcycles on patrol
in a French Village
in 1918.

One of the most famous motorcycle stories to come out of World War I involved a Harley-Davidson and a Yank from Chippewa Falls, Wisconsin, named Roy Holtz. It began on November 8, 1918, while rumors were circulating among the Americans that peace had been declared. Corporal Holtz, a motorcycle dispatch rider stationed in northern Belgium, was ordered to take his captain out on a night mission. The roads were muddy after days of rain, as well as being torn up by artillery fire.

Following orders, Holtz started out on his Harley-Davidson with his captain in the sidecar. Although it was dark, Holtz knew the countryside well and warned his captain that they were going in the wrong direction—toward enemy lines. The captain disagreed, politely at first, and then vehemently, so they continued.

Soon they saw the lights of an old farmhouse, and Holtz was ordered to get directions. Angry, he plodded to the door and pounded on it fiercely. When it opened, he stepped inside to face the glare of enemy soldiers. As he feared, they had blundered into a German division headquarters, and

FPG

The returning
war dead.

Riding his Harley-
Davidson, Roy Holtz
was the first Yank to
enter Germany.

the two were immediately captured. "See what you and your blasted directions got us into," Holtz told his captain, who was now very subdued. Now, of course, they realized that the rumors of an armistice were false.

They were questioned, but treated decently. Holtz was even given four glasses of schnapps in an effort to loosen his tongue, but the Germans finally gave up.

Three days later, on November 11, 1918, the war did end. Holtz and his captain were released and headed back toward their own headquarters, arriving just as their outfit was ready to move out. And, on November 12, he became the first Yank to enter Germany. . .aboard his Harley-Davidson.

At the time, Roy Holtz was unaware that his picture had been taken. The photo prints were discovered a few days later in a German photography shop by a fellow dispatch rider, who forwarded them to Harley-Davidson. In 1943, the photo was published in Harley-Davidson's *Enthusiast*. When Holtz heard about it, he came to the *Enthusiast* office to see it—for the first time since it was taken in 1918.

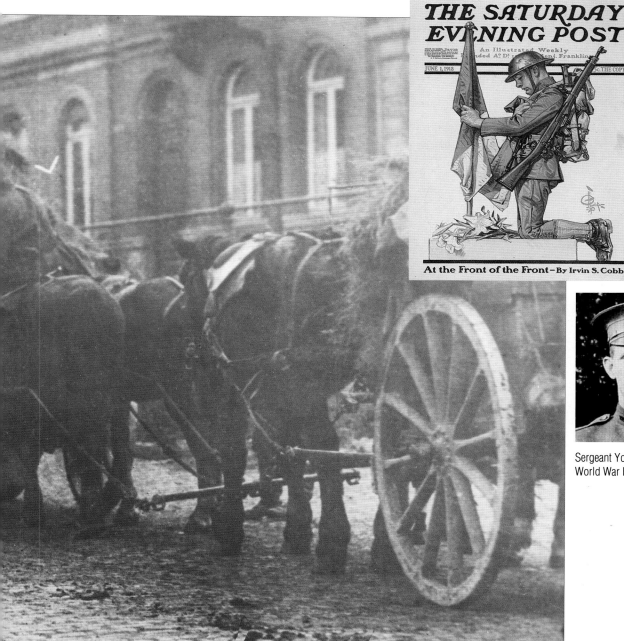

Sergeant York was a World War I hero.

The people of Harley-Davidson served their country well during World War I, receiving several commendations from the military for their loyalty and dedication to the war effort. William Harley served as a member of the Motorcycle War Service Board and contributed to the government's decision to give motorcycles a B-4 classification, which meant the industry was deemed essential and was able to procure needed materials for production.

In all, 312 employees entered military service during the war, and all but three returned—those having paid the ultimate price for their country. Harley-Davidson invited all veterans to return to the company and resume their old jobs, or jobs of equal worth. Most did just that.

The conversion back to civilian production was relatively smooth and simple for Harley-Davidson. The only reminder of the war was the army green that had replaced the popular pre-war gray. It continued as the standard motorcycle color for some years after the war.

In an undoubted effort to acquaint youngsters with Harley-Davidson, a full line of bicycles was introduced in 1917, playing off the motorcycle's reputation for quality, dependability, balance and, of course, Americanism. Offered in the "soldier color" of olive drab, the nonmotorized Harley-Davidsons were advertised as "a true brother to the Harley-Davidson motorcycle." While attractive and well-made, the Harley-Davidson bicycles were expensive for the times—$30 to $45 retail—and disappeared from the product line a few years later. However, these bicycles began a policy of involving the rider's family in Harley-Davidson products that continues to this day.

A bicycle race held in Plaza del Congress, Buenos Aires, Argentina.

Of Course It's a Harley-Davidson

That's the bike red-blooded fellows choose—choose it because it stands the "gaff," because it's a bike they can always be proud of.

If you want a bicycle that has the sturdy build and the ruggedness to withstand all kinds of hard riding; you, too, will choose a

Harley-Davidson Bicycle

It's a beauty, too. Classy lines and a cleancut construction. Well designed frame and "soldier" color. A fit running mate for the famous Harley-Davidson motorcycle.

Dad knows—bring him with you when you come in to look at the new models. They're here now.

(Dealers Name)

HARLEY-DAVIDSON
MOTORCYCLES
BICYCLES

"Gee Dad! buy Me a HARLEY-DAVIDSON"
WE HAVE A COMPLETE LINE OF HARLEY-DAVIDSON
BICYCLES IN STOCK

(Dealer's Name Here)

An impeccably restored Sport Model.

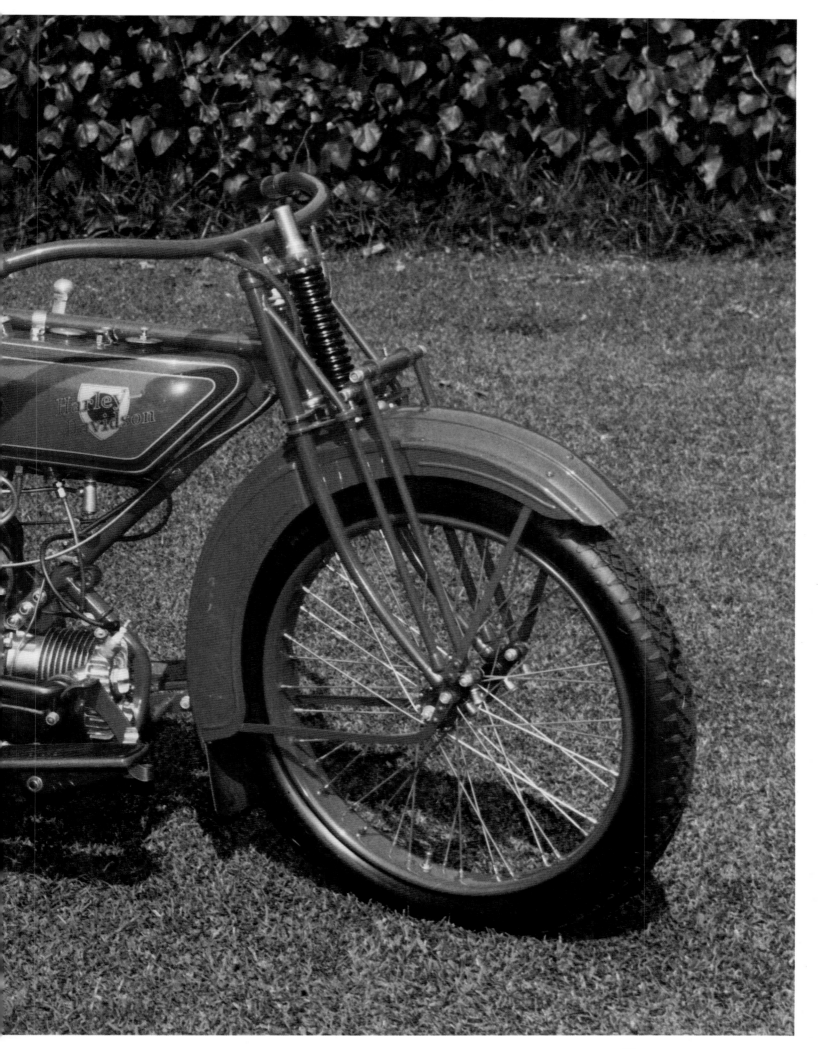

Since British motorcycle manufacturers had been out of the civilian style business for practically all of 1914-1918, Harley-Davidson's position in the world market steadily improved. By 1919, Harley-Davidson motorcycles were sold in nearly every civilized country in the world, and some not so civilized. Some 2,000 dealers world-wide delivered machines in such diverse areas as Tasmania, Japan, Fiji Islands, Ceylon, Iceland, South Africa, all of Europe and—before the 1917 Bolshevik Revolution—even Russia. Fully one-sixth of Harley-Davidson's production was going to foreign enthusiasts, and an important part of the company's business has been in exports ever since.

A 1918 Harley
with covered
sidecar.

A 61 cubic inch Model J.

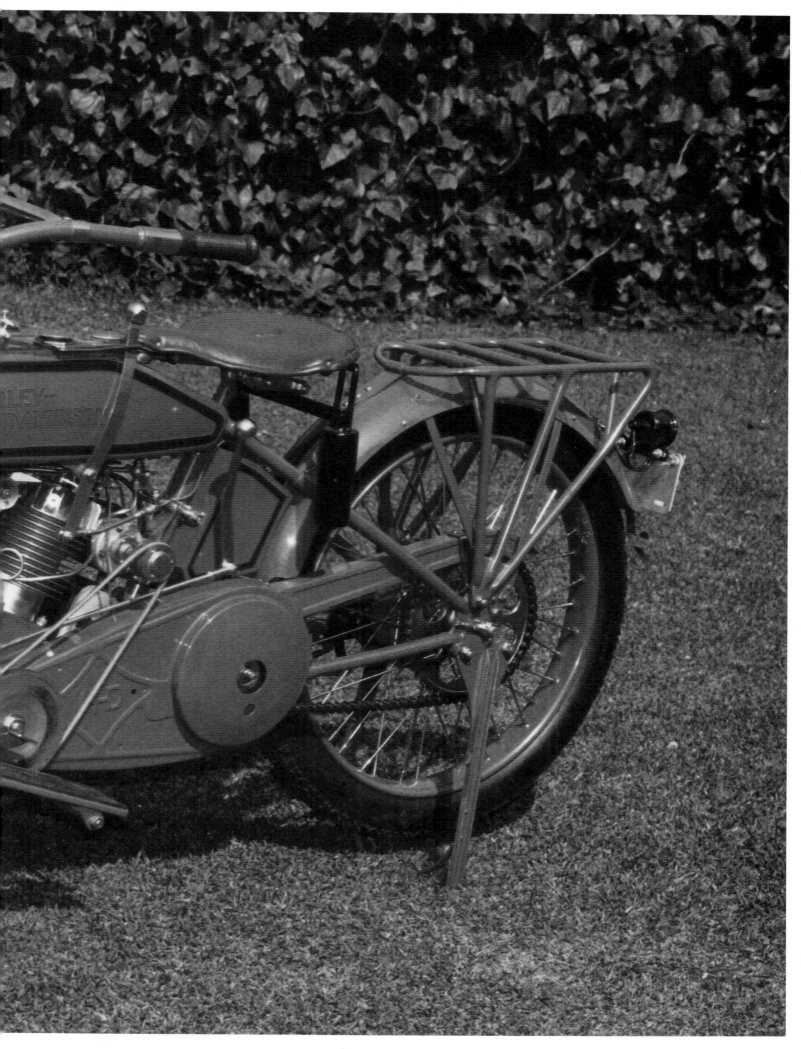

Also in 1919, Harley-Davidson produced its most radical motorcycle to date—and perhaps ever—the Sport Model. Unlike the conventional motorcycle with its popular V-twin engine, the Sport Model was powered by a 37 cubic, inch longitudinally opposed, fore and aft, twin-cylinder, six-horsepower engine. Intended for solo rather than sidecar riding, it soon earned a reputation as being a smooth running, dependable mount and was widely acclaimed by both owners and the motorcycle press. Nevertheless, its very design offered little in the way of future refinements and improvements, and the Sport Model was dropped four years later. In its day, though, it was a great competitor that set many records, including a 74 hour, 58 minute run from Canada to Mexico, piloted by Hap Scherer.

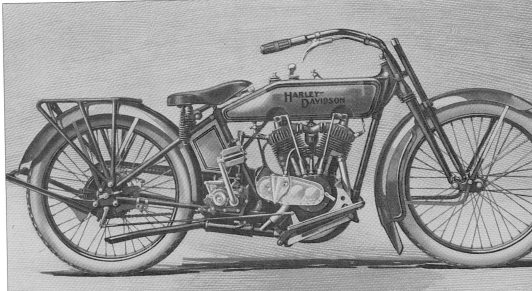

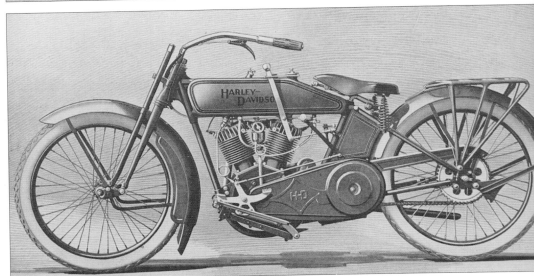

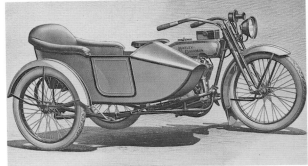

1919 also marked the introduction of the 20J V-twin. This 1920 model was special because it carried its very own, Harley-Davidson-produced electrical system.

As the decade wound to a close, the little Milwaukee company founded by four young imaginative men had grown to be one of the great powers in the motorcycle world. Inhabiting over 400,000 square feet of manufacturing space in 1919, nearly 1,800 Harley-Davidson employees were involved in the production of 22,685 motorcycles and 16,095 sidecars.

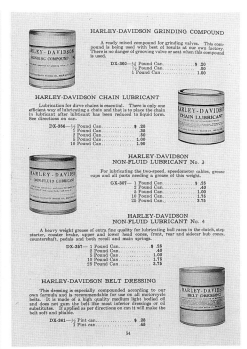

THE 1920'S

Roaring Into The Twenties

THE 1920'S

The "war to end all wars" was over. The world was at peace. Industry had returned to peacetime pursuits, and the economy was percolating. The year was 1920 and prosperity had returned to the land. Consumers went on a buying frenzy to own those luxury items denied them while America's attention was turned towards defeating the Kaiser and his armies.

The motorcycle publications that year were filled with optimism regarding the health of the industry. Motorcycles were hard to come by and factories were working to capacity. The general consensus in the motorcycle industry was that it would take at least two years for supply to catch up with demand.

Warren G. Harding, 29th president, died in office; succeeded by Vice-President Calvin Coolidge.

The World's Champion

THAT is the name and the fame the Harley-Davidson motorcycle has gained. It is preferred for its performances all over the world—and adopted by the United States government as standard after its wonderful war work on the fields of France. Let that be *your* standard to go by when you buy a motorcycle. Won 200 mile World's Championship road race, 200 mile National Championship. Come here and see the 1920 Harley-Davidson. See why it is the World's Champion.

40 to 60 miles on a gallon of gasoline, 250 miles on a quart of oil.

The Woman's Out-Door Companion

GERTRUDE HOFFMANN owns a motorcycle—it is the feature-refined, woman-kind

Harley-Davidson

And many other women are getting the joys of motorcycling and the great good of the great out-o'-doors aboard the driver's seat of Harley-Davidsons.

Motorcycling among women has become accepted as much as horseback riding in days gone by, and the Harley-David-son responds to the guiding hand of woman as did the kindest tempered steed of old.

If you are an out-door girl or woman you'll glory in the "git" and the "go" of motorcycling.

Come here and see the 1920 Harley-Davidson, the World's Champion.

Dealer's Name and Address

Don't *Haul* Parcels Use Motorcycle Side Van

DON'T use tonnage trucks for poundage delivery. You're carting away profits every trip you make. You're 'way over your head in over-head. Use a

Harley-Davidson

Motorcycle with roomy side-van or parcel car. Bring the weight and size of your delivery system down to the weight and size of your deliveries. One or two, or a fleet of Harley-Davidson Motorcycles with side-van or parcel car are the most practical for parcel and package delivery. 40 to 60 miles on a gallon of gasoline, 800 to 1000 miles on a gallon of oil, and three small tires instead of four. Come here and see the Harley-Davidson side-van outfit, and with the facts and figures we have see how it fits your business.

Dealer's Name and Address

This Way To Work and Back

DON'T take the slow, stuffed street car any longer to work and home. Let the breezy Harley-Davidson Motorcycle take you back and forth—and it won't take as long. It's easy to own a

Harley-Davidson

Terms of payment can be arranged here to suit your convenience. You can ride 40 to 60 miles on a gallon of gasoline, 250 miles on a quart of oil, with practically no cost for tires or repairs. Street car fare and the time you will save will pay for the keep of a Harley-Davidson.

Be motor merry, motorcycle between work and home, go motor-miles to your heart's content, get the great good of the great out o'-doors—buy a Harley-Davidson Motorcycle, THE WORLD'S CHAMPION. Come here and see the 1920 model.

The National Champion.

In the Twenties, Harley-Davidson motorcycles were promoted for many forms of transportation, from general use to business purposes, and as "The Woman's Outdoor Companion."

In racing, Harley-Davidson was king, and the winner's circle was its throne. At Ascot Park in California, on January 4, 1920, a quartet of Harley-Davidson riders, led by the great Otto Walker, swept first through fourth in a performance that set the pace for motorcycle racing that year and the next. In February, the legendary Red Parkhurst, racing a 61 cubic inch Harley on the storm-roughened beach at Daytona, established new speed records for the one kilometer and the one mile at over 103 mph each. He also set new marks for two miles and five miles of 99 and 98 mph, respectively. Next, astride a 61 incher coupled with the brand new "Bullet" racing sidecar, Parkhurst dialed off another string of records. In all, twenty-three speed records fell to the Harley-Davidson onslaught that day. By May of the next year, Harley-Davidson also owned all the dirt track records for the one, two, five, ten, twenty-five and fifty mile races, in addition to being the first motorcycle to average over 100 miles per hour in a race.

Silent screen comic Harold Lloyd.

Red Parkhurst, with teammate Fred Ludlow in the "Bullet" sidecar, led a rampage of record-shattering wins on the beaches of Daytona in 1920, which saw 23 new records fall to Harley-Davidson in one day.

OTTO WALKER CAPTURES ASCOT RACE

A Sunday crowd of 25,000 turned out on January 4, 1920 at Ascot Park to watch a quartet of Harley-Davidson riders clinch the first four places in the fastest race run to date at the Los Angeles track. The big event was a 100-miler that saw the best riders in the country going head-to-head for first-place honors.

While the other competitors were riding the potent eight-valve racing machines, the Harley-Davidson contingent was powered by more conventional pocket-valve machines. Smooth riding, consistent performance and superb work by the Harley-Davidson pit crew were contributing factors as Otto Walker led teammates Ralph Hepburn, Red Parkhurst and Fred Ludlow to a clean sweep of the 1920 season opener, a clear sign of things to come.

LESLIE "RED" PARKHURST

By 1920, Harley-Davidson motorcycles were devouring the competition on race tracks all over the country as event after event fell to the machines from Milwaukee. Of all the daring young men campaigning on Harleys, undoubtedly one of the most popular was Leslie "Red" Parkhurst, a red-headed competitor with a perpetual grin.

Born in Denver, Red got the racing fever early on and began competing on the notorious motordromes of the era. Motordromes were huge oval racetracks built of pine planks, laid side-by-side like a wood floor. With their steeply-pitched sides, they were famous for high speeds and spectacular crashes that could incapacitate or kill both rider and spectator alike. Little wonder that they earned the nickname of "murderdromes."

Red heard of a new motordrome being built in Milwaukee and headed east, where he soon caught the attention of Harley-Davidson's racing department, newly formed in 1914. Recently married, Parkhurst gave up the dangers of the motordrome in favor of campaigning the new Harley racing motors on conventional tracks.

Victory after victory, and record after record fell to the amiable redhead, as he and his fellow teammates toured the country. At a track in Rockford, Illinois in 1915, he took his most serious spill. According to the doctor who attended him, Red's brain was shifted to one side in his skull, which resulted in an unbalanced mental condition for a short time. Fortunately, there were no lasting effects, and he returned to the tracks again to continue his winning ways. When America went to war, racing more or less came to a halt, and Red got a job as a superintendent at a large coal company in Milwaukee. Over the next two years, Red's oft-repeated statement was: "You'll never get me back into motorcycle racing."

But by the spring of 1919, Harley-Davidson was preparing some powerful eight-valve engines in anticipation of racing again, and after a talk with Harley racing engineer Bill Ottoway, Red was hooked one more time. At the first race of the season at Portland, Oregon, which signaled the revival of postwar motorcycle racing, it was the big grin of Red Parkhurst that was featured again in the winner's circle.

Red led a one-two-three Harley sweep in Marion, Indiana, followed by personal victories in the five, ten and twenty-five mile events in his hometown of Denver.

While many racers regularly jumped from one make of motorcycle to another, Red Parkhurst steadfastly refused all offers, regardless of how lucrative they appeared, preferring to campaign on the machines he had started on. His loyalty to Harley-Davidson earned him the respect of everyone connected with the sport.

At the height of his career, when he was probably the oldest and undoubtedly the most popular racer in the country, Red chose to retire from racing and work for Firestone Tire & Rubber Co., in Akron, Ohio. He cited a responsibility to his wife and child as his main reason for leaving professional racing. While no longer a competitor, he nonetheless retired as one of the early stars of motorcycle racing, and still frequented races on behalf of Firestone for years to come.

Red Parkhurst, right, led a 1-2-3 sweep of the Marion, Indiana race in 1919, followed by Harley-Davidson teammates Otto Walker, left, and Ralph Hepburn.

Despite the rosy outlook at the beginning of 1920, business took a decided downturn a few months later. The automobile industry had overproduced, companies had been paying inflated prices for goods and labor—which drove retail prices up, and banks were overloaded with loans. Consumers adopted a wait and see attitude, creating excessive inventories. To stimulate sales, Henry Ford cut prices on his cars, which put a scare into related industries, and motorcycle sales slumped.

At a national dealer convention in Milwaukee, in November 1920, company president, Walter Davidson, addressed the problems of flagging sales and pledged to make the dealers stronger than ever. A new emphasis on business management was to be the driving force behind Harley-Davidson. Dealers were educated on the need to advertise more, to provide better service, to enhance the rider's enjoyment of the sport by increasing their performance in accessory sales and to improve the somewhat negative public image of motorcyclists. These areas of improvement, as defined by Walter Davidson in 1920, are still stressed by Harley-Davidson today, some seven decades later.

The Motorcycle & Allied Trades Association, the industry's self-appointed watchdog, launched a massive campaign to both make dealers think more seriously about running their stores and improving the public image of the sport and its legion of enthusiasts. To this end, Harley-Davidson ran full page ads calling those who ride with open mufflers "boobs" and calling on concerned motorcyclists everywhere to take action "lest the entire wholesome sport of motorcycling be banished, like a leper, by legislation." The future of the sport, it was felt, was dependent on acceptance by the public at large.

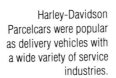

Harley-Davidson Parcelcars were popular as delivery vehicles with a wide variety of service industries.

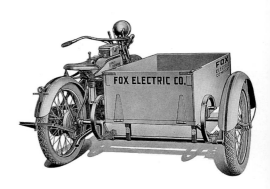

HARLEY-DAVIDSON SETS WORLD RECORD

World motorcycle racing history was created on the international scene in January 1920, when Domingos Lopez won the Brazilian Kilometer Championship Sidecar Race riding a Harley-Davidson motorcycle with sidecar. His average speed of 80.77 miles per hour set a world record at the time for the fastest officially recorded sidecar speed. Another Harley-Davidson racing sidecar rig took second place in the event, which saw all the major U. S. motorcycle makers competing.

At the South American Tourist Trophy Race in Argentina later that year, Harley-Davidson riders scored another one-two victory in the sidecar event, and swept the solo competition by capturing the top five places.

By 1920, Harley-Davidson was the largest motorcycle manufacturer in the world, both in floor space and in number of machines produced. It was one of the largest advertisers in the western part of the country, with a budget for 1920 of a quarter of a million dollars, a huge sum in those days. *The Enthusiast*, Harley-Davidson's free magazine, was being mailed to 50,000 people monthly, and plant tours were conducted on a daily basis, a practice that continues today. Harley-Davidson boasted dealers in 67 countries worldwide.

Two champions! Jack Dempsey had his picture taken on the Single while training in Colorado.

FPG

Jack Dempsey lost crown to Gene Tunney in controversial fight, September 23, 1926.

HARLEY-DAVIDSO

Sport Model

Makes Every Path a Highway

Swift--Silent Easy-Riding

HARLEY-DAVIDSON CHUMMY CAR

40 to 60 Miles per Gallon of Gasoline

Do You Know What it Costs to Operate a Harley-Davidson

The power, speed, comfort and other features of the Harley-Davidson resemble so closely those of the motorcar that, without investigation of facts, one is inclined to estimate the upkeep cost of a Harley-Davidson Motorcycle as on a par with that of the automobile.

Such is, however, far from being true. The Harley-Davidson upkeep cost is remarkably low as proven by the fact that this World's Champion Motorcycle, in ordinary hands, will travel 40 to 60 miles per gallon of gasoline and 800 to 1000 miles on a gallon of oil. Motorcycle tires are smaller than automobile tires, and therefore cost less.

These are figures worth memorizing considering that motor fuel and lubrication costs are rising. The Harley-Davidson offers great sport, comfortable travel and dependability at an extremely low cost.

Let us show you the latest Harley-Davidson models. No obligation if you drop in to see them.

We can arrange an easy payment plan to suit your own convenience.

Sales of 61 cubic inch V-twin motorcycles comprised the bulk of Harley-Davidson's sales in 1921 as production plummeted to the lowest number in almost a decade, just over 10,000 machines. Sidecars were still very popular, so, to satisfy the need for more power and give sales a needed shot in the arm, the first Harley-Davidson 74 cubic inch engine, which developed 18 horsepower, appeared in 1922. Advertised as the Superpowered Twin, it was designed for sidecar or tandem riding, while the proven 61 incher remained for solo riding. The 1922 machines were sophisticated for the times, employing 38 different types of high grade metals in their construction and undergoing a rigid test and inspection before being shipped. Gone was the army green color. Three coats of brewster green with gold striping, varnished and baked, was the new color for 1922. However, just a few years later, the company returned to olive green with maroon striping.

Emphasis was placed on economy of operation, not only for the consumer but for municipal and commercial uses as well. A new model, the 21-CD, was developed for commercial use with a single-cylinder engine designed for ease of maintenance, economy and longevity. Ads soon boasted 80 miles per gallon and a penny-a-mile operating costs. Numerous ads and flyers extolled the virtues of using Harley-Davidson motorcycles for businesses and municipalities. By 1924, 1,400 police and sheriff's departments were using Harley-Davidson motorcycles, as were countless private businesses.

Illustrations from a 1921 promotional flyer titled "My Harley-Davidson with the Pal Car" promoted the "good fellowship" of the Harley-Davidson sidecar with the theme: "No matter where my trail may be, My Pal will always ride with me."

Keep Warm!

Articles That Add Greatly to the Comfort and Pleasure of Winter Driving

Early in the game, Harley-Davidson realized the importance of providing riders with clothing and accessories which were unique to the sport and unavailable except through Harley-Davidson dealers.

Lamb Lined Moleskin Vest

IX-340—Made of fine gray moleskin cloth with sleeves of genuine cowhide leather. Body is lined with lambskin 3 inches from front and bottom facing. Collar and wristlets are of knitted brown wool. Pockets are leather trimmed. Length 25 in. Sizes 36 to 44 inclusive.
$13.50

JX-285
One-Finger Style

Mackinaw

HX-331—Classiest Mackinaw on the market—and the warmest. Made up in a handsome plaid of a hard finish, all wool, wind resisting, heavy Mackinaw cloth. Length 34 inches. Sizes 36 to 44 inclusive.
$17.50

Boy's Mackinaw

HX-331 B—Just like the above in sizes 12, 14, 16 and 18 years.
$15.00

"Flexicuf

Ideal for winter
warm lamb linin
lambskin.

Cuffs are the ne
lined and extra
heavy mackinaw

Leather used is t
hide. In producti
ving is used in
strength and dura
particular stock i

Made in an extr
dom of the hand.

Fit is perfect and

For Fall Driving

Sweater Coats
Sweaters
Leather Coat
Windproof Vests
Leather Helmet

Extra Heavy All Wool Sweater Coat

IX-306—Blue heather with special storm collar of a new type. Knit in the Shaker stitch. Sizes 36 to 44 inclusive.
$26.50

Medium Weight All Wool Sweater Coat

IX-305—Blue heather. Knit in the Shaker stitch. Comes with a large full roll storm collar. Sizes 36 to 44 inclusive.
$13.50

Slip-Over Sweater

IX-303—Green heather. Knit in the Shaker stitch of pure wool worsted yarn. V neck. May be worn over a blouse or vest. Sizes 34 to 42 inclusive.
$10.00

Sweater with Shawl Collar

JX-304—Very snappy. Blue heather with Oxford Gray collar, wrists and bottom. All wool and knit in the Shaker stitch. Extra heavy. Sizes 36 to 44 inclusive.
$13.50

Leather Lined Windproof Vest

IX-338—Lined with genuine cowhide leather. Outer material is a Leatho-Suede cloth. Has leather sleeves with knitted brown wool wristlets. Collar may be buttoned. Length of vest is 25 inches. Sizes 36 to 44 inclusive.
$15.00

Reversible Leather Coat

IX-318—Fine for fall and winter use. Genuine tan grain leather with a smooth finish on one side and an olive Galardine cloth on the other. Comes double breasted with convertible collar, slash type pockets and an all-around belt with buckle. Length 40 inches. Gives equal satisfaction whether riding or walking. Sizes 36 to 44 inclusive.
$65.00

Leather Helmet

IX-298—Made of soft tan grain leather insuring comfortable fit. Lined with khaki cotton serge. Has cups over the ears and strap at the top which facilitates removal from the head. Exposed edges bound with tan silk binding. Fastens with strap and elastic. Sizes 6½ to 7½ inclusive.
$8.00

Leatho-Suede Vest

IX-337—An unlined vest made of soft, pliable Leatho-Suede cloth which looks and wears like leather. Collar and wristlets are knitted of brown wool. Three patch pockets. Sizes 36 to 44 inclusive.
$9.00

Ask About Them

OCTOBER

ACCESSORY FEATURES

New Popular Articles For Winter Riding

HARLEY-DAVIDSON MOTOR CO.
MILWAUKEE, WIS.

Taking advantage of Prohibition, Al Capone built a bootleg booze empire throughout the Twenties.

96

In the lean years of the early Twenties, Harley-Davidson began taking a harder line on virtually every aspect of the business. Racing was temporarily abandoned in 1923, although privateers worldwide continued to campaign on Harleys. The company not only produced large catalogs of accessories and clothing, but took an aggressive stance against the use of non-genuine parts in its motorcycles. Taking a page from an advertising tactic so popular today, Walter Davidson sent a personal message to potential buyers, via a direct mail flyer, touting the benefits of the 1924 line of Harley-Davidson motorcycles and inviting them to take advantage of a Pay-as-you-Ride Plan. No stone went unturned in the company's efforts to revitalize the sport, as dealers were given tips on how to advertise and promote their products and how to organize rallies, start clubs and sponsor competitive events. Involvement in the sport was seen as a way to not only attract new riders to motorcycling, but to also keep existing enthusiasts active and interested.

How far did you go yesterday?

THAT'S the first question the gang will ask you when you get back on the job Monday morning. You want to be able to tell 'em right to the dot and you want to tell 'em your highest speed too. That's just what you can do if your bus is equipped with a Corbin Speedometer. If some of the fellows doubt your word just tell 'em to cast their lookers over your Corbin and the argument is settled. You're getting a real speedometer when you buy a Corbin. Total mileage, trip mileage, maximum hand, 80 or 100 mile dial, luminous dial if you like, and everything.

Your dealer can fix you up to-day

Leather Togs

are now sold by your

Harley-Davidson Dealer

Coats   Jackets
Helmets   Breeches
Belts
Sheepskin Saddle Covers

"You'll like them"

Some Class!

That's what everybody will say when you step out in this Harley-Davidson racing jersey. It's the same jersey the Harley-Davidson racing stars and hill climb men have been wearing the past few years. The color is a knockout, dark green body and orange sleeves. It's also got three inch high letters that will tell 'em a mile off what motorcycle you ride. You are getting real value in this jersey. Sizes 36 to 44.

Specify

No. KX 256-K

When you go o that big trip—

take along a can of Harl Davidson summer oil and tr your motor right. Any old won't do the work in your cooled motor. When you miles from nowhere you'll glad you took along a can of good Harley-Davidson summ oil. Now supplied in flat gal cans that fit snugly under yo sidecar seat. Has a handy sp that makes it easy to pour. fore you go on that big vacat trip drop around to your dea and get a can or two of genu Harley-Davidson oil.

One gallon ca

$1.65

AT FACTORY

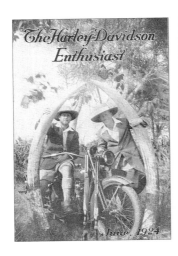

John Barrymore's role as Hamlet was another legendary performance by a member of one of America's most famous acting families.

Now we've got it for you!

WE take a big personal pride in presenting these new 1924 Harley-Davidsons to you motorcycle riders— the finest bunch of red-blooded outdoor sportsmen in the world.

Bill Harley and I and my brothers have ridden motorcycles, built them and lived with them for 21 years. We know that these new Harley-Davidsons will give you more pleasure and greater value than you ever thought possible in any motorcycle or sidecar. You'll find them by far the best motorcycles that have ever carried our name on the tank and you know what that means.

I ask only this of you. Step into your Harley-Davison dealer's place and look over these 1924 models, go for a ride and see for yourself. If you haven't met our dealer, get acquainted with him. You'll like him. He's your kind of a man. Harley-Davidson dealers are picked men. I know most all of them personally and I want you to feel this is a personal introduction from me to your Harley-Davidson dealer. Just tell him I asked you to come in to ride one of these new Harley-Davidsons.

Walter Davidson
President
HARLEY-DAVIDSON MOTOR COMPANY

For over 21 years Walter Davidson and Bill Harley have personally tested and tried out on the road every succeeding model of the Harley-Davidson before it has been offered to you. Many of the improvements you find in these new Harley-Davidsons, have come from just such roadside talks between Walter and Bill.

"Flesh and the Devil" was the first of many films to pair John Gilbert and Greta Garbo as a romantic duo.

Rudolph Valentino became an all-time screen immortal when he starred as "The Sheik."

Clara Bow, the movies' "IT" girl.

Refinements to the Harley-Davidson motorcycle continued throughout the Twenties. An alemite lubrication system, with 12 fittings on the motorcycle, appeared in 1924, and grease guns became the rule. Drop-forged, steel-frame fittings were developed in 1925. The Teardrop gas tank, so much a part of the unmistakable Harley-Davidson look, made its inaugural appearance that year, providing a more modern look than its boxy predecessor. Designated the "Stream-Line" models, these new offerings featured a truss-loop frame, speedster muffler, lowered riding position and a lower price. A brand new 30.50 cubic inch single, a 12-horsepower model, intended initially for foreign markets, was hailed by the press as an innovative and powerful lightweight motorcycle. Two years later, a device the motorcyclist of today generally thinks of as a "must," the front brake, came into use. At the time of its appearance, it met with some degree of rider skepticism. A carburetor air cleaner was added the same year. By 1928, production had increased to over 22,000 motorcycles.

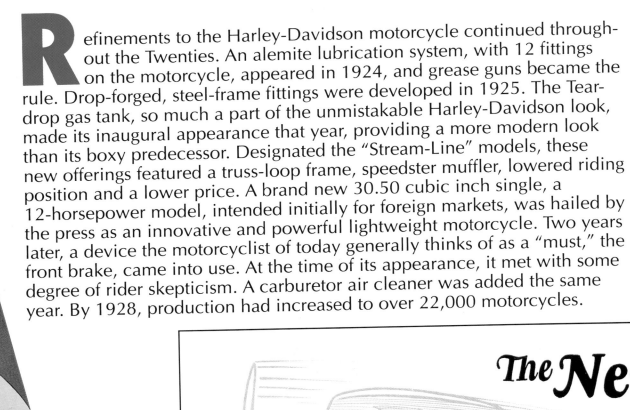

The New

1925

SPEED in every line—strength in every cu[rve]
—low hung for safety and easy control
better-sprung and bigger-tired for luxuri[ous]
comfort—that's Harley-Davidson's lat[est]
and greatest motorcycle, the "Stream-Lin[e]"

Never a mount like this before—so power[ful]
so speedy, so perfectly balanced, so roadwor[thy]
From every standpoint of performance, go[od]
looks and economy, the "Stream-Line"
a new standard. *And yet the price is redu[ced]*

*We have a real proposition for
dealers where we are not represented. Write for full particulars.*

New
Speedster
Muffler

"Stream-Line"

New

New

ng

p

New
ing
fort

New!

It's Here!
the Sensational
"Stream-Line"

The year 1928 also welcomed the second generation of the Harley-Davidson family when William H. Davidson, son of William A. Davidson, started with the company. He was followed the next year by Walter Davidson's sons, Gordon and Walter C. Davidson, and William J. Harley.

Charles E. Lindbergh became internationally known as "Lucky Lindy" after his first solo New York-Paris nonstop flight in 1927. It took him 33.5 hours.

Now

the 1927

HARLEY-DA

"Stream-Lin HARLEY-DAVIDSON

Newest and finest model of the World's Greatest Motorcycle—the 1925 "Stream-Line" Harley-Davidson! How the young bloods will itch to get this handsome, speedy, peppy thoroughbred out for a trial spin!

It's the biggest news of the motorcycle business—this year or for years past. Every prospect you've talked to—every man who ever wanted a motorcycle—will BUY when he sees the new "Stream-Line".

The "Stream-Line" will make 1925 a bigger year for thousands of dealers. Why not you? See new features on next page. Write—wire—phone!

HARLEY-DAVIDSON MOTOR COMPANY, Milwaukee, Wisconsin, U. S. A

Reduced Prices:

odel 25FE, magneto, equipped, 61" motor - - $295
odel 25JE, electric equipped, 61" motor - - 315
odel 25FDCB, magneto equipped, 74" motor - 315
odel 25JDCB, electric equipped, 74" motor - 335
odel 25QT, two passenger sidecar - - - - 130
odel 25LT, single passenger sidecar - - - - 100
Above prices are at factory and do not include war tax.

New Lower Price

1927—TWIN "74"—PRICE $320
(Electrically Equipped)

THE greatest Harley-Davidson of all — at new and lower prices! Improved — refined in many details — but no radical departures from the time-tried Harley-Davidson design. Old timers and beginners alike will recognize in these 1927 Twins the last word in engineering achievement. Powerful—speedy — built to hug the road — the most dependable and satisfactory mount that ever split the wind.

the 1927 twin

1927—TWIN "61"—
(Electrically Equip

ADDED to the greater value built into the 1927 Twins — added to improvements that every rider will welcome — prices are lower than ever before. Harley-Davidsons have always been outstanding values. Now, more than ever, the Harley-Davidson motor-cycle stands without a rival. In performance, in price, in rugged endurance, the 1927 Twins are the world's standard of motorcycle comparison.

HARLEY—DAVIDSO

"The Jazz Singer," starring Al Jolson, shown in New York City in 1927, was considered the first major "talking" motion picture.

Babe Ruth hit 60 home runs in 1927.

A New Wonderful 45 Twin

HERE IT IS! ...45 twin, the motorcycle ...at the world has been ...y-Davidson to build.

...cycle!—great acceleration ...power—quiet speed that ...he parades of cars far ...Above all a motor-...y to handle, a com-...pleasure to ride.

...you would expect in ...he Harley-Davidson ...he tanks. Features ...at stamp it the ...odern motorcycle engineering.

...put this 45 through its paces. ...'ll wonder how its price can pos-...so low . . . . $290 at the factory.

Two Bullet Headle... give more and better... —this means safer... riding. Handy to... switch on right hand... cuts out right light... depresses beam of... light, when desired. New Clear-the-way... has a pleasing yet... trating tone that... the road far ahead...

THE "45" twin

—a new HARLEY-DAVIDSON 1929

...sweeping ...ments for

RLEY

102

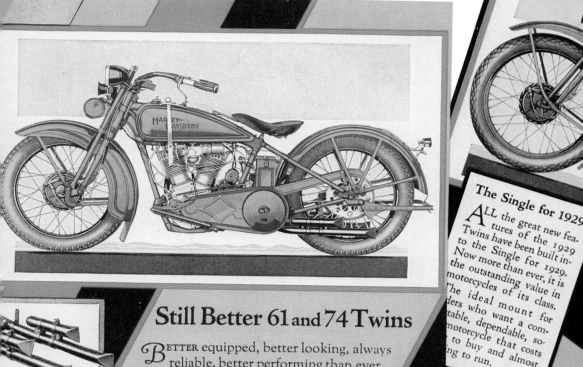

Still Better 61 and 74 Twins

BETTER equipped, better looking, always reliable, better performing than ever —the 1929 Big Twins are the finest motorcycles Harley-Davidson has ever built.

Safer night riding with two bullet type headlights, quiet exhaust with four tube muffler, instantaneous generator output control, a new electrical panel with built-in ammeter are features that keep these world famous twins far in the lead. And yet with all these advancements there is no raise in prices.

See your Harley-Davidson dealer today, look over and ride the new 1929 models. Their wonderful easy riding comfort and outstanding features will surprise you.

New 4 Tube Muffler changes the tone of the exhaust, blending it into a lower pitched tone that is agreeable to the ear. Muffler divides at the end of the exhaust pipe into two tubes, each carried to the rear at either side of the wheel. Each of these tubes in turn carries an additional outlet tube, providing in all four expelling tubes for the exhaust gases. This muffler is positively the most quiet muffler ever developed for motorcycles.

New Generator Output Controller—instantly regulates the generator output by means of an outside lever. With the always visible ammeter, this new feature should assure a fully charged battery at all times.

DAVIDSON

The Single for 1929

ALL the great new features of the 1929 Twins have been built in to the Single for 1929. Now more than ever, it is the outstanding value in motorcycles of its class. The ideal mount for riders who want a comfortable, dependable, so motorcycle that costs to buy and almost to run.

... and Prices

...ngle	$235.00
...pistons)	290.00
	310.00
...pistons)	325.00
...pistons)	320.00
...stons)	335.00
...n Two Cam	370.00
...ger Sidecar	100.00

...e at factory.

...N MOTOR CO.
...Wisconsin

Single Passenger Sidecar

HERE is the sidecar that will appeal to the man who wants to share his motorcycling joys. Luxurious comfort for the passenger. Easy to handle. Beautiful in appearance. Richly upholstered. Lots of room for touring luggage. Inspect it and you'll find it correct in design and right in every mechanical detail.

he DL 45-inch side valve twin came along in 1929 and became an immediate hit. Accenting its already sleek looks was a pair of bullet headlights, standard on the line that year. This motorcycle combined the power of the big twin and agile handling of the single. For 1929, Harley-Davidson offered V-twin engines in 45, 61 and 74 cubic inch displacements. In addition, a special twin-cam 74, powered by a version of the highly successful racing engine, was offered as "the fastest road model that Harley-Davidson has ever offered to the public."

The year 1929 was a momentous one. The American Motorcyclist Association (AMA) took the reins of overseeing the industry from its predecessor, the Motorcycle & Allied Trades Association. At a January sales meeting in Milwaukee, Walter Davidson reiterated the company's pledge to help the dealer market his products. An Open House Celebration was held at Harley-Davidson dealerships all over the country that summer. The number of police departments using Harley-Davidson motorcycles swelled to more than 2,900. And, the 1930 models were announced in August amid much critical acclaim and enthusiasm.

1925

Wyoming elects Nellie Ross as first U. S. woman governor.

John Scopes convicted of teaching the theory of evolution in public school in Tennessee "monkey trial."

First publication of *The New Yorker* magazine.

Scottish inventor, J. L. Baird, transmits human features by television.

1926

Dr. Robert Goddard demonstrates potential of rockets using liquid fuel; rocket travels 184 feet in 2.5 seconds.

Gertrude Ederle is first woman to swim English Channel.

Ford introduces 40-hour work week to check overproduction and limit unemployment.

1927

Trotsky expelled from Russian Communist Party.

1928

Alexander Fleming discovers penicillin.

Richard E. Byrd explores Antarctic.

America meets Mickey Mouse in first cartoon released by Walt Disney Productions.

1929

U. S. Stock market collapses; first phase of U. S. Depression.

St. Valentine's Day gangland massacre in Chicago.

f course, 1929 also brought the start of the Great Depression, and along with it, some heavy blows for the motorcycle industry. Dozens of manufacturers dropped out of sight. A shortage of dollars for individual transportation, combined with low pricing and growth in the automobile industry, were at least partly at fault. Then, too, motorcycling had evolved into largely a recreational activity, and people were reluctant to spend money on "leisure" pursuits. Harley-Davidson suffered along with everyone else, as industry-wide sales fell sharply.

However, the company prevailed where others couldn't, and the reasons are somewhat difficult to pinpoint. Certainly a strong dealer network, long established advertising programs, quality products, an affinity for the sport and the enthusiast, police and commercial use, conservative business management, and a strong export business were all contributing factors to Harley-Davidson's survival in the decade of the Twenties, later known as the darkest in the history of America.

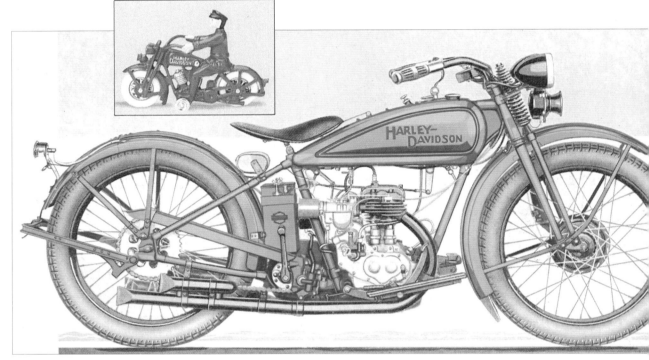

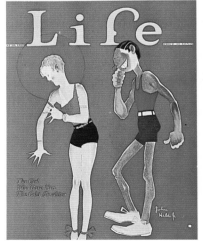

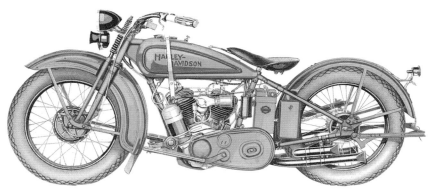

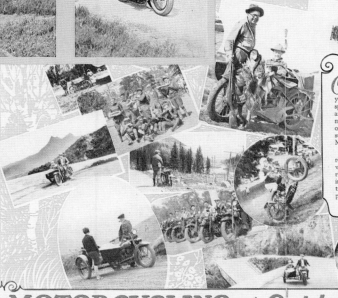

Over the hills and far away! Up hill and down dale with the speed of the wind. The healthful fresh air on your cheek. A purring mount that responds to your every wish — always anxious to do more. Ten, twenty, thirty miles slip by before you know it. Hundreds of miles in a day. New scenes, new pleasures — life that is worth living — that's Motorcycling, Outdoors' Greatest Sport.

Can't you hear that call of the open road? Come on for a joyous week-end, a vacation trip you'll never forget, a club run or tour, a wonderful hunting or fishing trip. Swing into the saddle of your trusty Harley-Davidson and leave the long parades of cars far behind.

Come On — Let's Go!

MOTORCYCLING ~ *Outdoors' Greatest Sport*

THE 1930'S

Growing Stronger Through Hard Times

THE 1930'S

Just like the beginning of the previous decade, the Thirties started on a high note of optimism, both for the sport of motorcycling and for Harley-Davidson. Motorcycle business, in general, was up 31 percent over the prior year, reflecting a fairly steady climb over the past years. Industry experts in January of 1930, like most people, had not fully realized the overall economic impact of the stock market crash of October. In fact, they believed that quick action on the part of President Herbert Hoover had repaired any damage.

The 1930 line of Harley-Davidson motorcycles was hailed as being virtually without comparison in the industry. Referring to the fact that the company was comprised of riders—including officers and shop men alike—*American Motorcyclist and Bicycle* magazine stated: "Dealers and riders will be in accord that the 1930 Harley-Davidson motorcycles achieve a closer relation to desires of devotees of the sport, the perfect motorcycle. No new feature has been added until it has been given an exhaustive road and bench test from a staff of competent engineers."

And, the 1930 models were loaded with features. The twin-cylinder and single-cylinder models all had new Ricardo removable heads, which provided for easier maintenance, improved efficiency and dramatic horse-power increases. The high compression 74 inch model, designated the VL, delivered 15 to 20 percent more horsepower than any previous engine of its size. The 74 also sported easily detachable, interchangeable wheels.

The entire line received larger front and rear brakes, larger tires, built-in front fork lock, a lowered saddle height, increased ground clearance and dual-beam headlights. The standard color was olive green with vermillion striping, but a forthcoming special paint program was announced to fill customers' requests for something different.

"Perfect Score Award" watch fob from the 1930 A.M.A. Annual Rally & Gypsy Tour.

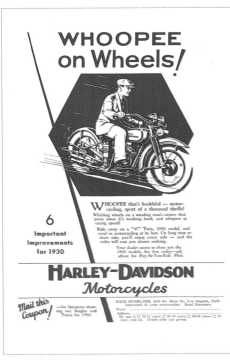

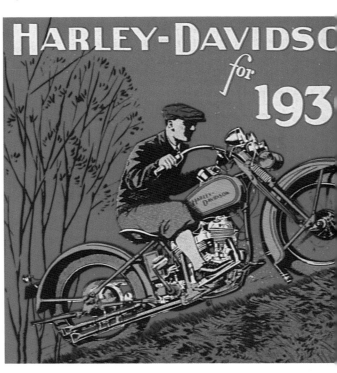

Harley-Davidson's advertising and promotion became even more aggressive in the Thirties, promoting both motorcycles and sidecars.

Any HARLEY-DAVIDSON *you want!*

Our Savings Club Plan

Pick out the model you want. You make a down deposit—as little as $2.50 is enough—and we give you your Savings Club Plan Pass Book shown above. Each week or pay day, you drop in and add to this deposit a certain amount or as much as you can. Your deposits are recorded, as made, in your book which you keep. When your deposits reach a certain total, depending on the model you select, you change over to the Pay-As-You-Ride Plan and ride out on your own mount.

$2.50 STARTS YOU!

So Easy to Own One

Pay-As-You-Ride Plan

On this plan you put down one-third the cost of the model you select and ride out. If you trade in an old motorcycle, the price we allow you counts in on the down payment. This down payment is recorded in your Pay-As-You-Ride Pass Book, which you keep. Then at regular periods you ride in to see us and make a payment as we have agreed upon. You pay as you ride and never feel the small easy payments.

⅓ DOWN~ and you ride out

"Garbo talks," said the publicity for Greta Garbo's first "talking" motion picture in 1930, "Anna Christie."

The NEWS and FASHION MAGAZINE of the SCREEN

PHOTOPLAY

JANUARY   25 CENTS

The High Price of Screen Love-making

Is Dietrich Through?

To launch the 1930 selling season, Harley-Davidson staged a nationwide open house on March 1 with over 400 dealers participating. Despite bad weather in some parts of the country, an estimated 50,000 customers visited dealerships to view the new models. Because of the enthusiastic response, industry experts felt that Harley-Davidson and the industry were "heading for record-breaking sales."

Indeed, they appeared to be right, as the outlook for Harley-Davidson looked rosy. Over 3,000 police departments were on Harleys. Literature for the export market was being produced in a number of languages, including German, French and Spanish. Hillclimbs and dirt tracks became the popular events, and Harley-Davidson racked up victory after victory.

As the economy deteriorated following the stock market crash, the industry reached out to stimulate business. The American Motorcyclist Association staged a nationwide Gypsy Tour, a longtime motorcycling tradition, to keep enthusiasts involved in the sport. Most dealers in the U.S. and Canada held some kind of event—including tours, rallies, polo tournaments, races, hillclimbs, field meets, rodeos, picnics, jamborees or anything else they could think of. The turnout of motorcyclists was tremendous. Unfortunately, sales continued to decline as enthusiasm for the sport failed to be an adequate substitute for cash. As money grew more scarce, it became increasingly difficult to attract new customers.

Calling on over 27 years of engine building experience, Harley-Davidson began marketing single-cylinder commercial motors called power units.

A caption from a 1930s *Enthusiast* reads: "The Special Delivery boys in East Liberty, PA, shoot the speedys straight with Harley-Davidson horsepower. The line-up shows the clan in low gear, clutches set, throttles throbbing. . .ready to GO PLACES."

Advertising materials were printed in many languages to promote Harley-Davidson.

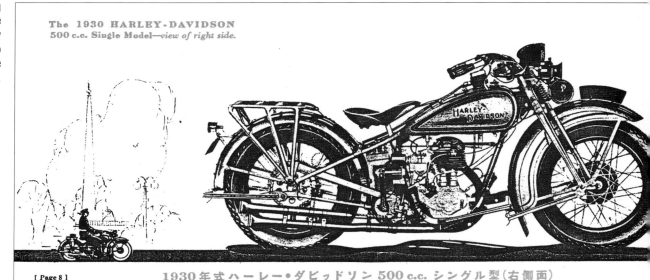

The 1930 HARLEY-DAVIDSON
500 c.c. Single Model—*view of right side.*

[Page 8]

1930年式ハーレー・ダビッドソン 500 c.c. シングル型（右側面）

114

DAVIDSON WINS "COW BELL CLASSIC"

The New American Motorcyclist and Bicyclist for October 1930, told how Bill Davidson was the winner in the Jack Pine Tour, nicknamed the "Cow Bell Classic." Entitled "Bill Davidson and the Cow Bell," the story read:

"Bill Davidson piled up a grand total of 997 points out of a possible 1,000 to win first honors in the annual 'Cow Bell Classic.' The individual class winners in the Jack Pine Tour were all Harley-Davidson mounted.

"Oscar Lenz, winner of the coveted bovine gong in 1923-25-26-27, gave Davidson a great battle for high honors. His score of 996 was good for second place in the Class A Solo, while his two brothers, also Harley-Davidson riders and boosters, were copping the gravy in their respective classes."

"Here we see the 1930 Jack Pine winner and his famous trophy. Bill is the son of William Davidson, vice-president and works manager of the Harley-Davidson Motor Company. In the face of the keenest competition, Bill came through to victory, putting his stock 45 through 420 miles of 'hell' in northern Michigan to win the Class A Solo event in this grueling two-day contest of brains and brawn."

THE NEW 1930 500 c.c. SINGLE MODEL

1930 年式 "500 c.c. シングル型"

小型 500 c.c. モーターも 750 c.c. 型と同様の改良を以て欧米同級車中の代表的單車乗用車として實に驚異的賞讚をうけて居ります。此の新型 500 c.c. のフレームは全く中型 750 c.c. のものと同型の低床式フレームにして新型フォークは自動的に發電出量を増加する新式ゼネレーターと共に、1930 年式 500 c.c. の主要特徴であります。尚モーターはリカルドー・ヘツド式を採用し、新型リム、大型バローン・タイヤ、獨特のハーレー・ダビツドソン・シート・ポスト、盗難防止装置、前方二聯式チェーン、自動給油装置等は何れも中型 750 c.c. 同様でありまして此等の理想的新設計によつて皆様は御愛乗に際し充分なる御滿足を御味ひになる事が出來ませう。

A January 1931 ad promoted Harley-Davidsons as the vehicle to help reduce auto accidents with police safety patrols.

To stimulate sales, Harley-Davidson embarked on an aggressive marketing campaign designed to turn its legion of riders into salespersons. Riders who convinced friends to buy Harley-Davidson motorcycles received bronze, silver or gold medals, with the best "salesperson" in the country receiving a large cash prize. A later contest similarly awarded points for each sale, which were redeemable for leather luggage, radios, movie cameras and other handsome prizes.

While always an important part of the business, commercial sales of Harley-Davidson motorcycles and products took on a heightened significance as quality, economy of operation and longevity of use became ever more important to Depression-stricken companies seeking to stretch their dollars. Drawing on its reputation as an air-cooled engine builder, Harley-Davidson reintroduced an industrial motor, or power unit, for commercial uses.

In late 1931, Harley-Davidson introduced the three-wheeled Servi-Car, intended primarily for use by garages and service stations for pickup and delivery of their customers' cars. With its economical 45 cubic inch engine, large capacity rear box and automotive-type rear differential, it was offered to the major automobile franchises as the ideal vehicle to service customers who were reluctant to drive to their local garage for work on their cars. A serviceman could ride to the customer's house on the Servi-Car, attach it to the rear bumper of the customer's car with a tow bar and drive back to

Mae West's feature film career, which often ran afoul of censors, began in the 1932 production of "Night After Night."

116

the garage. When the work was completed, the car was delivered, and the serviceman returned to work on the Servi-Car. A task normally undertaken by two men could now be done by one.

It was soon apparent that the Servi-Car was also an ideal vehicle for police departments. Because of its stability and ease of operation, it proved to be perfect for traffic control and enforcing parking restrictions and rapidly gained widespread acceptance.

Tame by today's standards, Boris Karloff's 1931 performance as the monster in "Frankenstein" shocked movie audiences.

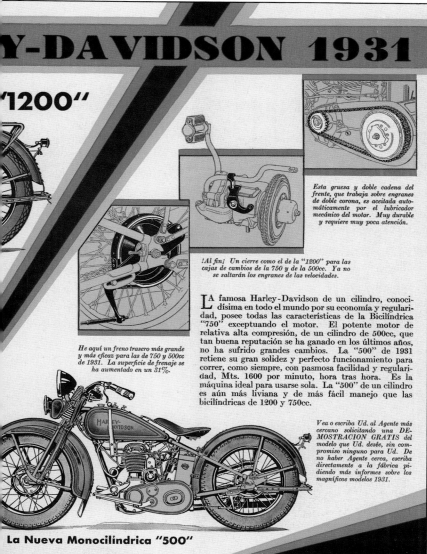

Esta gruesa y doble cadena del frente, que trabaja sobre engranes de doble corona, es aceitada automáticamente por el lubricador mecánico del motor. Muy durable y requiere muy poca atención.

¡Al fin! Un cierre como el de la "1200" para las cajas de cambios de la 750 y de la 500cc. Ya no se saltarán los engranes de las velocidades.

He aquí un freno trasero más grande y más eficaz para las de 750 y 500cc de 1931. La superficie de frenaje se ha aumentado en un 31%.

LA famosa Harley-Davidson de un cilindro, conocidísima en todo el mundo por su economía y regularidad, posee todas las características de la Bicilíndrica "750" exceptuando el motor. El potente motor de relativa alta compresión, de un cilindro de 500cc, que tan buena reputación se ha ganado en los últimos años, no ha sufrido grandes cambios. La "500" de 1931 retiene su gran solidez y perfecto funcionamiento para correr, como siempre, con pasmosa facilidad y regularidad, Mts. 1600 por minuto, hora tras hora. Es la máquina ideal para usarse sola. La "500" de un cilindro es aún más liviana y de más fácil manejo que las bicilíndricas de 1200 y 750cc.

Vea o escriba Ud. al Agente más cercano solicitando una DEMOSTRACION GRATIS del modelo que Ud. desée, sin compromiso ninguno para Ud. De no haber Agente cerca, escriba directamente a la fábrica pidiendo más informes sobre los magníficos modelos 1931.

La Nueva Monocilindrica "500"

Despite the company's best efforts, sales of new motorcycles continued to slip for the first several. years of the decade. With a surplus of cars on the market, a used Ford could be purchased for as low as $50, further eroding motorcycle sales. By 1933, industry-wide sales of motorcycles reached an all-time low of 6,000 units. Harley-Davidson produced 3,700 motorcycles that year, a far cry from only a few years earlier.

But Harley-Davidson has always been a resilient company. A policy in 1920 of teaching dealers how to advertise and promote their products, plus a total involvement in the sport, ranging from rider involvement programs to an aggressive stance on the marketing of parts and accessories, provided a substantial base to help the company through the lean years. Advertising in the *Enthusiast* magazine, and dealer ad slicks, promoted an extensive line of aftermarket products, from leather riding suits to luggage racks to motorcycle lubricants. In all instances, the company stressed the importance of using genuine Harley-Davidson parts, accessories and clothing, and in seeing a dealer for service.

Racing activities continued throughout the Depression, and names like Windy Lindstrom and Joe Petrali carried Harley-Davidson to victory time and time again. Racing was an inexpensive spectator sport that helped divert people's minds from the harsh realities of a depressed economy, and it was Harley-Davidson in the winner's circle that helped keep the loyalty of motorcycle enthusiasts intact.

Even though Harley-Davidson suffered a tremendous decrease in sales by 1933, it nonetheless tried to keep as many employees working as possible. Even if they only worked two days a week, they were still working while many Americans had no income at all.

The effects of the hard times were visibly apparent in the type and volume of advertising materials the company produced. In the Twenties, Harley-Davidson created large, colorful brochures, oftentimes with original paintings as illustrations. It was not unusual for several different brochures, all elaborate, to be produced in the same model year. In addition, large ads were carried in virtually every issue of every motorcycle magazine. By the Thirties, product literature had shrunk to little more than flyers with black and white or two-color illustrations. Even the amount of materials available for dealers shrank in volume compared to the previous decade. This was a bitter pill to swallow for a company that continually exhorted its dealers to promote their sport, their business and their products. Although reduced in scope, Harley-Davidson realized the value of advertising and continued it on a scale that was probably larger than sales justified at times. Obviously, they realized they were advertising for the future.

HARLEY-DAVIDSON
THE WORLD'S FINEST MOTORCYCLE

Above,
stars of the silver screen in the Thirties included Clark Gable, Gary Cooper, Cary Grant, Robert Taylor and Tyrone Power.

At left,
stars of the 1933 Harley-Davidson line were the new 74 Twin, 45 Twin, 30.50 Single, 21 Single and 74 Twin Sidecar.

119

1930

Ghandi's civil disobedience challenges British rulers.

More than 1,300 banks throughout U. S. shut down in economic crisis.

Oscar-winning movie "All Quiet on the Western Front" is released.

1931

Al Capone sentenced to 17 years for tax evasion.

U. S. unemployment estimated at four to five million.

New York's Empire State Building, world's tallest, opens.

1932

Amelia Earhart is first woman to fly solo across Atlantic.

Franklin D. Roosevelt elected president in Democratic landslide.

Charles Lindbergh Jr. kidnapped, later found dead.

1933

Prohibition recognized as a failure and repealed by 21st Amendment.

1934

Hitler becomes Fuhrer of Germany.

Joseph P. Kennedy named first chairman of Securities and Exchange Commission.

At the Depression's depth in 1933, Harley-Davidson made a radical departure from tradition, in both colors and tank graphics, in a further effort to stimulate sales. Gone were the block letters on an olive green background. They were replaced with Art Deco tank designs and vibrant new color options. Also available, for a $15 charge, was a chrome-plated package that included handlebars, chain guard, exhaust pipe and muffler, and several other major cosmetic pieces. Harley-Davidson had hit on the concept of factory custom parts and accessories.

By 1934, sales had climbed back to about 10,000 units, a number that would remain fairly consistent, year after year, to the end of the decade.

The Servi-Car quickly found acceptance among police departments as a practical and reliable traffic and parking enforcement tool.

Give 'em an "EAGLE EYE"!

Visibility—Unobstructed View—Uninterrupted Vision!

To the motorcycle officer, the boulevard ahead unfolds in an endless panorama. Side streets hold no secrets. No window frames to make him "lose" a car. No reason to rely on the "judgment" of a rear vision mirror . . . The motorcycle officer "sees all," and because he has full vision, he is a vitally important factor in traffic control — accident prevention — loss of life.

That's why we say — "give your traffic squad an eagle eye" — the latest Harley-Davidsons — with or without radios and sidecars. Sturdy, reliable, economical — the Harley-Davidson Police model has grown up with traffic control problems and is truly "The Police Motorcycle."

Ask your Harley-Davidson Dealer or write us for complete details and special Police literature.

HARLEY-DAVIDSON MOTOR CO.
Milwaukee, Wisconsin

HARLEY-DAVIDSON
The Police Motorcycle

TAKE TO THE OPEN ROAD

WITH A SONG in your HEART

WHEN springtime comes, be ready to take to the open road with a 1936 Harley-Davidson. Make every leisure hour a joy to be long remembered.

The new '36 models are something to get steamed up about. Motor improvements bring performance almost unbelievable. Balance that makes riding effortless. New streamlining, airplane-like in grace. Color combinations that fairly sparkle. The snappiest streamlined sidecar you ever saw. . . . All available in the 45's, 74's and a new 80 cubic inch Twin.

Don't wait. See your nearest Harley-Davidson dealer Now! Ask him for a Free Ride—let him explain his Easy Pay Plans—and send in the coupon.

MAIL THIS COUPON

Ride a **HARLEY-DAVIDSON**

HARLEY-DAVIDSON MOTOR CO.
Dept. P, Milwaukee, Wis. Send colorful folder illustrating and describing the 1936 model. Postage stamp is enclosed to cover cost of mailing.

Name.....
Address.....
My age is ☐ 16-19 years, ☐ 20-30 years, ☐ 31 years and up, ☐ under 16 years. Check your age group.

Harley-Davidson motorcycles were used as emergency firefighters by the U. S. Navy at Floyd Bennett Airport in New Jersey in the early Thirties.

Winners of first place in the Atlanta, Ga., 24-Hour Race. William Bracy, standing, and O. C. Hammond in the saddle of the stock 45 Harley-Davidson with which they piled up 1366 miles.

24 Hour Race won by HARLEY-DAVIDSON

Bert Baisden and his 1934 Harley-Davidson with which he and his team-mate scored second with a total of 1359 miles.

Third place winner, Jack Roberts, who with his relief rider, made a total of 1313 miles in the grind around the clock.

ATLANTA, Georgia, July 15—In one of the most grueling and hardest fought races ever staged in the history of motorcycling, Harley-Davidson riders captured the first five places in the 24-Hour Race held on the historic one-mile Lakewood dirt track.

William Bracy, piloting a '33 stock 45 Harley-Davidson and relief rider, O. C. Hammond, captured first place with the stupendous total of 1366 miles — an average of nearly 57 miles per hour. A close contender most of the race, Bert Baisden, on a '34 stock 45 Harley-Davidson and relief rider, Todd Haygood, rolled up 1359 miles. Jack Roberts, on a '33 stock 45, and Harley Taylor, as relief rider, came in third with 1313 miles. Lt. Ronnie Wilson of the Augusta, Ga., Police Department came in fourth and George Gunn, Atlanta, fifth.

A furious pace was set in the race right from the start. Baisden made the first one hundred miles in eighty-eight minutes. All the time these riders handled the throttle as though they were in a twenty-five mile race instead of a twenty-four hour grind. It was a marvelous exhibition of the ability of the riders and an outstanding demonstration of the staunchness and the stamina of the Harley-Davidson motorcycles.

HARLEY-DAVIDSON MOTOR CO.
MILWAUKEE, WISCONSIN, U. S. A.

RIDE A WINNER!

Child star, Shirley Temple, made over 25 movies in the Thirties, while sultry Jean Harlow made the cover of *Time*, captioned: "Feathers Make Fine Fans."

SERVI-CAR for 1934

The NEW DEAL Delivery Unit

WHY travel a ton of car or truck to deliver packages? SERVI-CAR will handle five-hundred pound loads at a fraction the cost of light trucks or autos

Ideal for druggists, merchants, and delivery services. Easily handled by anyone who can drive a car. Sturdy air-cooled motor and standard-differential rear axle. Speedy, rugged, distinctive.

Phone for our representative, or drop in. We are open evenings

HARLEY-DAVIDSON Motorcycles

Sport glasses "designed and made for motorcyclists" were among the many accessories, clothing, tools and dealers' supplies in the 1933 Harley-Davidson dealer catalog.

From left: Arthur Davidson, Walter Davidson, William Harley and William Davidson inspect one of the new 61 inch OHV ELs just coming off the assembly line.

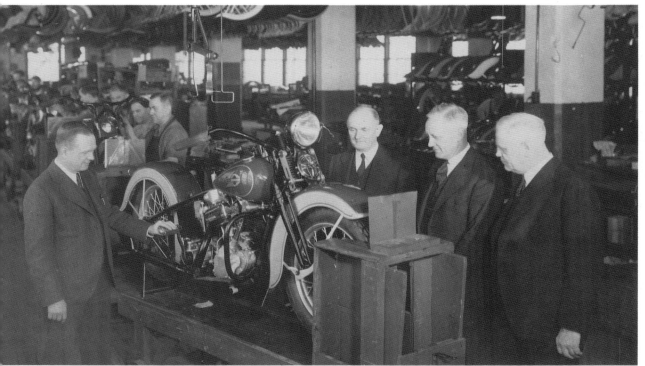

As money became increasingly more scarce, people were unable to buy motorcycles, and enthusiasts kept their interest alive by going to the races. As in most sports, a star soon rose to outshine all competitors.

Joe Petrali emerged in the Thirties as the one to beat in nearly all types of motorcycle competition, but few succeeded. Symbolic of his racing dominance was his outstanding performance on the mile and half-mile dirt tracks in 1935. A perennial crowd pleaser, Petrali handily won every National Dirt Track Championship that year, a total of 13 events, to mark the first time in history that one man and one brand of motorcycle had accomplished such a feat. In the process, he set four new A.M.A. records and was crowned the 1935 Dirt Track Champion. Rarely has one person dominated a sport as thoroughly, and as long, as Joe Petrali.

Joe Petrali is shown (clockwise, from upper left): on his 30.50 cubic inch Peashooter; demonstrating classic Petrali style with the rear tire off the ground of the rough track at Union, NJ; in a posed studio photo astride the record-setting Daytona bike; hitting the timer cord with his rear wheel as he clinched the 1935 hillclimbing title.

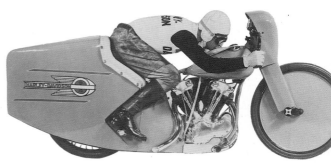

The Marx Brothers in "A Night at the Opera."

122

JOE PETRALI

Every sport has had its legendary heroes. Golf had Bobby Jones; boxing had Jack Dempsey; baseball had Babe Ruth; football had Red Grange; and car racing had many: Barney Oldfield, Ralph DePalma and Eddie Rickenbacker, to name a few. The sport of motorcycle racing had its own hero, as well, a star whose championship performances have never been matched and not even approached: Smokey Joe Petrali.

Joe Petrali was born in San Francisco on Washington's birthday, February 22, 1904. He first became attached to motorcycles at the early age of seven, when an adult neighbor allowed Joe to shine his early-day Flanders motorcycle. When Joe was 12, the neighbor let Joe solo on the Flanders, and Joe's love affair with motorcycles was torrid from that time on. He persuaded his father to let him acquire a used single-cylinder Indian, which Joe promptly converted and tuned for competition, and he enjoyed great success riding this machine in everything from gasoline economy runs to outlaw race meets in Northern California. Indeed, he was so good that soon he was invited to ride one of the Indian factory team's racing models on the board track at Fresno. Although Joe was only 16 years old, he finished a convincing second against the best factory riders in the sport at that time.

After this spectacular start, Joe bounced around for a time. While racing and working in cycle shops, he was always learning something new about engines and fuels. In addition, Joe had long been experimenting with alcohol and carburetion.

Then, on the 4th of July in 1925, on the board track at Altoona, Pennsylvania, it happened! Almost unknown in the east, Joe showed up a few days before the race as a member of the Indian factory team. Somehow, Petrali's Indian had gotten lost enroute, and he was without a mount. Then Ralph Hepburn, a Harley-Davidson team regular, broke his hand in a spill while practicing on his Harley-Davidson on the day before the big Independence Day race and wasn't able to ride. Petrali made a deal with Hepburn and showed up at the starting line on Hepburn's hastily repaired Harley-Davidson. The July 8, 1925 issue of *Motorcycling* magazine carried the race story under this title: "DARK HORSE WINS AT ALTOONA. PETRALI WHO CHANGED CAMPS WINS 100-MILE NATIONAL CHAMPIONSHIP. BOARD TRACK SPEED RECORDS SHATTERED."

Speed records were indeed shattered! Joe Petrali clipped an amazing 13-4/5ths seconds from the old record, and became the first rider to cover 100 miles in less than one hour in a motorcycle competition. Joe's time was 59:47-1/5, more than 100 miles per hour.

For the remainder of 1925, Petrali and his 1000cc flying Harley-Davidson continued to win and break records at super speeds, and at the year's end he was declared National Champion. However, before the year was over motorcycle racing underwent a momentous change with the introduction of a new 350cc class, which immediately became the favorite, because these tidy racers were made available to private buyers on an off-the-dealer's-floor basis. It marked the end of an era of costly super-factory teams, with a half dozen star riders on special racing machines and an army of mechanics for each team. However, it didn't end the super performances of a star like Petrali, who continued as a one-man team, briefly with a 350cc Excelsior in the late 1920s, and permanently with Harley-Davidson after 1930.

Throughout the early Thirties, Petrali successfully raced his 350cc Harley-Davidson Peashooter against other one-man teams on Indians and various British-powered 350s. Success piled on success, and in 1935 Petrali achieved the ultimate: he scored a grand slam by winning all of the 13 American Motorcycle Association National Championship dirt track races on his Harley-Davidson Peashooter, setting four new records in the process.

In 1937, on the beaches of Daytona, Florida, Petrali became the fastest man on two wheels, setting a blistering record speed of 136.183 mph on a specially streamlined Harley-Davidson powered by one of the new 61 cubic inch OHV V-twin engines. The same day he also set a similar record for 45 cubic inch motorcycles, also on a Harley-Davidson.

Always the consummate racer, Petrali was also a fierce competitor on the hillclimbing circuit, racking up national championship titles for five consecutive years, 1932 through 1936.

During 1938, motorcycle factory support of racing, which had already shrunk to almost nothing because of the continuing Depression, faded out completely. The days of the fast, reliable 350cc racing models and their crack riders came to an end, replaced by a new racing class and a new generation of riders. It was known as Class C, and provided for private owners to compete on stock 750cc road bikes.

In the years from 1925 to 1938, the swift and superb-handling 350cc Harley-Davidsons —along with similar Indians, Excelsiors and a variety of foreign-powered 350cc models —wrote thrilling motorcycle history. It was an epochal era that provided motorcycle racing fans with a great deal of pleasure and excitement.

Still at the peak of his career, Joe Petrali retired in 1938 to become the flight engineer and chief service and maintenance man for Howard Hughes. Petrali was on hand in 1947 when Hughes successfully, albeit briefly, flew his mammoth wood amphibian transport plane, dubbed the Spruce Goose. Later, he went on to become an official for the United States Auto Club and, fittingly, was the USAC timer who officially recorded Harley-Davidson's land speed record at Bonneville in October of 1970.

Following his successful record-shattering ride on the beach at Daytona, Petrali was greeted by well-wishers. William Harley is at left with the hat and glasses.

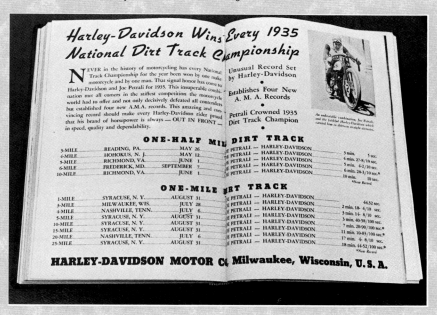

n September of 1935, Harley-Davidson announced its lineup of new models for the coming year. With the exception of the new 80 cubic inch side-valve model—including a high performance version capable of nearly 100 miles per hour—the line for 1936 reflected mainly refinements and improvements of the 1935 models, and, of course, carried new graphics.

The 1936 line did, however, have two striking new additions. In place of the long-used, speedboat-style sidecar was a redesigned sidecar body, which more accurately reflected the styling trends of the times. The side door had been eliminated and, in its place, a large step had been added for ease of entry. Richly grained black upholstery, large windshield, accent striping and stainless steel trim all served to make the 1936 sidecar a handsome complement to the new motorcycles.

The other addition to the line was the startling 61 cubic inch, overhead-valve model called the EL. It laid to rest the rumors which had circulated regarding the new engine Harley-Davidson was developing. Speculation had ranged from the downright amusing to the ridiculous, as people tried to guess what the new Harley would be.

FPG

Notorious criminal, John Dillinger, met his death while resisting arrest in 1934.

The 1936 EL model launched a
whole new generation of
Harley-Davidson motorcycles.

Inally, at the National Dealers' Convention in the fall of 1935, the EL was introduced with a caution to dealers that it would be a limited model, and they should concentrate on selling the rest of the line. In fact, the EL was put on the market with little promotional fanfare. At the time, the press felt that the EL was an experiment in marketing, although calculated and well-planned. Approximately 2,000 EL models were built for the 1936 model year.

In addition to the overhead-valve engine, which produced almost double the horsepower of the side-valve 61, this newest member of the Harley-Davidson family boasted a number of features not found on any of the other 1936 models. Cradling the engine was a double-loop, truss frame topped by a smoothly restyled, welded teardrop gas tank, shorter and more gracefully rounded. On top of the gas tank, a teardrop instrument cluster was mounted with an integrated speedometer and gauges. Nestled under a sleek wrap-around oil tank was a new hand-shift, four-speed transmission. The first oil circulation system also debuted on the EL. To one degree or another, all these features also found their way into most other models in the 1937 line.

The 1936 EL was a landmark motorcycle for Harley-Davidson because it proved to be the direct ancestor of the models being offered today. Many of the styling ideas and product features pioneered on the EL are used in varying forms on contemporary motorcycles. From the shape of the gas tanks to the wraparound oil tank, these are styling trends that have become synonymous with Harley-Davidson over the years and have indeed been copied extensively by competitive brands.

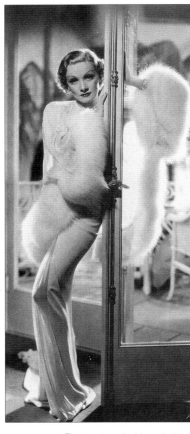

Marlene Dietrich, shown here in the 1936 production of "Desire," began her American film career in 1930 in "The Blue Angel."

The teardrop dashboard of the revolutionary 1936 EL model.

Florence Burnham, well-known speedboat racer, preferred a chrome and white 1936 Harley-Davidson EL when getting about on dry land.

1936 saw President Franklin Delanor Roosevelt re-elected to his second term.

FPG

Nelson Eddy and Jeanette MacDonald sang their way into the hearts of millions in "Rose Marie."

OFFICER DOTSON GETS HIS MEN!

That was the caption of a May 1935 Harley-Davidson *Enthusiast* article, telling how "Courageous motorcycle officer William Dotson of Savannah, Georgia, single-handedly captures four escaped convicts," and emphasized: "Fellow officers mighty proud of Dotson."The story, reproduced exactly as written, continued:

"Midnight! On the Coastal Highway near Savannah, Motorcycle Officer W. Dotson, acting on a hot tip, crouches over the bars of his trusty Harley-Davidson in the shadows of a wayside filling station. Serious business ahead tonight. Four escaped convicts, heavily armed, are reported heading in Dotson's direction in a high-powered, stolen car. Dotson has not long to wait.

"Far down the road a low hum gradually grows to an angry roar—Dotson tenses himself—that roar means something. No ordinary motorist would take a chance here at that speed. Suddenly the roar dies down, and the driver evidently is about to stop for gasoline. Dotson and the convicts see each other at the same instant. Gears clash as the car, a late model V-8 of popular make, plunges forward into the darkness with Dotson in hot pursuit of the fleeing prisoners.

"Faster and still faster speeds the car, but Dotson, with siren screeching, begins closing in. For five miles the chase continues towards Savannah. The speeding car reaches 76 miles an hour but

otson, cool and calculating, lets the driver go until the Savannah city limits come into sight. Dotson pulls his service revolver and bangs e rear tire.Then he swings alongside the driver and forces the car over to the curb at gunpoint. He disarms the convicts; two of them ved their striped shirts to avoid suspicion. He confiscates an axe, a pistol and a double-barreled, hammerless shotgun loaded with Two of the convicts are still wearing shackles.

me other motorcycle officers arrive. Excited motorists crowd around—at a safe distance. The four prison-breakers are taken to the barracks and held until they can be returned to their Lanier County prison cells.

necessary here to point out the details leading to the prison break nor how the car was commandeered by the desperate criminals in dash to freedom. The fact which stands out in the whole thrilling encounter is Officer Dotson's personal bravery and courage. Under disadvantageous circumstances, he chose to perform his duty and to protect the residents of Savannah, knowing as he did that the were well armed. To Officer William Dotson, who typifies the spirit of the motorcycle patrol, we take off our hats. He's a man. A real believe no finer tribute can be paid him. But aside from Dotson's fine job, there was another factor—something so important that Dotson could not have made his great capture—we mean his dependable Harley-Davidson, a 1934VLD. In the great test, when Dotson erfect, unfailing performance his trusty machine responded. And so, once more we salute Officer Dotson and his motorcycle.

In order to prove the power and performance of the new engine—subsequently dubbed the "Knucklehead" because of the configuration of its rocker boxes, Harley-Davidson headed down to the beaches of Daytona in March of 1937 for an assault on the world one-mile straightaway speed record. Limited to engines of no more than 61 inches, the record of 132 miles per hour had stood since 1926. Factory engineer, Harvey Syvertson, showed up with the curiously streamlined Harley-Davidson machine for which Joe Petrali, not surprisingly, had been selected as rider.

With a disc front wheel, streamlined forks, front cowl and fully enclosed rear body, the "Knucklehead" represented the first use of streamlining in the United States. Equipped with one carburetor for each cylinder, the V-twin was fueled by a mixture of alcohol and benzoyl, producing a whopping 65 horsepower at 5,700 rpm.

After a few days of untimed practice runs, Petrali and the streamliner rolled onto the sand on March 13. It was soon discovered that the rear streamlined tail produced a high-speed wobble, so it was removed for the event. To qualify for a record, two one-way passes were required to neutralize any effects the wind would have on speed. Joe roared down the beach, and on the return run, his speed was sufficient to set a record of 134.83 mph.

Next, he mounted a 45 cubic inch *un*streamlined Harley-Davidson and set a new record of 102.04 mph for that class. Returning to the pits, he said: "I'd like to take another shot with that 61. There's still more in it." And the streamlined motorcycle was rolled out for another two-way run, this time aiming at his own newly established mark. When the sand settled, Joe Petrali had added one more triumph to his long list of accomplishments by establishing a still higher record speed of 136.183 miles per hour.

Mickey Rooney and Judy Garland teamed up for many musicals beginning in the Thirties.

The 1936 61 cubic inch overhead valve engine quickly earned the nickname of "Knucklehead" because of the rounded shapes of the polished rocker boxes atop the heads.

FPG

FPG

Hindenburg disaster, May 6, 1937.

When Douglas "Wrong Way" Corrigan, famed flyer who flew solo from the U. S. to Ireland, visited Milwaukee in 1938, he was escorted by a group of Harley-Davidson police motorcycles and enthusiastically welcomed by thousands. Seeing the 61 inch OHV Harley-Davidsons everywhere he went, former Harley owner Corrigan was prompted to seek a ride on one of the new 1938 models.

Fred Astaire and Ginger Rogers made a perfect dance team in Hollywood musicals.

All-around athlete, Olympic champion and pro golfer, Babe Didrikson Zaharias.

FPG

Just one month later, a cloud was cast over the jubilation at Harley-Davidson when William A. Davidson, vice president and co-founder of the company, passed away on April 21, 1937. Much respected in the industry and well liked by all who knew him, his loss was sorely felt.

Continuing the policy of evolution and refinement, the Harley-Davidson line received updates and improvements late in the decade that enhanced its attractiveness and performance. Rather than making radical changes, the company chose to improve and refine its established products. By 1939, the Harley-Davidson lineup was clearly the most popular in the country. By the end of the Thirties, fully 67 percent of all the motorcycles registered in the U.S. were Harleys.

Like much of the nation, the company had faced the toughest times in its history. And through innovation, sound marketing and solid leadership, Harley-Davidson—while not unscathed—had emerged as the strongest, most popular motorcycle manufacturer in the country.

At a time when the Soviet Union was a large purchaser of Harley-Davidson motorcycles, two young members of the Leningrad Motor Club visited the Milwaukee factory. In the background, left to right: Arthur Davidson, B. H. Bellenson, Walter Davidson and William S. Harley. On December 15, "Gone With the Wind" premiered in Atlanta, Georgia.

IS VIVIEN LEIGH A REAL-LIFE SCARLET

WILLIAM A. DAVIDSON

While William Davidson may have been the last of the four founders of Harley-Davidson to join the initial venture, he brought to the little company a wealth of experience and judgment that went far to assure its future success. As a skilled mechanic, he had been the toolroom foreman at the Milwaukee shops of what later became the Chicago, Milwaukee, St. Paul and Pacific Railroad. He was already a family man, and even the automotive industry provided an uncertain future in those days. But the concept of building a newer form of gasoline propelled transportation intrigued him, and he joined his brothers and William Harley with a dedication for the project, which would become the joy and commitment of his life's work.

As works manager, his desk was always piled high with parts from various stages of the manufacturing process: a semi-finished hub, bearing, shaft or rod. He knew the steel from which it was made, the processes it had undergone and those which were necessary for completion. His was the responsibility of purchasing presses and the other equipment needed to continually improve the manufacturing process, as well as meeting the rapidly growing demand for production of Harley-Davidson motorcycles.

Yet, he was not one to allow his fascination with the technical processes of manufacturing to isolate him from his fellow man. William Davidson was known for his compassion for others, particularly employees who needed advice or a helping hand from time to time. From machinists to dealers, bankers to politicians, he was willing to share his time. And while many people say their door is always open, William A Davidson not only said it but lived by that credo. Well respected throughout the community, he passed away April 21, 1937, at the age of 66.

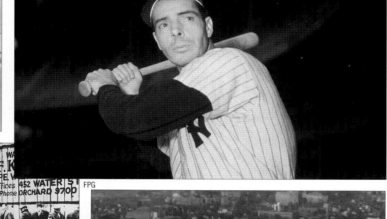

FPG

Clockwise from upper left: symbol of the National Recovery Act; the stars of MGM's "Wizard of Oz"; FDR on the cover of *Vanity Fair*; a Harley-Davidson "lucky charm"; Joltin' Joe DiMaggio; the New York World's Fair; Jesse Owens; Bette Davis; signs of hard times; bank robbers Bonnie and Clyde; and a Servi-Car on the job in Hackensack, New Jersey.

This Immense Plant is Devoted Exclusively to the Manufacture of Harley-Davidson Motorcycles

THE 1940'S

To War Once More

THE 1940'S

"**A**s 1940 looms ahead and we stand on the threshold of a new season," reads a 1940 Harley-Davidson news bulletin, "it is not amiss to recall that the public does not bestow its favor upon a product by whim or fancy. Only an article of superior value and outstanding merit can hope to win buyer approval year after year. But this favor has imposed an obligation. That which would be passably good is not good enough for the motorcycles bearing our nameplate. It is this challenge that spurs the Harley-Davidson organization to build better and still better.

"Supplied with the latest and best in manufacturing equipment, fortified by ample capital, directed by men of vision and long experience, we can confidently draw back the curtain on Harley-Davidson's offering for 1940.

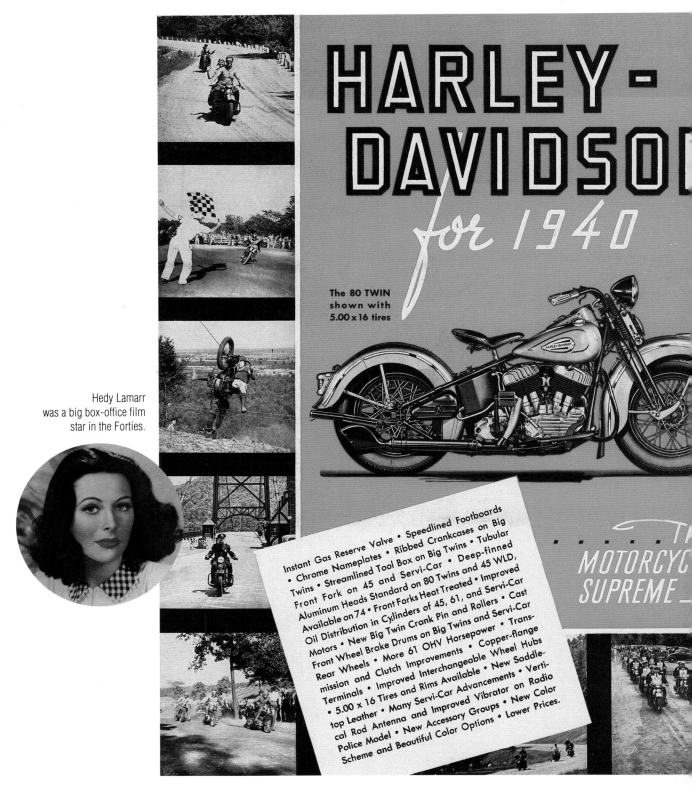

Hedy Lamarr was a big box-office film star in the Forties.

HARLEY-DAVIDSON for 1940

The 80 TWIN shown with 5.00 x 16 tires

THE MOTORCYCLE SUPREME

Instant Gas Reserve Valve • Speedlined Footboards • Chrome Nameplates • Ribbed Crankcases on Big Twins • Streamlined Tool Box on Big Twins • Tubular Front Fork on 45 and Servi-Car • Deep-finned Aluminum Heads Standard on 80 Twins and 45 WLD, Available on 74 • Front Forks Heat Treated • Improved Oil Distribution in Cylinders of 45, 61, and Servi-Car Motors • New Big Twin Crank Pin and Rollers • Cast Front Wheel Brake Drums on Big Twins and Servi-Car Rear Wheels • More 61 OHV Horsepower • Transmission and Clutch Improvements • Copper-flange Terminals • Improved Interchangeable Wheel Hubs • 5.00 x 16 Tires and Rims Available • New Saddle-top Leather • Many Servi-Car Advancements • Vertical Rod Antenna and Improved Vibrator on Radio Police Model • New Accessory Groups • New Color Scheme and Beautiful Color Options • Lower Prices.

"In a sweep of the eye we can see that these 1940 Harley-Davidsons are NEW! They are distinct, different, streamlined, and breathe the spirit of speed and power."

On this upbeat note, Harley-Davidson launched the decade of the Forties with a renewed sense of optimism. It had survived the previous decade, which had proved so devastating to so many companies, to release the most advanced, powerful and attractive line in its history. In addition to the well-accepted 61 inch OHV, the line now boasted increased power for the 80, 74 and 45 cubic inch models by virtue of deeply-finned aluminum heads that dramatically improved cooling, reduced weight, and provided greater power and performance.

Cosmetically, the new models received semicircular floorboards and a streamlined tool box, both still popular today, plus a stylish metal name-plate and optional 5" x 16" balloon tires and rims. Reflecting the growing militarism of the times, the 1940 models were offered in five colors, with names like Flight Red, Clipper Blue and Squadron Gray.

Police business continued to be a large part of Harley-Davidson's market in 1940, with over 3,500 cities using their products. Motorcycle clubs were also becoming more and more popular, with many members attending large rallies and meets, where they paraded their riding skills and elaborate uniform styles. For many years, Harley-Davidson accepted motorcycle clubs' ideas or sketches and produced custom embroidered emblems to be sewn on uniforms, shirts or jackets.

FPG

...cycle mounted officers exemplify the spirit of public service. They are real ...ians of life and property. Motorists ...destrians alike respect their presence. ... prevent accidents and tragedies. ...are "Sentinels of Safety" whose alert-... and efficiency in solving countless

traffic problems build public confidence for police departments. It is significant that an overwhelming majority of the nation's motorcycle officers are mounted on dependable Harley-Davidson Police Motorcycles ... Have your dealer bring over a 1940 model for your inspection.

HARLEY-DAVIDSON MOTOR COMPANY, *Milwaukee, Wisconsin*

137

radually, events in other parts of the world came to have an impact on Harley-Davidson and, indeed, the nation at large. Japan's aggression in Asia, and especially Hitler's actions in Europe, awakened Americans to the necessity of preparing for eventual war. The German Panzer divisions' startling success in smashing through the French Army in 1940 gave renewed importance to the mechanization of the U. S. Army.

In the newly formed U. S. armored divisions, motorcycle reconnaissance units were created to probe for enemy traps, mines and ambushes; secure

Chrome nameplates of sweeping design were featured in the 1940 Harley-Davidson line, which included (clockwise from upper left): the 61 OHV Twin, 74 Twin, 80 Twin and 45 Twin.

bridges; and establish forward positions for each division's 400 tanks and 300 scout cars. To meet this need, the Army ordered steadily increasing numbers of 45 WLA Harley-Davidsons, the military version of the 45 WLD model, and other military branches also followed suit.

As England and Russia came under the onslaught of Germany's military might, their motorcycle industries were converted to the production of war-time materials. To round out the military units of our essential Allies and relieve their beleaguered industries, Harley-Davidson motorcycles were shipped to both countries and gratefully accepted.

FPG

FPG

At the end of 1940, with America not yet directly involved in the war, Harley-Davidson announced the new 1941 model line with a 74 cubic inch version of the EL model as flagship. Like other 1941 models, the mighty 74 offered a number of improvements, including a more efficient oil pump, a better clutch, an easier-to-read speedometer and, of course, new color options.

Conditions deteriorated around the globe and friendly countries grew scarce. America offered more support to its Allies and the likelihood of going to war increased. More and more of Harley-Davidson's production was siphoned for military or police use, and raw materials became harder to find. Unable to get enough civilian motorcycles to meet their needs, dealers were urged to sell additional machines to the police, citing the need for increased protection at vital defense industries. Harley-Davidson also continued a high level of advertising to local police forces, both to support national defense and bolster dealers' sales efforts.

The availability of civilian motorcycles decreased and racing activities were curtailed. Club events became more important to the sport. In the *Enthusiast*, the free magazine published by Harley-Davidson, more clubs were featured in an effort to keep motorcycling interest alive. In October 1941, an all-women motorcycle organization, called the Motor Maids, was formed as an auxiliary of the American Motorcyclist Association, acquainting the public with the fact that motorcycles could be handled safely and properly by female riders.

Genuine Harley-Davidson Oil was promoted in this 1940 poster.

Glenn Miller's unique style was making a strong impact on popular music.

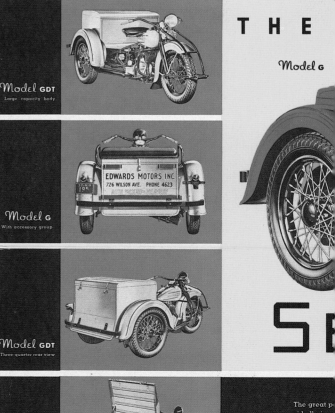

Enjoy Motorcycling More

With

HARLEY-DAVIDSON ACCESSORIES

Everything for the Motorcyclist
APPROVED MOTORCYCLE ACCESSORIES
for 1940

IF YOUR DEALER CANNOT SUPPLY YOU . . . WRITE DIRECT TO

HARLEY-DAVIDSON MOTOR CO.
MILWAUKEE, WISCONSIN, U.S.A.

IN U. S. DOLLARS F. O. B. MILWAUKEE, WIS., U. S. A. ALL DUTIES, TAXES, TRANSPORTATION, EXTRA.
QUOTED SUBJECT TO CHANGE WITHOUT NOTICE

HARLEY-DAVIDSON

I-CAR....

Servi-Car with automotive establishments everywhere is based on its ability to de-
...uce greater profits. By building greater volume it increases revenue from every
...nd service facilities. It saves rent and storage space by solving the pressing prob-
...n serviced. Through promotion efforts it will help iron out the slack and rush
...ote shop efficiency. Out on the streets, it gives you splendid advertising that
...per or billboard space. Running cost is unbelievably low, only one man is required
...car can handle it. The convenience it affords customers builds good will and in-
...n your business will prove one of the most profitable investments you ever made.

A 32-page catalog
offered "everything
for the motorcyclist"
in Harley-Davidson
accessories.

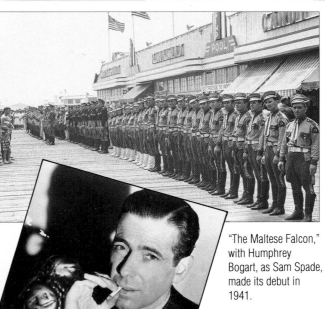

Motorcycle clubs
often sported
striking uniforms,
as evidenced by this
gathering in 1941 at
Seaside Heights,
New Jersey.

"The Maltese Falcon,"
with Humphrey
Bogart, as Sam Spade,
made its debut in
1941.

NORTH AFRICAN DESERT PATROL

By Edward Duncan

A Long Range Desert Group of the Middle East Forces lines up for inspection. The men wear the Arab headdress, a necessary piece of equipment for all who must battle the rigors of the desert. Author Duncan is at the right, nearest the camera.

When I arrived in the Middle East in February of 1940, I little dreamed that I would be assigned to the task of leading patrols and doing dispatch riding for our forces on a Harley-Davidson motorcycle. That same summer, the L.R.D.G. (Long Range Desert Group) was being formed in Cairo. An L.R.D.G. patrol consists of one officer and about fifteen men in five or six motor vehicles. From the beginning, it was clear that navigation on the desert would be a full-time job which the patrol commander could not undertake in addition to his other work, and therefore, it was necessary that each patrol have an official navigator, either an N.C.O. or a Private.

Within the frontiers of Egypt, desert navigation presented no problems, because we were in the possession of fairly good maps. But the maps of the Libyan Desert, beyond the Egyptian border, presented another problem. Naturally, there were no roads but vast stretches of sand for hundreds of miles, from the Egyptian border to the Mediterranean Coast of Libya.

And that is where desert navigation came into the picture. The L.R.D.G. was faced with the task of teaching new navigators, and it took time to train these men. Navigation instruments were hard to obtain as desert navigation is entirely different from sea navigation. The need for navigation, however, as distinct from map reading, came about from the nature of the country.

The interior of Libya in which the L.R.D.G. operated is the most deserty desert in the world—arid and featureless to a degree which the dweller in a northern climate can hardly appreciate. If you were to eliminate rain, you would also remove the natural landmarks by which the inhabitant of Europe or America, with map in hand, could find his way over the country, across streams, lakes, hedges, woods, rivers and valleys. The man-made landmarks—such as roads, villages, towns, railroads and canals—depend directly or indirectly on water for their existence. Thousands of years of heat, cold, wind and blowing sand have formed the desert landscape, smoothing down the features of the past geological eras into vast plains of sand and gravel for hundreds of miles, until it looks like a sea of sand over which movement by patrol trucks in any direction is very restricted. Lack of landmarks compels the deep-sea mariner to rely on sun, stars, compass and log to show him where he is. In the desert, almost equally devoid of recognizable features, the sand sailor must use the same methods. As I have already said, navigation instruments were hard to obtain, so I used to ride on ahead of the patrols for hundreds of miles guided only by a wrist compass which was very much in error. But the speed and distance I could cover on my Harley-Davidson 61 OHV enabled me to make up for such errors, something which a patrol truck could not do. With the kind permission of *Enthusiast* readers, I would like to recall some of my desert experiences with the hope that they may prove interesting.

Among the greatest terrors of the desert are the sandstorms, often called Khamseens, averaging about fifty per month. I always carried at least six pairs of goggles. During a sandstorm, the sand was blown at such an intensity that it penetrated the glasses, rendering them useless. I had a light canvas cover over the engine to keep the sand out of the carburetor, but on top of the fuel tank, it was never unusual to see about two inches of sand. The heat, on an average, was about 142 degrees in the shade. I always left the sand on the fuel tank to prevent the sun from beating down directly on it. I often used to wonder why my spare two gallons of gas which I carried did not catch fire.

One patrol took me into the interior of the Gilf Kebir and into the still little known Eghei Mountains between the Kufra Oases and Tibesti where, as far as I know, not more than a dozen white men have ever been. This region of the desert is still unexplored. I passed through this section at night, and when I laid down to sleep beside my faithful Harley-Davidson, I used to look at my mount and think of what would happen to me if it had broken down, for I was at least four or five hundred miles from civilization. I carried only one water bottle and army rations.

On numerous occasions, I have ridden down sandy slopes for 15 or 20 miles without using any gas whatsoever. As I rode through this blazing inferno, I thought about the people in the United States, for instance, who die from heat waves when the thermometer barely gets over 100 degrees. Here the heat was so intense, I had to wear gloves to prevent my hands from blistering on the handlebars. My shirt had a white coating of salt on it formed by perspiration. You can thus imagine how much I loved my old faithful Harley-Davidson because of the terrific heat and sand it was going through and how it stood up after endless hours of grueling riding. And even though I loved her, I never spared her one bit when it came to the business of pushing on day after day through the scorching sea of sand.

From that hell on earth, I eventually arrived in Alexandria, Egypt, several hundred miles away, and then on to Cairo, another 250 miles. After what I had been through, the temperature was most pleasant and the riding was excellent. Shortly thereafter, I left Cairo for Alexandria again and then I had to journey by water over to Piraeus in Greece when we went to help the Greeks. From Piraeus, I rode through to Mount Olympus in extreme cold and deep snow, and then across the Thessaly Plains to Larissa where General Freyberg, in command of the G.O.C.N.Z. Troops, had his headquarters at that time. From there, I rode through a railroad town called Trikkala, which at that time was occupied by the Germans. I never discovered it until I was half way through. Without warning, the German motorcyclists got after me in a hurry. I made up my mind not to be captured, although my map showed that I would have to ride through a mile-high pass near Metsovo, in and across the Pindus Mountains along a rough Greek road. A blinding snowstorm was raging at the time. How far the Germans followed me, I do not know because I soon lost them. But I am sure they must have sent a radio message to other German motorcyclists near the pass. As I arrived at the pass, I noticed that the road sloped downward in the direction I was going, so I shut off the motor of my Harley-Davidson and was nearly through the pass when the Germans got after me again. By their uniforms, I could see that they belonged to the Adolf Hitler Division of the Elite Guards. They were on motorcycles and immediately it became a battle of motorcycles. A few shots were fired at me but took no effect. And then began a grueling race over a very rough road to Lamia, the gate to the mountain pass of Thermopylae where the Germans hoped to cut me off. But they only wasted their time, for the wonderful power I had under me and the ability of my dependable Harley-Davidson to stand up to the terribly rough roads brought me through safely. Much of the time during that wild chase I was fairly bouncing out of the saddle.

After leaving the pass behind, I followed the road down the mountainside to a shallow river which had about a foot of water in it with the river bed full of gravel. I managed to slip and slide across to the road on the opposite shore which I then followed until I came to the foot of Salamis. From Salamis I got my Harley-Davidson back to Alexandria in Egypt. I went on to Cairo, another 250 miles, and was in time to see Captain James Roosevelt fly his plane over our base camp and Maadi.

Then I went into action with our troops when we entered Fort Capuzzo and then on to the Mediterranean port of Bardia where I was taken prisoner for six weeks by the Italians. They abused my faithful Harley-Davidson something terrible. When I was recaptured again by our own troops, I got my dear old faithful Harley-Davidson back once more. Although she had had a rough spin of it, I had no trouble in getting her going again. From Bardia, I went on, still following the troops to Sidi Azeiz, Sidi Omar and Sidi Rezegh.

This is all barren desert up the coast and hundreds of miles inland all the way to Tripoli and Algiers. After Sidi Rezegh I went on to Gambut, which we captured, then to Bel Hammed, Bir Hachiem, Tobruk, Derna, Sollum and Bengasi, then through the Halfaya Pass, called Hell-fire Pass by our troops because it has a blistering heat of 150 degrees in the shade and is covered with loose gravel and boulders varying in size from 6 inches to 2 feet in diameter. It is several miles in length, and it is painful even to look at. As a matter of fact, it looks well nigh impossible for a man to pass through, let alone a motorcycle. But when I got going on my faithful Harley-Davidson, she took it all right, although she bucked and jumped and turned around to go back to where she had come from.

After going through Halfaya Pass, I went back to the base again for a rest. I also gave my Harley-Davidson an overhaul. Most of the paint had worn off of her and the engine looked as if it was overheated, for it had already done thousands of miles. But when I started it again, I had no trouble. Then when we started our big offensive at El Alamien to drive the enemy out of Africa, I was up there again as usual. She was still going extremely well as I followed the troops' advance right on up to Bengasi. From there I went on to Tripoli and then to Gaves. Several miles farther on, I entered the town of Sfax, and about 30 miles farther, I reached Kairwan, a few miles from Sidi Ahmed Airdrome, then in enemy hands. After we had driven them out of the airdrome, with the help of your P-38s and B-25s, a few miles farther on, I entered Ferryville. Then, after more severe fighting, we entered Tunis and Bizerte where we finally had the Germans run out of Africa. From Bizerte, I went over the road through mountains to Tebourba where I met an American, Colonel Zanuck, who was watching a tank battle taking place between your troops and the Huns. The climb was about 6,000 feet above sea level.

Unlike most military motorcycle riders who rode the side-valve 45WLA Harley-Davidson, Edward Duncan used a 61 OHV Model, like this one, equipped with a sidecar.

From Tebourba, I went on farther to Bone, at which place your troops landed. From Bone I began my return journey. Before I started, I patted the tanks of my faithful Harley-Davidson and said, "Look here, old girl, we have a long way to go—possibly 3,500 miles or more. I am confident you will carry me through to safety." It was a long and tough ride but without driving her, I did it in about 16 days, thanks to the wonderful motor itself and the lighting system, even though the roads were terribly bad. I found the twin headlamps far better than a single one for night riding in a continent like Africa where a man might make a slip and shoot over a precipice.

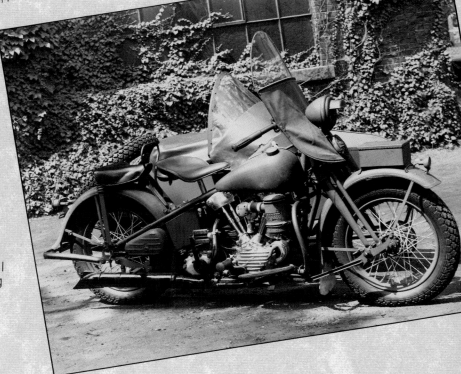

And that about winds up in a general way my experiences in North Africa on a Harley-Davidson. Some day I hope to come to the United States and see the place where these wonderful machines are made. That 61 OHV Harley-Davidson that I rode surely did its share for our Middle East Forces and aided materially in helping our forces eventually drive the enemy completely out of Africa.

War now seemed inevitable and production was devoted almost totally to the defense effort. The company discontinued plant tours in November. By December 7, 1941, when the Japanese Imperial Navy launched its sneak attack on Pearl Harbor, Harley-Davidson was building a motorcycle every five minutes. America was completely in the war, and so was Harley-Davidson.

In many ways, Harley-Davidson was fortunate in providing motorcycles for the armed services. By producing motorcycles instead of tanks or machine guns, all the manufacturing processes were kept intact, which ensured more rapid conversion to civilian production at the war's end. It also guaranteed a constant, although limited, supply of spare parts for civilian use. And, the extensive military use of Harley-Davidson motorcycles familiarized tens of thousands of riders with the company's products. In this instance, familiarity bred affection.

During the war, Harley-Davidson produced approximately 90,000 WL military models in various configurations, for use on virtually every front. It was reported in 1945 that the Russian Army utilized 30,000 Harley-Davidson motorcycles in advancing through Eastern Germany toward Berlin. Surprisingly, the Russians chose to copy the German BMW after the war and produced it for decades after.

World War II was also responsible for another unique Harley-Davidson twin. It was called the XA, and displaced 45 cubic inches. What made it unique was the configuration of the twin cylinders: the XA was a horizontally-opposed flat twin and the only shaft-drive Harley-Davidson ever produced. It was designed for use by the Allies in North African desert warfare, since sand had a nasty tendency to devour chains and sprockets. However, only 1,000 were produced before that phase of the war was over. Throughout the war, the Harley-Davidson banner would be carried by the popular, olive-drab 45 WLA models, which consistently proved up to the task.

A horizontally-opposed, shaft-drive Model XA was developed for waging desert warfare.

Greta Garbo retired from the screen after *Two-Face Woman*.

FPG

HARLEY-DAVIDSON
★ MOTOR CYCLES ★

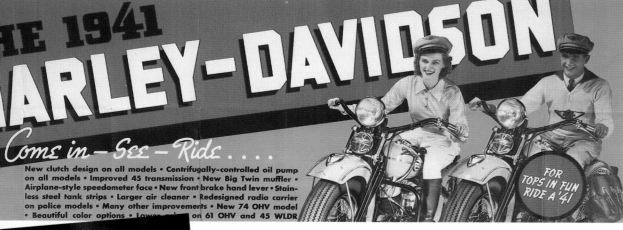

THE 1941 HARLEY-DAVIDSON

Come in — See — Ride....

New clutch design on all models • Centrifugally-controlled oil pump on all models • Improved 45 transmission • New Big Twin muffler • Airplane-style speedometer face • New front brake hand lever • Stainless steel tank strips • Larger air cleaner • Redesigned radio carrier on police models • Many other improvements • New 74 OHV model • Beautiful color options • Lower price on 61 OHV and 45 WLDR

FOR TOPS IN FUN RIDE A '41

Above, top to bottom: Pearl Harbor attack; FDR declares war; Army-Navy award to Harley-Davidson for exceptional performance in production of war materials; 1941 announcement banner; singer/film star, Deanna Durbin.

1940

President Roosevelt elected to unprecedented third term.

America prepares for war with first peacetime draft.

Estonia, Latvia and Lithuania annexed by U.S.S.R.

1941

Japan attacks Pearl Harbor, U.S. tools up for war production.

Ford signs first labor union contract.

Ted Williams hits .406 season batting average; Joe DiMaggio hits safely in 56 consecutive games.

FDR declares Four Freedoms essential: freedom of speech and religion, freedom from want and fear.

1942

First nuclear chain reaction demonstrated at University of Chicago.

Battle of Midway is Japan's first major defeat.

U.S. and British troops invade North Africa; Marines land in Guadalcanal.

1943

Rationed items include shoes, canned goods, meat, cheese, gasoline, sugar, others.

Mussolini deposed; U. S. troops invade Italy.

1944

Allies launch invasion of Europe at Normandy on D-Day, June 6.

President Roosevelt wins re-election to fourth term.

At home, the nation and Harley-Davidson adjusted to a wartime mode, as concessions were made in everyday life. The service school was transformed into the Quartermaster School for exclusive training of military mechanics. In 1942, the Daytona 200 Mile Race was suspended for the duration of the war. Aluminum for pistons became scarce, and dealers had to turn in old pistons before Harley-Davidson could get their equivalent weight to make new ones. Containers for liquids, like oil, were converted from metal to glass. Shop tools and chains were scarce, and dealers were asked to return empty oil drums to Harley-Davidson so they could be reused. Like the rest of the country, Harley-Davidson learned to cope with shortages.

From top, counterclockwise: The Service School taught military personnel the mechanics of Harley-Davidson motorcycles; Americans being sworn into service; women replacing men in defense plants inspire the song "Rosie the Riveter"; Harley-Davidson in the Army.

FPG

FPG

146

Gasoline was not only rationed, it was hard to find.

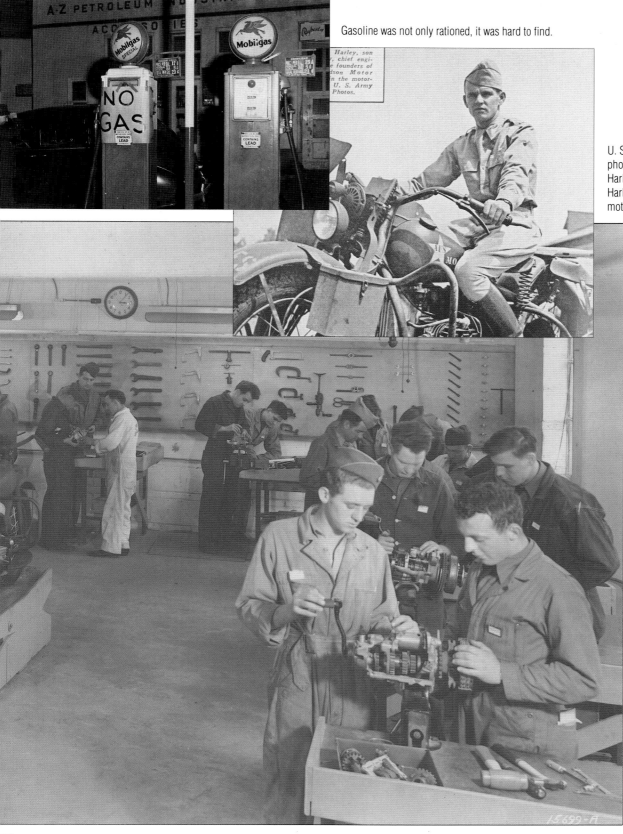

U. S. Army Signal Corps photo shows Lt. John E. Harley, son of William S. Harley, as an officer in the motorcycle department.

Far left: WWII cartoon.
Left: All-time classic "Casablanca" with Bergman and Bogart debuted in 1942.

O n top of the terrors and hardships of all-out war, personal tragedy struck closer to home in February 1942 with the death of Company President, Walter Davidson. He was succeeded by William H. Davidson, who previously served as a vice president. A year and a half later, William S. Harley also passed away. Of the four founders, only Arthur Davidson remained.

WALTER DAVIDSON

Early in life, Walter Davidson learned his trade as a machinist, working in railroad shops in Milwaukee and other cities. After lending his talents to help build the first Harley-Davidson back in 1903, it wasn't long before the demand for additional motorcycles convinced him to give up his work with the railroad and devote his full time to the young but growing Harley-Davidson Motor Company.

From building motorcycles to riding them was a short step for Walter Davidson, who soon became one of the most enthusiastic competition riders. In 1908, he was awarded a diamond medal by the Federation of American Motorcyclists for his winning score in the greatest endurance run of that day, made with a single-cylinder Harley-Davidson. The course of the two-day classic started from Catskill, N.Y., went on to Brooklyn, and around Long Island. Shortly thereafter, he established an economy record at Roslyn, Long Island, N.Y., covering fifty miles of hilly road on one quart and one ounce of gasoline. His competition achievements and many victories on hill, road and track did much to bring Harley-Davidson national recognition.

From the twin viewpoints of being a skilled machinist and a competitive rider, Walter Davidson always insisted on the importance of the highest quality standards in Harley-Davidson motorcycles. In later years, he was widely recognized for his expertise in business and, at his death, he was a trustee of the Northwestern Mutual Life Insurance Company, and was a director of the Milwaukee Gas Light Company.

WILLIAM S. HARLEY

At the age of 15, William Harley started work in a Milwaukee bicycle factory and soon became a draftsman. He and his boyhood friend and neighbor, Arthur Davidson, became dedicated to the development of a motor-driven bicycle for their own use. Combined with the expertise of Arthur's brothers, William and Walter, it became the concept for the first Harley-Davidson motorcycle and the company for which it was named.

After helping develop the first Harley-Davidson motorcycle, William Harley was still fascinated by the more technical aspects of engineering, and enrolled in the School of Engineering at the University of Wisconsin in Madison. He worked his way through school, waiting on tables and doing drafting in a local plant, and after graduation actively rejoined partners Arthur, Walter and William Davidson.

William Harley was also a real motorcyclist who rode some of the first Harley-Davidson motorcycles in many endurance contests, finishing well consistently. Testing out his own designs for years, he understood what the motorcycle public wanted, and his judgement had a profound influence on all motorcycle design.

Always an enthusiast, William Harley could always be counted on to be present at major events of the year, especially the annual races in Daytona Beach, Florida. For twenty-four years, he served on the Competition Committee of the American Motorcyclist Association. An avid outdoorsman and excellent hunter, he also found great fascination in photographing and sketching wildlife. He was active in both the American Motorcyclist Association and the Business Men's Sketch Club of Milwaukee.

NAMA PICTORIAL!

Upper left: Deep in the Panamanian jungle a motorcycle instructor, left, and students pose on their Harley-Davidsons in front of a palm-thatched native hut. They are: Pfc. D. Henderson, instructor, and Privates T. Garman, W. Klespies, J. Hendricks and W. Hall. Lower left: Instructor Henderson plunges into a jungle stream. In the rear is Pvt. Garman and farther back is Pvt. Klespies. Upper right: Over rugged jungle trails Pfc. Henderson and the motorcycle students come bouncing along. Lower right: Three members of a Cavalry Reconnaissance unit cross a jungle river on their Harley-Davidsons. They are Sgt. Lester Parker of Hornell, New York, Cpl. John Jacaway, Springfield, Illinois, and S/Sgt. John Randle, Evanston, Illinois.
U. S. Army Signal Corps Photographs.

Bette Davis and Paul Henreid in *Now Voyager*.

PANAMA PICTORIAL

Left page: In the upper left photo Lieut. R. Reppa writes message to be dispatched by S/Sgt. Randle. At the right two messengers traverse a difficult jungle trail. Below: Three riders line up for a picture in the jungle clearing. They are: S/Sgt. Randle, left, Sgt. Parker and Cpl. Jacaway. Right page: S/Sgt. Randle demonstrates how messengers deliver messages from headquarters on the fly to the leader of an armored vehicle. Below: Cpl. R. Berry of Virden, Ill., skillfully maneuvers his Harley-Davidson through the rocky bed of a jungle stream. On the right Sgt. Parker and Sgt. Randle and their sturdy Harley-Davidsons are shown at the entrance of a dense jungle trail. U. S. Signal Corps Photographs.

Harley-Davidsons continued to be a police favorite in the Forties. This photo from a 1942 *Enthusiast*, captioned "Harley-Davidson in the Lone Star State," shows Texas highway patrolmen on Harley-Davidsons near Houston , examining the credentials of a motorist.

Introducing Officer Bill Curry of the Topeka, Kansas, Police who marks parked cars so fast that even "Believe-It-or-Not" Ripley was amazed.

MARKED CARS SO FAST RIPLEY DIDN'T BELIEVE IT

Harley-Davidson even rated space in Bob Ripley's "Believe-It-or-Not," according to a May 1942 *Enthusiast* story which read as follows: "You have to do something unusual to rate space in Robert Ripley's famous 'Believe-It-or-Not' Column. And that's just what Officer Bill Curry of the Topeka, Kansas, Police Department has been doing for years. Officer Curry's specialty is marking parked cars and he estimates his yearly total at around five million. He figures he can mark and check 16,000 to 18,000 cars a day.

"So fast and adept is Officer Curry that when a representative of Ripley's 'Believe-It-or-Not' heard about the fantastic number of cars marked, he shook his head. Obligingly the officer asked the representative to get in his car and follow Curry on the Police ServiCar. They moved over to a side street and the officer got busy. He speeded up to 20 miles an hour and stick and chalk flashed in and out beneath the cars. The representative tagged along behind, wide-eyed. He followed the speedy officer for half a day. Then the amazed representative called a halt. He had seen enough. In recognition of the officer's unbelievable speed in marking cars, he was given prominent mention on Ripley's radio program."

KEEP PITCHING AMERICA

WIN THE WAR
3¢ 3¢
UNITED STATES POSTAGE

FPG

Winston Churchill flashes his famous "V-for-victory" sign.

GENUINE
HARLEY-DAVIDSON MOTOR CYCLES
PARTS and ACCESSORIES

This Part Is MADE OF PROPER MATERIALS MADE TO FIT PERFECTLY . . . GUARANTEED SATISFACTORY

THE CONTENTS OF THIS PACKAGE HAVE PASSED THE MOST RIGID INSPECTION
HARLEY-DAVIDSON MOTOR CO., MILWAUKEE, Wis. U.S.A.

GENUINE
HARLEY-DAVIDSON MOTOR CYCLES
PARTS and ACCESSORIES

GENUINE
HARLEY-DAVIDSON MOTOR
BEARINGS

"HELL ON WHEELS" division. Tommy guns spitting, they lead tanks into action

IRON PONIES

They're the mounts of the 1942 Rough Riders, toughest and fastest of land-army troops

IN THE last war motorcycle troops were "messenger boys."

In this one they are the fastest-moving land branch of the Army.

The medicos' best customers, they suffer more crack-ups in normal work than the tank crews, plane crews and parachutists combined. And although their members are being knocked off regularly, war or no war, they have a peculiar brand of fatalism which impels them to perform even the most routine mission with dash and abandon.

These modern Rough Riders go through a rigorous eight-week course at Fort Knox, Ky. Many of them are famous as dirt track and hill-climbing performers; all have had long experience on cycles. Few soldiers can qualify for the cycles — and not many want to!

The only way to get an appreciative taste of their job would be to ride with one of these wheeled cow-punchers at 40 miles an hour in a total blackout along a rutted country road crowded with fast-moving tanks which take up two-thirds or more of the available space. Your first trip is guaranteed to turn your hair gray!

Roughly — and the word is used advisedly! — they have four missions: scouting and patrolling; traffic control for large troop and supply movements; liaison and courier work; and, finally, as a small harassing force to do the work that horse cavalry used to do.

That New Job

IN THIS mechanized era, the second task is vital, but it is the fourth which has made the motorcycle man so different from his 1918 predecessor.

In a tank attack the cycles may either follow right behind the big monsters, tommy guns blazing; or they may precede the tanks if the situation warrants. (Each armored division has about 200 cycles.) On scouting work they must be keyed for surprise attack and quick action, since theirs is usually the first contact with the enemy. In such a situation it is breath-taking to see a swiftly moving squad of cyclists plunge headlong off the road like a band of Hollywood stunt men, spilling their wheels in the grass or brush while they unlimber their sub-machine guns and cover the enemy until the tanks lumber up.

Strangely enough, one of the outstanding developments in this wild-and-woolly branch of the service is a new type of motorcycle infinitely quieter than the standard commercial cycle.

So the enemy will soon find hell descending on him without so much as a "put-put" of warning.

— PAUL W. KEARNEY

TOUGH. He takes hardest knocks in the Army

QUICK. Enemy sighted, split-second dismount

NON-STOP. Even rivers can't slow him down

Teddy Roosevelt could probably not have pictured the "Rough Rider" described in a 1942 issue of *This Week* magazine.

Films co-starring Spencer Tracy and Kathryn Hepburn were big box-office hits, even back in the Forties.

In April 1943, Harley-Davidson was presented with the prestigious Army-Navy "E" Award by Under Secretary of War, Robert P. Patterson, for exceptional performance beyond the normal execution of duty in the production of war materials. With the award, Company President William H. Davidson received a large banner for Harley-Davidson to fly along with the American flag.

On behalf of Local No. 209, Union President, Leonard Hackert, said: "The employees of Harley-Davidson are working long, hard hours. We're buying war bonds and accepting shortages. Most of us are staying on the job, day in and day out, often working on days when we aren't well—days we would lay off in peace time. That's the way we are dealing blows to our enemies. By winning this grand award, the boys in our Armed Forces and our Allies are saying, 'Thank you for your production.' And they may rest assured that we, the employees of Harley-Davidson, will never let them down."

SAN DIEGO MOTORCYCLE OFFICER GETS HIS MAN

The following article from a mid-Forties issue of the *Enthusiast* illustrates Harley-Davidson's longtime promotion and recognition of Harley-Davidsons as effective law enforcement tools.

"Seldom are the thrilling captures made by the Nation's motorcycle officers, in line of duty, given the publicity they deserve. This is regrettable because their effective law enforcement work is not always fully appreciated by the public. Therefore, it is with satisfaction that the recent experience of Officer Vic R. English, San Diego, California, is briefly recounted here.

"As Officer English was leaving the police station on his Harley-Davidson 74 OHV one day recently, he was informed by Lt. F. E. Wolfe that a car, stolen in Van Nuys, was reported heading south toward San Diego. Officer English proceeded to Gillette Street and waited. Soon the car was spotted and the chase was on! Faster and faster roared the desperate driver, aware now that he was being followed. Officer English, crouched low over the tanks, siren screaming, and red pursuit light flashing, began to close in on the car. The needle of the

Officer Vic English is shown on the 74 OHV Harley-Davidson, which he piloted through the streets of San Diego in the successful pursuit of a fleeing law breaker.

speedometer raced across the dial to 50—60—70—80—90 miles an hour and still it moved! As the frantic driver approached Juniper Street, a girl stepped down off the curb. The car driver applied his brakes, swerved to miss the pedestrian, went into a skid and slid broadside into a signal standard. Officer English quickly came to a stop, took the uninjured driver into custody, and another traffic menace was soon deposited in a safe place. The officer's prompt, courageous action undoubtedly prevented a more serious and perhaps even a fatal accident. A salute to Officer Vic English and to the other motorcycle officers who, like him, are determined to make our streets and highways safe."

Right: Roddy McDowall starred in the original "Lassie Come Home" in 1943.

Far right: Bob Hope, Dorothy Lamour and Bing Crosby helped lift the spirits of the nation with their series of "Road" movies in the Forties.

Upper left: Harley-
Davidsons in action at
U. S. Army training camps.
Above: "Pin-up girl"
Betty Grable.
Left: Harley-Davidson
Motorcycle Oil was
packaged in glass during
wartime because of the
defense industry's
urgent need for metals.

Far left: A May 1942
Milwaukee Journal
photo of (left to right):
Gordon Davidson,
William H. Davidson,
Arthur Davidson,
William S. Harley.

At right: The Model XS was a version of the XA with a sidecar. The wheel of the sidecar was powered by a driveshaft running off the rear hub of the motorcycle. Very few XS models were actually built.

Bottom right: An American Army motorcyclist in England uses his Harley-Davidson as a shield while firing during maneuvers. Bottom left: "Marcus Welby" star, Robert Young, was a Harley-Davidson enthusiast back in the Forties.

Celebrities on Harley-Davidsons included (clockwise from upper left): Clark Gable and Ward Bond; Gene Tierney; Tyrone Power and Preston Foster; John Payne; Van Johnson and Keenan Wynn.

The Enthusiast

A MAGAZINE FOR MOTORCYCLISTS

JANUARY 1943

By the end of the war, Harley-Davidson employees had three silver service stars added to their banner, signifying three more "E" Awards to their credit.

During World War II, Harley-Davidson received countless letters from soldiers recounting their wartime experiences on motorcycles. There were so many that the *Enthusiast* ran regular columns and photographs of the accounts of our men and women in uniform. In those troubled times, Harley-Davidson made it a point to keep sending *Enthusiasts* to those men and women, to let them know that they weren't forgotten and to keep their interest in Harley-Davidson alive.

History, as everyone knows, has a habit of repeating itself. Just as in World War I, when Private Ray Holtz, on his Harley-Davidson, was the first American in Germany, another Harley rider was one of the first Yanks to enter Germany in World War II. Censorship of the time prohibited using his name or the date, but in his letter recalling the event, the Army private added: ". . .and I'll try to be the first Yank to ride into Berlin."

Many servicemen's letters praised the performance of the WLAs, and closed with: "I can't wait until I get home and get my own new one." After the end of the war in 1945, however, it still wasn't easy to get motorcycles for civilian use. Material shortages, coupled with general strikes in many related industries, caused a scarcity of new machines. It wasn't until 1947 that Harley-Davidson resumed full civilian production of motorcycles, parts and accessories.

Right: During World War II, Harley-Davidson supplied 90,000 WLA 45s to the armed services of America and its allies. Below: Following the death of President Franklin D. Roosevelt, on April 12, 1945, Vice President Harry S. Truman became president.

Left: U. S. military veterans return home from combat after World War II.

Harley-Davidson kept experimenting during the war years in attempts to expand the serviceability of the product line. An experimental power plant for a Canadian mini-tank utilizing dual OHV 74 engines (below left) and a shaft-drive, flat twin 50 cubic inch ServiCar (shown here) were tested but never put into production.

1945

Germany surrenders May 7.

1946

First meeting of United Nations General Assembly in London.

1947

Jackie Robinson breaks major league baseball's color barrier with Brooklyn Dodgers.

Captain Chuck Yeager pilots first aircraft flying faster than speed of sound.

1948

President Truman's re-election victory over Thomas E. Dewey amazes nation.

U.S.S.R. begins Berlin land blockade; broken by U.S.-British airlift of supplies.

Gandhi assassinated in New Delhi by Hindu fanatic.

1949

North Atlantic Treaty Organization (NATO) begins, signed by 12 nations.

National Basketball Association formed via merger of two existing leagues.

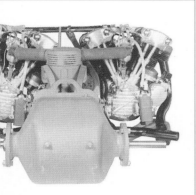

Pan American World Airways used a side-valve 750 package truck to make rush deliveries of priority packages in Miami.

Harley-Davidson's exhibit at the 1944 Navy War Bond Show in Milwaukee proudly displayed the company's "E" Award banner with the first of three silver service stars.

Above left, in 1945, atomic bombs dropped on Hiroshima, August 6, and Nagasaki, August 9; on August 15, Japan surrendered. Below left, the official Japanese surrender on the deck of the U.S.S. Missouri.

At right, after the Japanese surrendered, Americans celebrated V-J (Victory over Japan) Day.

The 1947 models were the first new Harley-Davidsons introduced since Pearl Harbor, and were eagerly sought by enthusiasts. They were basically updated 1941 models, but they did feature significant improvements, such as a new taillight, redesigned instrument panel, hydraulic shock absorber, and additional chrome and accessory groups. They also boasted streamlined new nameplates created by the noted industrial designer—and later, the builder of Excalibur cars—Brooks Stevens.

The year 1947 also saw Harley-Davidson produce a larger and more comprehensive catalog of accessories and clothing. It offered nearly everything imaginable for that time, from batteries, leather saddlebags and chrome dress-up accessories to riding breeches, ladies' wear, leather helmets and goggles. Appearing for the first time was a black leather jacket, which sported chrome zippers and snaps, a belted waist and zippered sleeves, available in men's or women's styles. The forerunner of today's Cycle Champ jacket, it quickly became the traditional outerwear for American motorcyclists.

When racing resumed after the war, the supremacy of Harley-Davidson continued. 1947 saw Harley-Davidson take checkered flags in the National TT, National Miniature TT, and other Nationals at Richmond, VA; Springfield, IL; and Milwaukee. Seven of the top 10 finishers at Daytona rode Harleys. In 1948, Harley-Davidson riders won 19 of 23 National Championship races. The following year, they took 17 of 24.

While the races were being won, a certain segment of the riding public began to exhibit some unpopular practices, like using unmuffled engines, weaving in and out of traffic, and cutting up at rallies and events. Perhaps this was due to a release of pent-up post-war energy, or a reflection of the virtually unrestricted motorcycle riding customs of combat—now unleashed on civilian roads. Most notable of these events occurred in Hollister, California, where the rowdy behavior of a motorcycle group was publicized out of proportion by the national news media. The Hollister event later became the basis for the Marlon Brando movie, "The Wild One." Incidentally, Brando rode a British motorcycle in the movie.

The Jack Pine Endurance Run, dominated year after year by Harley-Davidson, was a grueling test of man and machine.

Two of John Garfield's postwar movie hits were "The Postman Always Rings Twice" and "Body and Soul."

The outcry over this aberrant behavior became so loud that the American Motorcyclist Association, as well as manufacturers like Harley-Davidson, waged concentrated campaigns to clean up the image of the sport. By 1948, there was a very real fear that the actions of a few could force legislation that would affect everyone. Fortunately, then like now, the majority of the motorcyclists respected the laws and operated their motorcycles in a responsible manner. While the undesirable element was not totally eliminated, reason prevailed, and the sport survived intact.

Rita Hayworth, Lizabeth Scott and Lana Turner typified the glamorous film star of the late Forties.

159

In 1948, big things were happening in the world of Harley-Davidson. At a national sales conference held in Milwaukee in November 1947, dealers from all over the United States and Canada—and as far away as Cuba and India—were delighted to hear details of a brand new 125cc, single-cylinder model for the young or inexperienced rider. Weighing only 170 pounds, the two-stroke Model 125 averaged 90 miles to the gallon and could be operated for two cents per mile. It was the first in a long line of postwar, lightweight motorcycles offered by Harley-Davidson.

Of further interest were new, more advanced 61 and 74 OHV engines with such innovative features as aluminum heads; hydraulic valve lifters, previously found only in airplane and luxury car engines; and lifters that operated in an oil mist. Topping the new heads were one-piece, chrome-plated rocker covers that eventually earned the engine the nickname of the "Panhead."

The 1948 models also sported additional chrome, eight optional equipment groups, and a host of new accessories for motorcycling enjoyment. Harley-Davidson was striving to fill every need of the motorcyclist.

The most exciting announcement of that meeting occurred after a nighttime train ride to a "secret destination" in the Milwaukee area. Leaving the 14 train coaches, the dealers were stunned to find themselves in a recently purchased 260,000-square-foot building in a Milwaukee suburb, the newest facility of Harley-Davidson. The one-story plant on Capitol Drive was initially operated as a large machine shop to support manufacturing, but was subsequently converted to production and assembly of engines and transmissions.

1948 proved to be the biggest year to date in Harley-Davidson's 45-year-history, as the company turned out motorcycles in record numbers to fill the built-up demand created by curtailed wartime production.

Inset at left: Distinctive valve covers eventually earned the new overhead-valve engine the nickname of "Panhead."
Left: The Model 125 was introduced as a lightweight, economical motorcycle for less experienced riders.

Dealers at the 1947 Convention in Milwaukee were surprised when a train ride to a "secret destination" proved to be a sneak preview of Harley-Davidson's recently purchased plant on Capitol Drive. Company President, William H. Davidson, is at far left in railroad car.

The next year saw more significant improvements in the company's products, especially on OHV models. Most important was a hydraulically-dampened, telescoping front fork called the Hydra-Glide Fork, which smoothed out bumpy roads and absorbed shocks. Also notable were skirted airflow fenders and rubber-mounted handlebars.

The economy was in high gear. Everyone was working. Crops were abundant. Harley-Davidson was advertising like never before, and future prospects never seemed brighter.

Gary Cooper and
Patricia Neal in
Ayn Rand's *The
Fountainhead*.

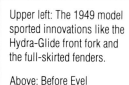

Upper left: The 1949 model sported innovations like the Hydra-Glide front fork and the full-skirted fenders.

Above: Before Evel Knievel's time, this daredevil attempted a "12-man jump."

The 1950's

Celebrating Our
Golden Anniversary

The 1950's

The Fabulous Fifties debuted on a note of optimism in the country as the aftereffects of World War II were relegated to history. At long last, scarcities of raw materials were no longer an issue and a booming economy cranked out consumer goods at a record pace, all of which competed with the motorcycle dealer for the customer's dollar. The Fifties became a market for eager consumers and with so many products available to enhance the average American's everyday life, it became more difficult to attract new buyers to the motorcycle marketplace.

Recognizing the need for a more aggressive marketing stance, Harley-Davidson dealers were encouraged to get out from behind the counter and work more closely with their potential customers. They were urged to advertise and promote not only their products, but the sport of motorcycling in general. For the first time ever, each dealer was supplied with a demonstrator motorcycle, and advised of the importance of giving demo rides to prove the comfort, power and performance of the new Harley-Davidson motorcycles. Also, by the 1950s Harley-Davidson was continually expanding its already considerable line of accessories and clothing in order to maintain the interest of enthusiasts already involved in the sport.

To help combat some negative images generated by certain motorcyclists, the 1950 models sported new mufflers that produced a deeper, mellower tone compared to the harsh, staccato sounds of earlier years. This quieter, more pleasing exhaust note was created despite a ten percent increase in power developed through redesigned and enlarged cylinder inlet ports on the 61 and 74 OHV engines.

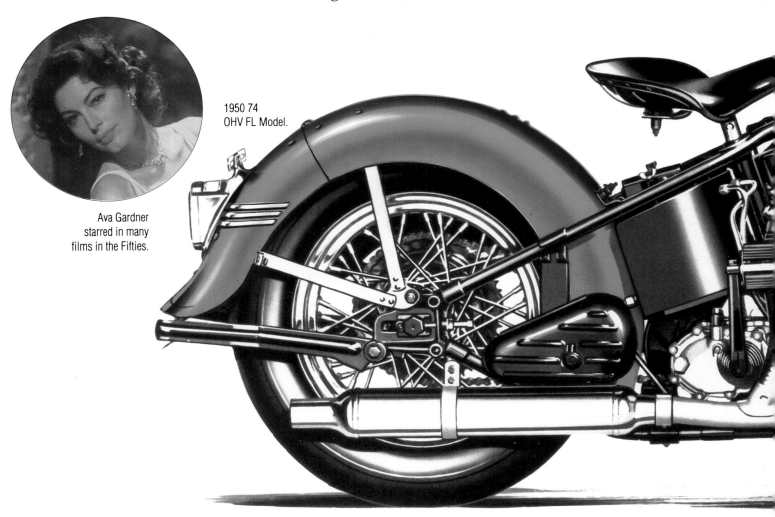

Ava Gardner
starred in many
films in the Fifties.

1950 74
OHV FL Model.

In the postwar motorcycling world, racing continued to play an ever-increasing role as Harley-Davidson riders scored victory after victory in all types of two-wheeled competition. Gerald McGovern won the 1950 Jack Pine Endurance Run, marking the twenty-first win for Harley-Davidson in the twenty-four times the event had been held. Bill Huber won Langhorne, Roger Soderstrom took the checkers at Peoria, and Larry Headrick scored double wins at Springfield and Milwaukee, just to name a few. In all, Harley-Davidson riders took 18 of 24 National Championships in 1950, establishing six new racing records in the process.

Clubs, too, enjoyed increasing popularity as organized motorcycling attracted more and more riders. Many of the clubs worked diligently at improving the motorcyclists' image through civic activities such as organizing fund raisers, providing escort services, arranging muffler inspections, helping the needy and working for civil defense.

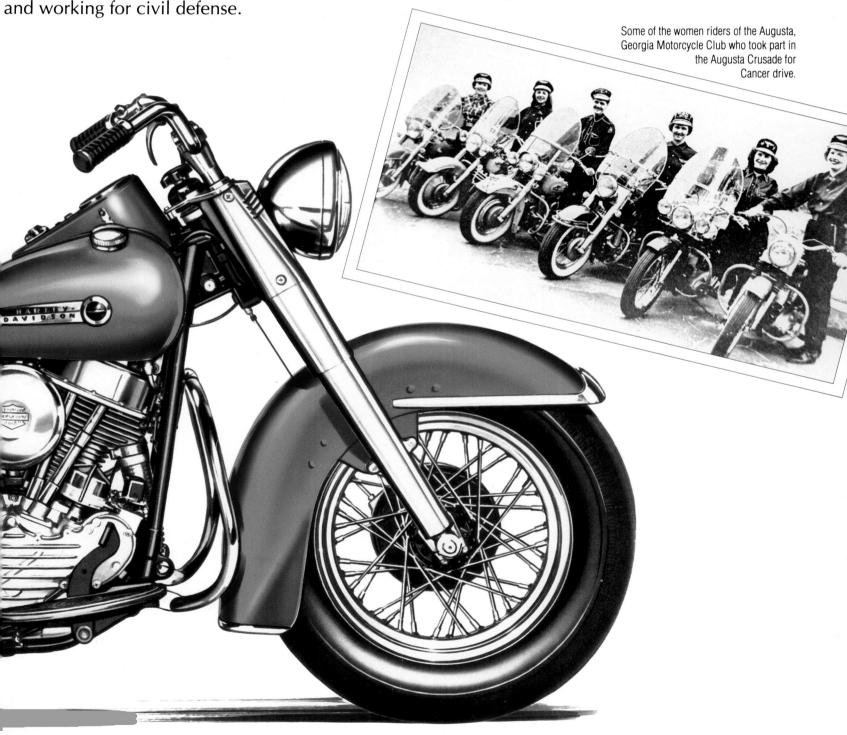

Some of the women riders of the Augusta, Georgia Motorcycle Club who took part in the Augusta Crusade for Cancer drive.

*B*ecause of international tensions heightened by the 1950 Communist invasion of South Korea, America was gripped by the fear of nuclear war. Several cities staged mock civil defense exercises in which motorcycle club members played key roles in keeping the lines of communication open after a simulated nuclear attack. When all other forms of communication failed, motorcycle dispatch riders kept information flowing. In every instance, the motorcyclists were praised for their dedication and performance.

A sad note was rung in the final days of 1950 when Arthur Davidson, secretary and general sales manager and the sole surviving founder of Harley-Davidson, was killed along with his wife in a tragic automobile accident. The task of running the company had now been fully passed to the second generation of Harleys and Davidsons.

Opposite page, top center; An arresting picture! In the Fifties, it was a pleasure to get "curbed" in Sullivan County, N.Y. Instead of issuing tickets, a special corps of Courtesy Copettes on motorcycles presents a list of cardinal safety rules of Sullivan County and explained how safety pays. The method was said to be successful *and* popular.

ARTHUR DAVIDSON

Teaming up with boyhood friend William S. Harley, Arthur was the first of the Davidson brothers to join in the production of the original Harley-Davidson motorcycle. And as the new Harley-Davidsons gained in popularity and production increased, it was Arthur who took charge of sales, covering the country from coast to coast and establishing a sound network of dealers. Arthur also appreciated the importance of competent mechanics to serve Harley-Davidson owners, and the Harley-Davidson Service School is a tribute to his foresight.

In the early days of advertising, Arthur was quick to recognize it as a new force in selling and always insisted that the merits of Harley-Davidson products be promoted constantly before the public. When the trend toward installment buying was recognized, the Kilbourn Finance Corporation was organized in 1923, and he served as its president for many years. He also served the last six years of his life as president of the American Motorcyclist Association and helped develop many of the policies and programs instituted to enlarge its scope and influence. During those same years, he was also president of the Motorcycle and Allied Trades Association, an organization of members of the motorcycle industry.

Always interested in youth activities, he served in many capacities with the Boy Scouts of America and received scouting's highest award for distinguished service. He was also a board member of the Milwaukee Boys' Club and active in the Y.M.C.A. A great lover of the outdoors, he was a lifetime member of the Izaak Walton League. Because of his keen business and financial insight, Arthur Davidson served as a director for several firms, such as the Koehring Company, the Kellogg Seed Company and Wisconsin Pharmacal Company.

While many young Americans celebrated the spring of 1950 with formal dances, others entered South Korea to help fight the North Korean Communist invaders.

Smartly Styled

Cycle Queen Jacket
THE LADIES' CHOICE

Here's an ideal jacket for the gal on the Buddy Seat — a tailored *match-mate* to the Cycle Champ. Styled from brilliant black leather with action back for a feminine fit..............only $26.95

See it today at your
Harley-Davidson Dealer

HARLEY-DAVIDSON MOTOR CO.
MILWAUKEE 1, WISCONSIN

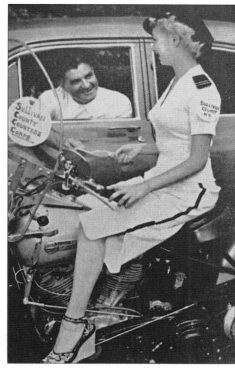

Smartly Styled

The Cycle Champ
BLACK HORSEHIDE JACKET

Riders everywhere agree that the famous Cycle Champ is *tops* for warmth, comfort and appearance. The jacket is made from genuine horsehide with form-fitting, action back..............$32.95

See it today at your
Harley-Davidson Dealer

HARLEY-DAVIDSON MOTOR CO.
MILWAUKEE 1, WISCONSIN

Rise 'n Shine COME OVER TO OUR **HARLEY-DAVIDSON SPRING OPEN HOUSE** TELL YOUR FRIENDS ★ BRING A BUDDY.............

the early Fifties, a number of newspapers around the county employed young riders on Model 125's to deliver their papers, like this group of boys from the Denison Herald in Texas.

As good as the new Harley-Davidsons had become, 1951 saw even more innovations, with chrome-plated piston rings on the OHV motors and—an industry first—hydraulic rear brakes on the Servi-Car, which was still an important boon to police and business concerns. The Model 125, the junior Harley-Davidson, also received an update with a telescoping Tele-Glide front fork patterned after that of its bigger brothers.

Perhaps the biggest news in 1951 was the founding of the Harley-Davidson Mileage Club. Based on mileage accumulated since January 1, 1951, Harley-Davidson owners could earn recognition for their riding achievements by receiving a handsome pin and membership card in three classifications: 25,000 miles, 50,000 miles and 100,000 miles. Remarkably, by the end of the Club's fourth year, 73 members had already topped the 100,000 mile mark.

"The Honeymooners" was a TV favorite.

The Fifties were *Howdy Doody Time.*

Long before the TV series, Harley-Davidson promoted "Happy Days."

THROUGH NORWAY ON A HARLEY-DAVIDSON

Steve and Karen Slaby of Detroit toured Norway in 1952 on a Harley-Davidson 125. Fully loaded with gear and two passengers, the spunky little 125 had a gross weight of 570 pounds, yet was able to handle the mountainous terrain and gravel roads with little difficulty. In one instance, the pair was forced to navigate an almost continuous grade for 50 miles, riding in first or second gear, resulting in the engine getting so hot it even ran with the ignition turned off. Nonetheless, the motorcycle never failed them and they were able to enjoy the remarkable scenery of that beautiful northern country.

General Douglas MacArthur returned to his boyhood home of Milwaukee.

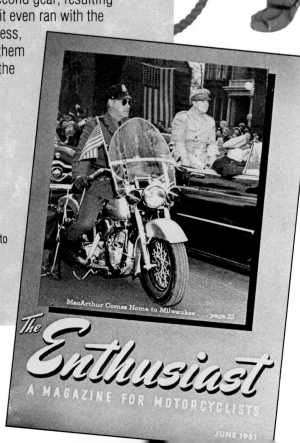

MacArthur Comes Home to Milwaukee · · · page 22

The Enthusiast
A MAGAZINE FOR MOTORCYCLISTS

JUNE 1951

*I*n 1952 the venerable 45 WL, which had been in the line since the Thirties, was dropped in favor of an excitingly different motorcycle called the Model K. Powered by an all-new 45 cubic inch side-valve motor, the Model K represented the most modern and technologically advanced Harley-Davidson ever produced. Features included an integrated four-speed foot-shift transmission, hand-operated clutch, hydraulic-suspension front and rear, and sleek, sporty looks. The K was an instant success on the streets, and its sporty racing brothers, the KR and KRTT, were equally successful on the nation's race tracks. At the 200-mile 1953 National Championship race on the sands of Daytona Beach, it was Paul Goldsmith on a pepper red KR who took the lead just before the halfway point and held it all the way to the checkered flag, winning by a margin of over two miles and setting a new course record.

The next year saw two models disappear from the model line. Succumbing to increasing demands for the more powerful 74 OHV, the 61 OHV was dropped. To appeal to riders seeking a lightweight motorcycle with a little more power, the Model 125 was replaced by a 165cc model. It still averaged an impressive 80 miles per gallon and yet, could travel up to 60 miles per hour, a necessity for the increasingly faster traffic of the times.

More significant was the fact that 1953 marked the fiftieth year of business for Harley-Davidson. To commemorate the event, a handsome logo was designed, depicting a "V" symbolic of the engine configuration, crossed by the company name and accompanied by the legend: "50 years—American made." This logo, in the form of a brass medallion, would grace the front fenders of all 1954 models.

The 45 cubic inch Model WR dominated dirt tracks until it was replaced by the more advanced KR in 1952.

174

Honoring Harley-Davidson's Golden Anniversary September 3, 1953 were (left to right): John Harley, product engineer; Walter C. Davidson, secretary; William H. Davidson, president; Gordon Davidson, vice president; William J. Harley, treasurer and chief engineer.

*A*t a dinner honoring the anniversary, Company President William H. Davidson remarked, "Harley-Davidson looks back on its past with humble pride. Harley-Davidson looks to the future in eager anticipation of meeting tomorrow's challenge. Our assets are many as we start our second half century. Never have we had a finer array of models than our new Golden Anniversary line. No motorcycle manufacturer, anywhere in the world, has a range as complete as Harley-Davidson.

"The present Harley-Davidson organization owes much to the sterling example and sound pattern which the founders—the three senior Davidsons, William, Walter and Arthur, and William Harley, Sr.—so firmly established. Never has a finer business heritage been handed down from one generation to the next. Let me assure you that my generation holds this heritage in highest esteem and that we have the same unwavering faith in America's future as did our fathers before us.

"Harley-Davidson's achievements over the years, including the announcement of our splendid Golden Anniversary models, now in full production, are adequate evidence that we are firmly committed to an aggressive program of steadily moving forward. Harley-Davidson is sharply conscious of our ever-shifting economy, and the need for intelligent and constant change."

The reason for the company's need to remain vigilant was an influx into the United States of a number of foreign-made brands of motorcycles which, because of the lower labor rates in their home countries, made them cheaper than comparable Harley-Davidson models. Because of constant product line improvements, innovations and quality, plus rider loyalty and an outstanding racing record, Harley-Davidson was more than able to hold its own against the competition and remained the dominant force on the American motor-cycle scene. This was also a time that its oldest and best known competitor, Indian, ceased production, leaving Harley-Davidson as the only American manufacturer in an industry that once saw several hundred brands competing in the U. S. market.

1954. ® Walt Disney Productions

Fess Parker's portrayal of Davy Crockett created a national frenzy for coonskin caps.

Left: The tower of Milwaukee's City Hall welcomes Harley-Davidson dealers to a convention introducing the 1952 models.
Below: Harley-Davidson President, William H. Davidson announces the revolutionary Model K at a Milwaukee dealer convention.

177

*I*n 1954, the American Motorcyclist Association changed its method for naming the Grand National Champion, awarding it to the racer who accumulated the most points at a select group of dirt track, road racing and speedway Nationals held throughout the season. When the dust settled that year, it was Joe Leonard racing on the invincible Harley-Davidson KR model who earned the coveted Champion's number plate with its bold Number One. Trailing Leonard were fellow KR riders, Paul Goldsmith and Charlie West.

To satisfy the demands of the American riding public for more horsepower, the K evolved into the KH in 1954, growing to 55 cubic inches. In September of 1953, Don Pink won the twenty-seventh running of the Jack Pine on one of the new KHs and Bert Cummings won Class A Heavyweight top honors, also on a KH, proving the power of this new motor.

Since the early days of motorcycling, Daytona has always been the scene of hot racing action. 1955 was no exception as 19-year-old Brad Andres led a 1-2-3 Harley-Davidson sweep of the 200-mile road race, beating the old record set in 1953 by K-mounted Paul Goldsmith. In 1956, John Gibson also won on a KR, and Joe Leonard scored back-to-back, record-breaking victories in 1957 and 1958. Brad Andres brought his KR home to the checkered flag once again in 1959, rounding out a decade of Harley-Davidson dominance at this historic and prestigious event.

But it wasn't only the V-twins that could win for Harley-Davidson. On Labor Day weekend in 1956, a young rider named Leroy Winters from Ft. Smith, Arkansas, won the Jack Pine aboard a single-cylinder Model 165, defeating 526 other competitors in the process. This marked the first time a lightweight motorcycle ever won overall honors at the event, which was traditionally dominated by the bigger, more powerful twins.

A beautifully restored 1954 Model KH.

Kim Novak starred in the 1955 film production of "Picnic."

GRAND NATIONAL CHAMPION

Joe Leonard SAYS

"I always use
GENUINE
HARLEY-
DAVIDSON
OIL"

a championship winner like Joe Leonard uses nothing
Genuine Harley-Davidson Oil in race after race, you know it
must be mighty good oil. The oil that helps Joe win will also win
you dependable service under the most grueling conditions on or
off track or highway. It's the championship oil that is good to your
motor regardless of the rugged demands you may make upon it.

You are always ahead and you can't lose when you insist on the
Genuine Harley-Davidson Oil made expressly for high-speed, air-
cooled engines. Make your motor happy by always using it. This
championship oil is now available at all Harley-Davidson dealers.

HARLEY-DAVIDSON MOTOR CO.
MILWAUKEE 1, WISCONSIN, U.S.A.

THE Enthusiast
A MAGAZINE FOR MOTORCYCLISTS

MARCH 1955

Announcing the New
HARLEY-DAVIDSON *Hummer*

Leroy Winters made Jack Pine history in
1956 by winning the grueling 500-mile
off-road event on a Harley-Davidson 165.

e powerful KR racing
odel was unmatched
America's dirt
cks in the Fifties.

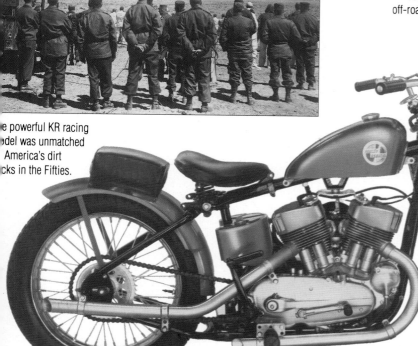

1955

U.S. agrees to help train
South Vietnamese army.

Supreme Court orders
"all deliberate speed" in
integrating public schools.

1956

First transatlantic
telephone cable begins
operation.

First aerial H-bomb tested
over Bikini Atoll.

1957

President Eisenhower
sends federal troops to
Little Rock, Arkansas to
enforce court-ordered
school integration.

The Space Age begins as
Russians launch Sputnik I
into orbit around earth.

1958

First U.S. satellite,
Explorer I, launched
at Cape Canaveral.

1959

Cuban President Batista
resigns and flees; Castro
takes over.

Alaska and Hawaii admitted
as 49th and 50th states.

Soviet Premier Krushchev
makes unprecedented tour
of U.S.

Organized club activities remained very popular throughout the Fifties.

"Rebel Without a Cause" featured James Dean, while Marlon Brando starred in "The Wild One."

The old Jack Pine winner, Oscar Lenz, presents cowbell and trophy to Gerald McGovern.

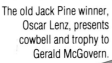

HARLEY-DAVIDSON
SPORTSTER *Takes* JACK PINE
LANSING, MICHIGAN
SEPT. 2, 1957

GERALD McGOVERN on HARLEY-DAVIDSON SPORTSTER
Wins Grand Championship of 500-Mile Jack Pine Endurance Run-959 points

CECIL LANE Riding HARLEY-DAVIDSON Wins Heavyweight Championship-948.37 points

ERNEST KIMBALL } on HARLEY-DAVIDSON Win Sidecar Championship-937 points
ROBERT KIRCHER

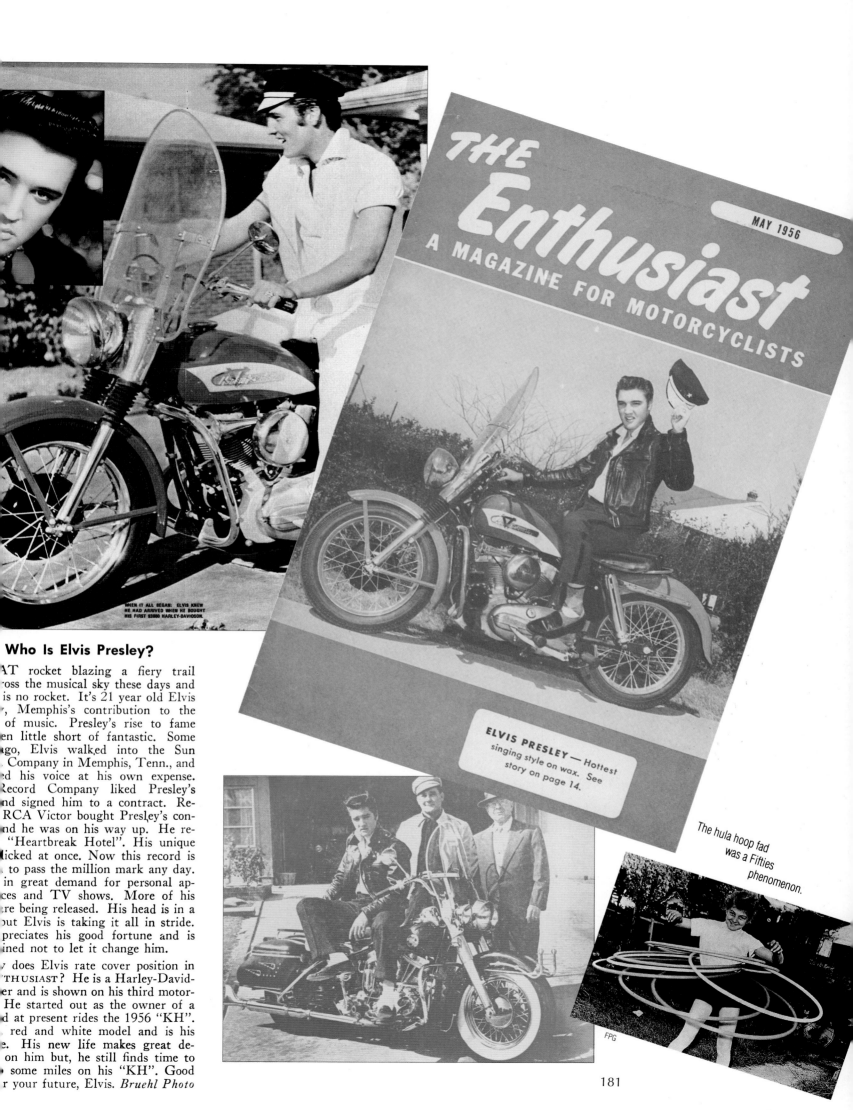

Who Is Elvis Presley?

...AT rocket blazing a fiery trail
...ross the musical sky these days and
...is no rocket. It's 21 year old Elvis
..., Memphis's contribution to the
... of music. Presley's rise to fame
...en little short of fantastic. Some
...go, Elvis walked into the Sun
... Company in Memphis, Tenn., and
...d his voice at his own expense.
...Record Company liked Presley's
...nd signed him to a contract. Re-
...RCA Victor bought Presley's con-
...nd he was on his way up. He re-
..."Heartbreak Hotel". His unique
...licked at once. Now this record is
... to pass the million mark any day.
... in great demand for personal ap-
...ces and TV shows. More of his
...re being released. His head is in a
...ut Elvis is taking it all in stride.
...preciates his good fortune and is
...ined not to let it change him.

...y does Elvis rate cover position in
...THUSIAST? He is a Harley-David-
...er and is shown on his third motor-
... He started out as the owner of a
...d at present rides the 1956 "KH".
... red and white model and is his
... His new life makes great de-
... on him but, he still finds time to
... some miles on his "KH". Good
... your future, Elvis. *Bruehl Photo*

WHEN IT ALL BEGAN: ELVIS KNEW
HE HAD ARRIVED WHEN HE BOUGHT
HIS FIRST $3000 HARLEY-DAVIDSON.

THE Enthusiast
A MAGAZINE FOR MOTORCYCLISTS

MAY 1956

ELVIS PRESLEY — Hottest
singing style on wax. See
story on page 14.

The hula hoop fad
was a Fifties
phenomenon.

FPG

181

*A*n exciting new model headed the 1957 line as the Sportster was introduced, with its 55 cubic inch overhead-valve engine. After not quite living up to the potential of its revolutionary engine, the following year the Sportster featured larger intake ports and valves, plus a 12 percent increase in horsepower, and a legend took life. The Sportster has since become regarded as the first of the so-called "Superbikes," and set the standard by which all others were measured for years to follow.

Gradual evolution and constant improvement continued to be the watchwords at Harley-Davidson as the company unveiled the striking 1958 Duo-Glide. With its powerful 74 OHV engine, hydraulic suspension, whitewall tires, chrome trim, two-tone paint schemes and hydraulically actuated rear brake, it was unquestionably the most comfortable and beautiful motorcycle on the road.

By the mid-Fifties, a new racing star began rising over the Harley-Davidson camp. Versatile, trackwise and sensational were the words used to describe Carroll Resweber, who proved virtually unbeatable as he carved his niche in the record books by winning the title of Grand National Champion in 1958 and 1959. That also made it six straight Number One plates for Harley-Davidson since the first was awarded in 1954.

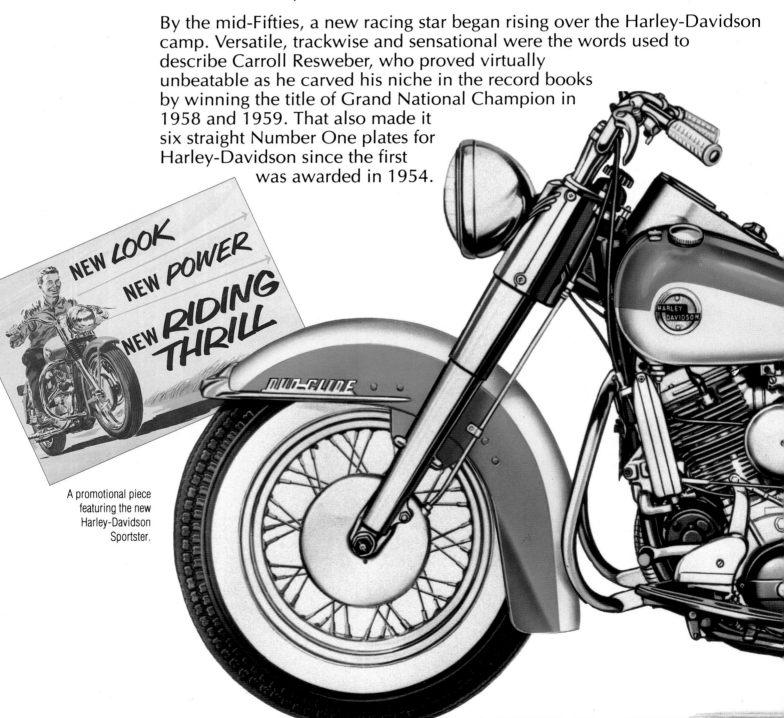

A promotional piece featuring the new Harley-Davidson Sportster.

182

the motorcycle
ENTHUSIAST
in action
THE MAGAZINE FOR MORE MOTORCYCLING PLEASURE

OCTOBER 1958

ROY ROGERS
RIDES AGAIN
see story page 2

In 1958, a CH version of the Sportster was offered for off-road competition. With its many high-performance components, the CH stood for "Competition Hot."

"Roy Rogers Rides Again" on a new mount: his Harley-Davidson Sportster.

Immortal airman, Charles Lindbergh, portrayed by Jimmy Stewart in "The Spirit of St. Louis," was an enthusiastic Harley-Davidson rider.

MONTREAL TO MEXICO

John Pitt was a 46-year-old native of Montreal, Canada in 1959. A real estate appraiser who also handled expropriation cases in court for various clients, Mr. Pitt got an itch to travel and discovered it took a Harley-Davidson Duo-Glide to scratch it:

Last June, I bought a new Oldsmobile 98 convertible and, although it's one of the finest automobiles I've owned, I was still missing something only an enthusiastic motorcyclist knows about and appreciates—that wonderful thrill of flashing speed only inches above the road surface; the pick-up and surge of power that leaves nearly all automobiles miles behind.

Feeling sort of fed up and not getting any younger, I suddenly decided in October to have a little fun and freedom. I called Harry Ison & Co. in New York City and bought a 1959 Harley-Davidson Duo-Glide. Postponing all of my business, I went to New York where Harry Ison's boys gave me a half hour's instruction and sent me on my merry way to Mexico.

What a grand trip! The weather was already chilly, so I took a southern route through Virginia, North Carolina, Georgia, Alabama, Mississippi, Louisiana, Texas—Mexico! Occasionally I hit terrible rainfalls and storms, but just kept going. Sometimes I'd only make 30 miles an hour because big drops of water felt like bullets when I went fast. Several times, in spite of the efficient rain pants, jackets and safety helmet, the water still trickled down the back of my neck—but that was all part of the fun.

The only way to really see Mexico is on a motorcycle. It gives you the feel of the country and an appreciation of truly magnificent mountains, awe-inspiring scenery, precipices, treacherous mountain roads and all the wonders you have to see first-hand to believe.

I went from Laredo, Texas, south to Monterrey, then west through Saltillo, Torreon and Durango. Then over the Sierra Madre Occidental Mountains and down to the Pacific Coast to Mazatlan. After the hot weather around Houston, I really was frozen at the six and seven thousand foot levels in the mountains.

The road from Durango to sea level was positively the worst bone-shaking experience imaginable. It was under construction and I wound a serpentine, tortuous passage through riverbeds, over huge boulders and through greasy clay, hugging precariously to cliff edges, and ducking under tons of overhanging granite that could have been dislodged by a rabbit. At times, it was completely blocked by an idle bulldozer or fallen trees. It took over nine hours to navigate 150 miles, but the Harley-Davidson performed well, and toward evening I got down to sea level. The Pacific Ocean, with its beautiful sandy beaches and magnificent breakers, was the most welcome sight I ever saw.

After a few days along the Pacific Coast of Mexico, I headed back to Monterrey and north to Laredo, Texas. I'd covered 4,500 miles, and in spite of the storms and the greasy mud, my wheels and chain accumulated, I didn't have one accident or a bit of mechanical troub On the return trip, a telephone message in Houston required me to return to Montreal. To my regret, I put the motorcycle up for the wint and flew home.

In May, a friend asked me to ferry his Piper Apache to Kerrville, Tex and I accepted. The next day, I was in the saddle again in front of St & Company's fancy show-windows all bristling with new Harley-Davidsons. They had really fixed my machine up well. I headed sou east and watched the front whitewall tire eat up the road. Boy, it felt wonderful to experience that surge of power, rush of wind and uniqu maneuverability that only a cycle can give.

Down around Galveston, it was so warm that I rode in shorts only. I through Baton Rouge, Atlanta, Charlotte, Richmond, Washington, D. stopping overnight at inns and motels. Finally, I rolled into Atlantic City, New Jersey, where my wife had driven our children down for a rendezvous. After a few days, I headed north again to New York City I was back after 7,000 miles and crossing the continent twice. Leavi New York, I was glad I wore the white coveralls and cycle boots, bec the air became mighty cold in the Adirondacks. Can't say I was over to return to Montreal, because it meant the end of my marvelous trip has very precious memories for me.

Pitt sits comfortably on his Duo-Glide atop a hill overlooking the town of Mazatlan, Mexico. Mazatlan is on the Pacific Coast about 15 miles from the Tropic of Cancer.

Elizabeth Taylor in "Cat on a Hot Tin Roof."

During the 1959 season, the Milwaukee Braves used a specially-equipped Topper with a sidecar to ferry pitchers from the bullpen to the pitcher's mound at County Stadium.

The first motorcycle hobby kit ever produced was the 1958 Harley-Davidson Duo-Glide.

Competing against 101 expert racers in the Daytona 200-mile road race, it was Harley-Davidson's Brad Andres, Number 4, who finished first. Congratulating him, 2nd place finisher, Tony Urquia, are William H. Davidson, right, and Walter Davidson, center.

DAYTONA MOTORCYCLE CLASSICS 1959

The north turn of the first lap of the 1959 200-miler on the beach at Daytona. A parade of six Harley-Davidsons, headed by Bart Markel, leads the pack.

*H*arley-Davidson closed the decade on a note of revolution rather than evolution as it introduced the Topper motor scooter. Advertised as "tops in beauty and tops in performance," the Topper was a handsome machine with its fiberglass body and two-tone paint. Powered by a 10 cubic inch two-stroke engine, the scooter boasted such features as automatic transmission, leading-link front suspension, rubber-mounted engine and two-wheeled brakes.

Innovative, maneuverable and fun to ride, the Topper nonetheless arrived on the scene a little too late in a declining scooter market. It faded from the product line after only a few years.

The Fifties were Fabulous, not only for the country but for Harley-Davidson as well. The company not only enjoyed a landmark celebration with its Golden Anniversary, but also launched a number of new and highly significant models and product improvements that would form the basic product line for years to come.

Doris Day in "Pillow Talk," the number one hit of 1959.

Harley-Davidson Topper Model A and AU starting at $430 f.o.b. Milwaukee — Denim Terry Topper. $5.95 — Ticking Surfer. $5.00 — Seersucker Quilted Terry Shawl Topper. $15.00 — Seersucker Quilted Terry Surfer. $10.95 — Sparkle Plaid Surfer Jac. $10.00 — Sparkle Plaid Surfer. $7.95

MAN ABOUT THE WORLD scoots about on nimble Topper... wears new

Topper is thrifty, easy to handle and parks anywhere. *Scootaway* automatic transmission is smooth and effortless — places Topper above all other scooters. Economy? The greatest — up to 100 miles per gallon. Perfect balance, hefty brakes and large wheels produce comfortable, safe ride. Fashioned in fiberglass, stainless steel and aluminum — for the modern man in motion.

New Surfers with a s... by the sea. Easy-car... back into action. Mc... a sun-basker, surf-r... baker type — add... your life. See them a...

TOPPER BY HARLEY-DAVIDSON

Harley-Davidson Motor Co., Milwaukee 1, Wisconsin

New! A *Scooter* by

HARLEY-DAVIDSON

Tops them all in beauty and performance
...it's the *TOPPER*

Fun-loving Jacks (and Jills, too) are jumping at the chance to meet the new Harley-Davidson Topper. And why not? There's not another motor scooter like it — combining clean, smart beauty with the newest mechanical secrets of success. Scootaway automatic transmission makes riding a snap... lowest center of gravity makes handling a dream. See the new Topper at your Harley-Davidson dealer. Or write for free, colorful folder.

HARLEY-DAVIDSON MOTOR CO., Milwaukee 1, Wisconsin, Dept. SC
World's leading manufacturer of lightweight motor vehicles

This advertisement will be seen by over 15,000,000 readers in the following magazines: SPORT, August; MOTOR LIFE, August; HOT ROD MAG, August; MOTOR TREND August; NATIONAL FUTURE FARMER, August-September; SCOOTER MAGAZINE, July; BOY'S LIFE, August; POPULAR MECHANICS, August; POPULAR SCIENCE, August, 1959.

Derby Helanca Shawl Topper, $10.95
Derby Helanca 3'er Surfer, $6.95

Punjab ADM Boat Knit Topper, $5.00
Punjab Surfer, $8.95

s and Toppers by McGregor

poise — colorful as a seascape — they're designed for fun
ol as ocean-spray — washes in a jiffy — bounces right
a mad colors to mate with carefree Toppers. If you're
clam-
fers to

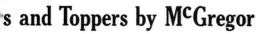

McGREGOR.

Also Boy-Sized, Boy-Priced. Made in Canada, too. McGregor-Doniger Inc., N.Y. 19, N.Y.

77 SUNSET STRIP

Kookie, lend me your *TOPPER*

See EDD "KOOKIE" BYRNES starring in "77 SUNSET STRIP" a WARNER BROS. TV

Tops under the Christmas tree this year...

because it's tops in appearance... tops in performance. There's so much new about the sensational Topper that we can only touch on the highlights. Things like automatic *Scootaway* transmission... finger-tip handling... silky-soft ride... sleek lines moulded in fiberglass... stop-on-a-dime brakes... 100 miles to the gallon economy.

Advice to Teenagers: When it comes to combs and scooters, never a borrower or a lender be. Instead, start dropping hints to Mom and

Dad about the new exciting Davidson Topper.

Advice to Parents: Harley-Davidson dealer more about young Amer most responsible transp or mail the coupon for

Harley-Davidson
MOTOR CO.
MILWAUKEE 1, WISCONSIN

HARLEY-DAVIDSON MOT
Dept. SC, Milwaukee 1, Wisc
Send me more inform
Harley-Davidson

Name _____
Address _____

Even Ed "Kookie" Byrnes of TV's "77 Sunset Strip" became part of Harley-Davidson's promotional efforts for the Topper motor scooter.

the motorcycle ENTHUSIAST in action

THE MAGAZINE FOR MORE MOTORCYCLING PLEASURE

DECEMBER 1

ENTRANCE Dino's Lodge PARKING

TOPPER SHARES SPOTLIGHT WITH "KOOKIE" ON TV
(See Story Page 2)

A fleet of radio-equipped 1958 Duo-Glides ready to be shipped to the California Highway Patrol.

This all-chrome Duo-Glide was ordered by a man in Venezuela from Arthur "Bub" Tramontin, Harley-Davidson dealer in Clifton, New Jersey, and was completely chrome from the nuts and bolts right up to the motor. The saddlebags and seat were hand-tooled. It took Tramontin approximately five months to complete it, and cost $3,500.

THE 1960'S

A Decade of Diversification and Change.

THE 1960'S

As the decade began, America was filled with a renewed feeling of optimism. Entering the White House with his attractive family was the nation's youngest President, John F. Kennedy. He was handsome, enthusiastic and full of vigor, and a new feeling of awareness was dawning in America.

Early in 1960, Harley-Davidson President, William H. Davidson, announced a program of overseas expansion to better serve the European market and substantially improve the company's position in the United States, particularly in the growing lightweight motorcycle market.

Harley-Davidson International, a wholly-owned Swiss-based subsidiary, was established to provide central control, administrative and technical assistance in the overseas marketing of motorcycles, parts and accessories, and scooters, particularly in Europe where the Common Market had recently been created.

Following a two-year study of motorcycle and scooter manufacturers in various foreign countries, Harley-Davidson purchased a half interest in an Italian firm, Aeronautica Macchi, and Aermacchi Harley-Davidson was formed. Already marketing its own line of touring and sport motorcycles for European enthusiasts, Aermacchi Harley-Davidson was to produce a line of lightweight Harley-Davidson motorcycles for the American market. The first of the Italian lightweights to be offered with a Harley-Davidson nameplate was the 1961 250cc Sprint.

Powered by a horizontal four-stroke, single-cylinder engine, the Sprint was a needed addition to round out the bottom end of the product line. Reliable and dependable, the Sprint's torque and power helped it slip comfortably into the product line, and it soon grew in popularity. At the same time, Harley-Davidson was also offering the domestically produced Topper motor scooter and the new 165cc Super-10—"keen wheeling for teen wheeling," according to the sales brochure.

The Aermacchi Harley-Davidson plant in Italy.

DUO-GLIDE FLH

DUO-GLIDE FL

DIFFERENT
DYNAMIC
DELUXE

'60 HARLEY-DAVIDSON
DUO-GLIDES

Robert Stack in
TV's "The Untouchables."

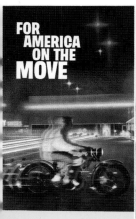

By 1960, there were more motorcycles registered in the United States than ever before, totalling well over a half million. Interest in the sport was on the upswing, and Harley-Davidson enjoyed a sixteen percent increase in business that year. William H. Davidson expected sales to continue growing, largely because the company was now able to offer motorcyclists a complete range of price and performance choices. Rounding out the top of the line were the stylish Duo-Glide and powerful Sportster models.

Harley-Davidson continued its racing successes into the Sixties, most notably with a resounding sweep of the 1960 Daytona road races. In the 200-mile National, it was veteran racer, Brad Andres, who scored his third Daytona victory while leading thirteen other Harley-Davidson racers to the top fourteen places. Tommy Seagraves led a top seven Harley-Davidson record-setting sweep in the 100-mile Amateur race, marking the third consecutive win in the event for Harley-Davidson.

The next year, the famed race was moved from the hard-packed beach to the newly opened Daytona International Speedway, where the 200-mile event consisted of 100 laps over a twisting infield course and spectacular high-

banked turns. Leading all but the very first lap, Roger Reiman piloted his Harley-Davidson KR racer to a win in that inaugural race. At the same time, five Harley-Davidson 165s swept the Lightweight Road Race, and Bob Hamilton proved the mettle of the new Sprint by scoring a win in the Class 5 Road Race.

In 1961, William J. Harley was named chairman of Aermacchi Harley-Davidson, and William H. Davidson's son, John, joined the company in the dealer relations department. Carroll Resweber, the transplanted Texan living in Cedarburg, Wisconsin, captured an unprecedented fourth consecutive title of Grand National Champion in motorcycle racing, a feat that has never been equaled.

John A. Davidson

The product line remained relatively unchanged for 1961; however, the next year saw several significant additions and changes. The 165 was enlarged to 175cc and offered in three versions, tailored to distinctly different riding tastes. The Pacer was a conventional street motorcycle; the Scat served a dual purpose as an on-road/off-road lightweight; and the Ranger was pure off-road, stripped of lighting and sporting aggressive tires.

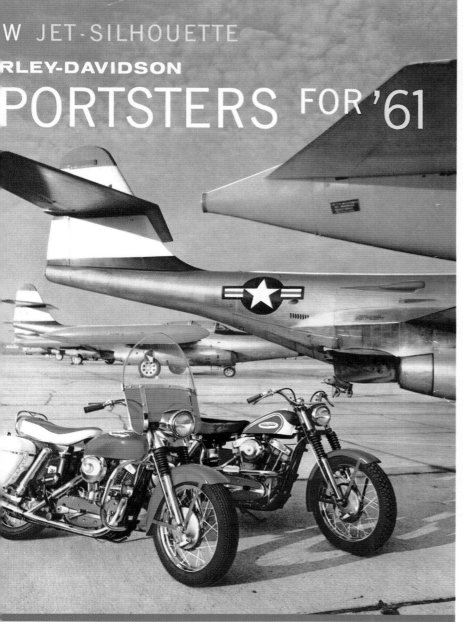

"Gunsmoke" was a top-rated television series.

At the 1960 International Sports and Vacation Show in the Los Angeles Coliseum, one of the top attractions was a demonstration of the Harley-Davidson XLCH Sportster's awesome power and climbing ability. Mounting a wooden ramp erected over the Coliseum seats, the Sportsters rode the 400 feet from the arena floor to the uppermost rim at grades of 45° to 55°.

The stunt had five riders performing three or four times a day for ten days, and was sponsored by the Rich Budelier Company, the L.A. Harley-Davidson dealer, to dramatize how safe a motorcycle can be when ridden properly by an experienced rider.

Right: An artist's sketch of the manmade hillclimb from the floor to the rim of the Los Angeles Coliseum. Below right: Metal trusses supported the wooden track above the seats.

ROGER REIMAN WINS 1961 DAYTONA 200

Roger Reiman of Kewanee, IL, led every lap but the first on his Harley-Davidson to win the 200-Mile National Championship on the Daytona International Speedway AMA road course. Reiman averaged 69.25 mph in the twisting, tortuous 100-lap road race. His winning time was 2 hours, 53 minutes, 17.51 seconds.

Harley-Davidson riders took three of the first six places. George Roeder was third and Bart Markel took fifth. In the time trials, Reiman was the top qualifier with a speed of 72.310. Carroll Resweber had the second fastest time—71.856. Larry Williamson, a Harley-Davidson rider from Peoria, Ill., took the first place spot at the start of the race, only to lose it to Reiman who kept the lead for the distance. Chief challenger up to the midway mark was Resweber on a Harley-Davidson. He held the number two position only 13 seconds behind Reiman for 50 laps! However, Resweber was forced out in the 51st lap. Lone former Daytona 200 winner in the field, Dick Klamfoth, had clutch trouble and only completed 28 laps. The number of riders in the front was whittled down rapidly. Larry Palmgren had the number three spot up to the 73rd lap when he went out. Garnet Koehler, a Canadian rider, was among the front five. Engine trouble sent him to the pits for two extra stops in the 86th and 89th laps. He finished eighth. As the race wore on, the fans realized that nothing could stop Reiman. He kept pouring it on, though, and ran the last 100 miles even faster than the first 100!

A crowd in excess of 7,500 attended the race, held for the first time on the Speedway's two-mile AMA road race course. It had six sharp turns which necessitated 3,000 gear shifts and at least 600 brake applications during the 100-lap event. There were 54 machines in the starting lineup. Only 27 survivors were still running when Reiman took the checkered flag. Of these, 15 were Harley-Davidsons! Once more, the superior power, performance and durability of the Milwaukee Brand had been proven in this gruelling test of man and machine!

THE REMARKABLE CARROLL RESWEBER

On August 20, 1961, Carroll Resweber accomplished what no man before him—or since—has ever equaled. On that date, Resweber won the 50-mile national race at Springfield, Illinois to earn his fourth title as Grand National Champion. The fact that he won his four titles in consecutive years make his feat even more remarkable.

Like fellow Harley-Davidson rider Joe Petrali in the Thirties, Resweber was almost unbeatable in the late Fifties and early Sixties. In 1961, for example, he won ninety-five percent of all the races he started.

Small of stature, the wiry Resweber was a transplanted Texan who moved to the small town of Cedarburg, Wisconsin, just north of Milwaukee. At a testimonial dinner in his honor after clinching his third title, over 300 residents of Cedarburg gathered to pay tribute to the champion and his accomplishments.

As a token of their esteem, the well-wishers presented Resweber with the keys to a fire-engine red 1961 Chevrolet. The car was purchased from a fund which received contributions from Cedarburg residents and industry, motorcycle dealers and racing friends from all over the United States and Canada.

After recovering his composure, the grateful Resweber told the crowd: "This is the greatest thing that has ever happened to me. All I can do in return is to say thank you! If I seem to be getting the best part of the deal, I hope all of you will understand."

But he did give them more than a simple "thank you." The next year he gave his fans the best year of his career, as he raced to his fourth and still unequalled national title.

Below, with his trophies providing the background, Carroll Resweber, second from right, is congratulated by Tom Vasey of the Cedarburg Chamber of Commerce. Looking on were Mayor Merlin G. Rostad (left) and Lin Kuchler, executive secretary of the AMA. Below right, Carroll Resweber—where he could usually be found in a race—out in front.

1960

America launches 17 space satellites and probes, including first weather satellite.

Francis Gary Powers shot down in U-2 spy plane over Russia.

1961

U.S. breaks diplomatic relations with Cuba.

Cuban "Bay of Pigs" invasion attempt to overthrow Castro is repulsed.

1962

John H. Glenn Jr. becomes first American to orbit the earth.

Cuban missile crisis: Kennedy blockades Cuba until Soviets agree to dismantle missile bases.

1963

President Kennedy is assassinated in Dallas; Lyndon B. Johnson becomes president.

Lee Harvey Oswald, Kennedy's accused assassin, shot by Jack Ruby.

U.S. troops in Vietnam total over 15,000 by end of year.

1964

Seven men convicted of conspiracy in Mississippi killing of three civil rights workers.

Seeking to expand its business interests even further, Harley-Davidson purchased a company in Tomahawk, Wisconsin, which had previously been devoted to the production of fiberglass boats. Because of the growing versatility of fiberglass in the motorcycle industry, it quickly became apparent that the company needed its own source to manufacture a growing number of components. In 1962, the Tomahawk Division was established.

It was also a time when Harley-Davidson decided to branch out into a totally unrelated field of leisure products and began production of three-wheeled golf cars. With their all-fiberglass bodies, they also became an end user for the Tomahawk plant, and the golf car bodies became one of the primary products manufactured there for nearly two decades. Harley-Davidson also produced a commercial version of the golf car called the Utilicar, which was ideal for use as a light-duty truck or personnel carrier. By the end of the decade, Harley-Davidson's fine gasoline and electric-powered golf cars had secured approximately one third of the U. S. market, and were used overseas as far away as Japan.

Other than the addition of an off-road version of the Sprint, 1963 saw no major changes in Harley-Davidson models, but subtle refinements were made in existing features to enhance riders' comfort and enjoyment. For example, the Duo-Glide—flagship of the line—received a fishtail muffler, brilliant Hi-Fi colors, huskier brakes and new backswept optional fiberglass saddlebags.

To help riders get the most out of the sport, Harley-Davidson marketed an extensive line of motorcycle accessories as well as motorcycle clothing and novelties. Using nothing but genuine Harley-Davidson accessories, a Harley-Davidson motorcycle owner could customize his mount to suit his own personal taste and riding style by installing his choice of a number of chrome racks, bars, lights, horns, windshields, or dozens and dozens of other items.

the motorcycle
ENTHUSIAST
in action
AUGUST 1962
THE MAGAZINE FOR MORE MOTORCYCLING PLEASURE

In the early Sixties, Harley-Davidson entered the golf car business with a reliable, well-built three-wheeled car that came to be a dominant force in the market by the end of the decade.

and now... another new Sprint by Harley-Davidson

a new 250 cc champion

the *Sprint* TT

a new Sprint model with real way ahead stay ahead power

the HARLEY-DAVIDSON *Sprint* TT

The New 250 cc Sprint H combines the lean, lithe lines of a thoroughbred with winning performance proven by the 1-2-3 finish in the AMA National Short-Track Championship at Santa Fe!

On road, track or trail the Sprint H packs the performance features to put you way ahead... and keep you there!

With a compression ratio of 9.2 to 1, oversize intake valve and port, the Sprint H has added zip. Its streamlined gas tank, bobbed fenders and hi-flo exhaust give it a distinctive custom look. Larger wheels for higher clearance get you through the rough stuff with ease!

Ride a Sprint H and FEEL the way ahead-stay ahead power. Try it today!!!

features

engine... With a compression ratio of 9.2 to 1, oversize intake valve and port, the Sprint H 250 cc overhead valve engine delivers 21 solid, reliable horsepower.

tank... A streamlined 2.6 gallon gas tank with bold red and white color styling make the SPRINT H a standout in appearance as well as in performance!

exhaust... Bobbed fenders for a distinctive custom look in a real road, track and trail machine. Thrill to the dynamic, virile note of its Hi-Flo tuned exhaust!

brakes... Brake back plates specially designed to keep out dirt and water. Large, safe 7" brakes are fast stoppers, every time!

wheels... Large 18" wheels mean greater ground clearance for scrambles track or grassy trails to take you through the rough stuff with ease.

frame... A sturdy, large diameter, reinforced, single strut frame is no matter how rough the going! Engineered for maximum strength.

SPRINT H EXTRAS • Specialized Crankcase Breather • Shrouded Air Cleaner • Tuned Exhaust System • Rubber-mounted Handlebars • Big ⅛ inch Control Cables
60 Watt Output Generator • New Improved Battery • Ball-end Control Levers

and... for road or show it's the *Sprint* with the custom look!

Commands attention wherever it goes! Distinctively different and smartly styled to take you out of the ordinary in motorcycling pleasure.

For you or two... the Sprint is completely engineered for full riding performance. Hydraulically damped front and rear suspension shares the load to give you a real joy ride.

Costs less to buy... costs less to ride with 70 miles-per-gallon economy. For style, spirit and really enjoyable motorcycling, it's the Sprint by Harley-Davidson!

and for the track ask your Harley-Davidson dealer about the *Sprint*

HARLEY

...mercial version of the golf car was offered ...er of configurations, shown here as ...ty carrier.

...Sprint, the first motorcycle resulting ...ey-Davidson's Italian merger, ...horizontal single-cylinder, ...r-stroke engine.

A new employee started that year, one who would have a deep, far reaching and lasting effect not only on Harley-Davidson but ultimately, the whole sport in America in future years. Fresh from a series of outside positions involving product design and styling, William G. Davidson joined the company as director of styling. The oldest son of William H. Davidson, he assumed responsibility for designing all subsequent Harley-Davidson models and many of their accessories. Riders nationwide would come to know him as Willie G.

With the company's diversification into the golf car business, Harley-Davidson felt a change in the company logo was warranted in 1964, to better reflect the broader scope of its leisure vehicle business. The familiar bar and shield trademark, which dated back to the first decade of the century, was dropped as the corporate logo. In its place, to identify the leisure vehicle business, was a stylized logo with the words "Harley-Davidson" flanked by two elongated triangles. Gone were the words "Motor Cycles." However, the old trademark continued to be used in various forms on motorcycles, parts and a wide range of consumer products for some time and was resurrected for corporate use much later.

JFK's tragic death stunned the nation and the world.

FPG

HARLEY-DAVIDSON

The third-generation William Davidson, William G. Davidson, joined the company as director of styling in 1963.

"Cleopatra," starring Elizabeth Taylor, cost and lost more than any film ever had before.

Sean Connery's series of James Bond films were big hits in the Sixties.

Late in 1963, the American Motorcycle Association sanctioned the use of fairings for streamlining motorcycles on road race courses, and the 1964 Daytona event marked their first use in a competitive event. Repeating his 1961 victory, Roger Reiman streaked to a thrilling win over an elongated 3.81-mile course in a record speed of nearly 95 miles per hour. The following year, Reiman was to repeat his win once again.

Capitalizing on Reiman's skill at controlling a motorcycle at high speeds, the company selected him to pilot its Sprint-powered streamliner in a 250cc class speed record attempt on the Bonneville salt flats of Utah in September. The old mark of 150 mph had stood unbroken since 1956. Despite a projected top speed of nearly 200 miles per hour, the streamliner's performance was hampered by poor surface conditions resulting from freakish summer storms. Nonetheless, Reiman managed to set new records for both the mile and the kilometer of over 156 miles per hour.

Under better racing conditions thirteen months later and powered by the new Sprint CR racing engine, George Roeder propelled the streamliner to an even higher mark of 177 miles per hour, the fastest speed any 250cc engine using gas or fuel had ever attained.

The engine used in Roeder's record attempt debuted in a 1965 model called the Sprint Scrambler. A competitive winner on the European racing circuit, it was added to Harley-Davidson's model line to fill a need for a competition —or pure off-road—high-performance 250. Also from the Aermacchi operation came a nifty little model called the M-50. A 50cc two-stroke in a step-through frame, it claimed an amazing 180 miles of breezy enjoyment per gallon.

Mickey Mantle and the Yankees dominated the American League in the early Sixties.

Teammates Roger Reiman (#1) and Mert Lawwill (#18) finished one-two in the 1965 Daytona 200 miler. Lawwill earned his own Number One plate for the 1969 season.

WORLD SPEED RECORD SET BY HARLEY-DAVIDSON SPRINT

One year and a month after Harley-Davidson set the 250cc world speed record at Bonneville, the Sprint streamliner returned to the salt and blasted the record up to an incredible 176.817 mph for the mile and 177.225 mph for the kilometer.

On October 21, 1965, under the guidance of top-notch racer George Roeder, the 250cc Harley-Davidson Sprint smashed all records in class A or class C runs with its two-way 177 mph average. The streamliner was powered by the new 1966 Sprint CR racing engine and burned standard pump gasoline. No 250cc bike had ever gone faster using gas or fuel. The historic speed runs were timed by the United States Auto Club (USAC) and sanctioned by the American Motorcyclist Association (AMA).

Clear, bright skies dried the flats for two weeks before the Harley Davidson Sprint was set to run. Under the direction of Stormy Mangham, airline pilot and record setter, the Sprint shell was brought up from Texas where it had spent the last year being refurbished and the updated Sprint engine was installed. Mangham was in charge of the 1964 Sprint record runs at Bonneville when Roger Reiman piloted the 15 cubic inch machine to 156.24 mph for the world's record.

At that time, the salt was mushy at all hours of the day, and the high-revving 250 could not get adequate traction to really let out. This time the salt was far from perfect, but it was considerably better than the previous year. By late morning, the old problem of water seeping onto the flats made good traction impossible, so most runs had to be made in the first few hours after sunrise.

On Tuesday morning, October 20, Roeder pushed the Sprint to a 170 mph two-way average to shatter Harley-Davidson's previous record. But it wasn't good enough for the crew on the salt. On the next day, the 14-foot Sprint streamliner was positioned 4-1/2 miles down the run from the timing traps and Roeder squeezed into the tight cockpit. Strapped down with only inches to turn his head, Roeder revved up the newly designed engine and was push-started down the course. The Sprint's five-speed transmission drove the bullet-nosed streamliner through the traps twice for the 177 mph mark average, and retained the Harley-Davidson 250's title as the fastest 250cc motorcycle in the world.

Below:
Nikita Khrushchev
and Fidel Castro.

For the first time, a Harley-Davidson motorcycle received an electric starter to crank its two massive pistons. Gone was the Duo-Glide; in its place was the Electra Glide. Riders never had it so good—not until 1966, at least.

That was the year Harley-Davidson doled out liberal doses of extra horsepower. The Electra Glide received an updated engine with redesigned "power pac" aluminum heads, which put out ten percent more horsepower. Because of the shape of their combustion chambers, these new heads earned the engine the nickname of "shovelhead."

Not to be outdone by its bigger brother, the Sportster also got a fifteen percent boost in power by virtue of a new carburetor and cams.

Added to the bottom end of the line was a Sport model of the M-50, as well as a new 175cc model. Called the Bobcat, this newest lightweight sported a

With Harley-Davidson accessories, a rider could tailor his Electra Glide to suit his own personal tastes.

Barbra Streisand and the Beatles made their impact on American Music.

unique one-piece molded ABS resin body which covered both the gas tank and the rear wheel. The Bobcat was the last of the domestically produced lightweights and, despite its modern looks, was gone from the line a year later. From then on, all the Harley-Davidson lightweight models were produced in the Italian plant.

More changes to the line for 1967 saw the XLH Sportster receiving an electric starter, while the M-50s got a boost in displacement to 65cc. The Sprint underwent styling changes to both the engine and its sheet metal, especially the H model which received a five gallon, road-race style gas tank. Companion to the Electra Glide was a smoothly-styled, more contemporary fiberglass sidecar. Except for the introduction of the 125cc Rapido, the model line changed little for 1968.

HARLEY-DAVIDSON'S BOLD NEW **BOBCAT** FOR 1966

Above: A promotional piece for the 1966 Bobcat; a cutaway view of the 1966 Big Twin engine; Julie Andrews in "The Sound of Music." Left: The 1965 Sportsters.

THE SUPER-HOT ONES FOR '65

WIDEN YOUR fun horizons

Far right:
Raquel Welch.

Hottest Thing Going On two Wheels

SPORTSTER H

electrifying!
PUSH BUTTON STARTING
positive, heavy-duty **electra glide type** with new 4-pole starter motor

Push the button . . . ZAP . . . and away you go. It's electrifying . . . it's unbelievable . . . it's new SPORTSTER H instant starting. Powerful 12 volt system, using a 32 ampere hour battery, leaps to your command to pulse SPORTSTER H's charging horses into action. Battery-oil tank combo is rubber mounted to isolate all vibration. Heavy duty system allows more power, too, for your favorite accessories. Make your fun more electrifying this year on a new SPORTSTER H.

NEW SPORTSTER H ELECTRIFYING STYLING — Stand back . . . take a look! Catch the sparkle of the new **twin tach-speedo** instrumentation. It's right up front where you can see it . . . but not the hidden drive cables. **New Headlight Nacelle** is really a beauty. An **Indicator Lamp Panel** is built right into the nacelle with aircraft design. New **Neat-Pleat All-Model Buddy Seat** has California styling that says ''class'' from the word go!

206

Above: "Spy" stories remained popular, as in TV's "The Man from U.N.C.L.E." Left: The 1967 Harley-Davidson model line.

NEW HOT AND SWINGING.... '67 HARLEY-DAVIDSON M-65's with 62% more horsepower

Above: "Bonnie and Clyde" shot 'em up on film, while Rowan and Martin broke 'em up on TV.

'67 electrifying HARLEY-DAVIDSON SPORTSTERS H&CH

FUN FOR YOUNG AMERICA AT ANY AGE

Never before has a lightweight sportcycle won so many hearts as the Harley-Davidson. Now, add the punch of more power and you've got a two-wheeled wildcat loaded with get-up-and-go! Safe power, too! Perfect for keeping up with traffic . . . ideal for long ride leisure. Yes, no matter what your riding pleasure, you'll love these neat and nimble lightweights . . . . they're a barrel of fun for everyone.

HARLEY-DAVIDSON MODEL M-65 and M-65 SPORT
Sleek for Sightseeing ■ Shopping ■ School ■ Work or Play

D RIDING LEATHERS
Lightweight, competition-styled garments of
select black leather. Nylon lined, form-fitting
for comfort and safety.
98140-60V Leather Shirt,
Sizes 34-48 . . . . $37.30
98145-60V Leather Pants,
Sizes 28-42 . . . . $39.50

The 1968 Electra Glide is unique in all cycling!

Introduce yourself to a one-of-a-kind experience. Ride the new Electra Gl
In this one motorcycle, you'll get the precise engineering of a formula racer
the handcrafted luxury of a custom roadster. Here too, are the stamina, bala
and ride that have made the 1200 cc Electra Glide the world's foremost cy
Now add electric starting, new instrumentation and futuristic styling. Th
Electra Glide for 1968. On display right now at the Harley-Davidson de
nearest you. A limited edition of unlimited excellence. Stop in for a test ride se

HARLEY-DAVIDSO

The Harley-
Davidson
accessories line
continued to grow
in the Sixties.

208

I CYCLE CHAMP AND CYCLE QUEEN JACKETS

Form-fitting, fashioned from choice black leather, both have quilted nylon lining, zipper closing, snap-down lapels, wind-tight sleeves, plenty of pockets.

98100-58V Champ, Sizes 34-48 (with belt) $47.50
98105-46V Queen, Sizes 32-42 (with belt) $43.75
98130-58VA Belt, Sizes 32-48 . . . .$ 2.75
Townsman Coat (not shown) — Black leather, hip length, belted coat, sizes 34-48, 98101-53V $49.75

The Beach Boys,
Sandra Dee and Troy Donahue in "A Summer Place."

209

Racing action continued hot and heavy with Harley-Davidson excelling in virtually every area of two-wheeled competition. From drag racing to hillclimbing to Bonneville record runs, it was the Sprints, Sportsters and KR racers from Milwaukee that set the pace and broke records on strips and courses all over the country.

Perhaps the greatest accolade to symbolize Harley-Davidson's dominance of motorcycle competition in the late Sixties was the nickname bestowed on its team of Class C dirt trackers and road racers. "The Wrecking Crew" was so powerful in 1968 that it won 18 of the 23 National Championship races held that year, wrecking everyone else's hopes of having a winning season.

The most stunning ride of the year was turned in by team road racing ace Cal Rayborn, as he rode his streamlined KR to victory at the Daytona 200 miler a full four miles ahead of the second place man. Rayborn's win was

The first lap of the 1968 Daytona 200 miler being led by the Harley-Davidson Wrecking Crew in its orange, black and white racing colors.

American astronauts take man's first walk on the moon.

FPG

one for the record books as he ran the race at an average speed of 101.290 miles per hour, the first motorcycle racer to crack the 100 mph barrier on the famed course. He also became the first racer to do it a second time when he won again in 1969, once more at an average speed over 100 miles per hour after having lapped the entire field.

The final year of the decade saw the Sprint engine receive an increase in size to 350cc along with its racing counterpart, the ERS, which took a first overall in the Greenhorn 500-mile National Championship Enduro in California.

Cosmetically, the dependable little Rapido received an update which gave it a cleaner, more modern look. Demonstrating the reliability and performance of the spunky little two-stroke, three adventurous motorcyclers made a trek of nearly 2,000 miles across the treacherous wasteland of the Sahara Desert on a trio of fully-loaded Rapidos in the early months of the year.

Peter Fonda and Dennis Hopper in "Easy Rider."

CROSSING THE SAHARA DESERT ON RAPIDOS.

Early in 1969, five American adverturers set out on the motorcycle journey of a lifetime, across the barren landscape of North Africa's fabled Sahara Desert. Their purpose was to make a photographic and cinemagraphic record of what was to become a long and arduous trek. Their motorcycles of choice were not thumping 250cc trail bikes, but rather the nimble 125cc Harley-Davidson Rapidos.

While all five men arrived in Casablanca in mid-January to start the journey, two of them would drop out and go home before the trip was even half over. The remaining three were Russel Rehm, Dick Ewing and Frank Fanger.

The plan was to set up their motorcycles and leave from Casablanca as soon as possible, in order to get across the desert before the March sandstorms began. As so often happens, the best laid plans don't always work the way they should, and the group faced two weeks of delays as they grappled with paperwork, indifferent officials and missing motorcycles. Four of the five Rapidos were being shipped directly from Aermacchi Harley-Davidson via the Italian port of Genoa and had not arrived on time.

With the bikes arriving from the docks by horsecart, the crew was finally able to begin assembly. In addition to normal setup, each bike was fitted with a high exhaust pipe so it could better negotiate the obstacles posed by desert travel.

Finally, the big day arrived on January 31. Up at 5:30 a.m., the men loaded—then unloaded and reloaded—the Rapidos, rearranging and discarding equipment in their attempts to balance the loads. Despite their best efforts, the bikes handled poorly that first day, causing several spills as they picked their way cautiously over the rugged roads. Fortunately, no one was seriously injured, and after that their skills at packing the little 125s got progressively better.

Heading northeast and then east through Rabat, Fex and Oujda, the travelers were treated to a variety of impressions as they witnessed everyday life in North Africa. Scenes such as town markets, vineyards, groves of fig and date trees, and Roman ruins all conjured up biblical images as they slowly motored eastward.

Pushing for Oujda, they encountered a cold front with 40° temperatures and driving rain. After 150 miles over miserable roads, the group opted for hot food, warm beds and clean sheets in the town's best hotel, rather than spending a night camping in the chilly weather.

Entering Algeria, they turned their motorcycles south and headed into the true desert. Crossing a plateau 3,500 feet high, they encountered an old, abandoned and shot-out fort where they spent the night under the stars. Their room for the night had apparently been used by wandering shepherds to pen their sheep, and smelled accordingly. But animal scents were the least of their worries. As they traveled, they continuously worried about the availability of gasoline and were plagued by the indifference of Algerian police and minor officials, who seemed more intent on making their lives difficult than speeding them on their way. They were constantly warned against taking pictures, and often were threatened with having their equipment and film confiscated.

As they rode southward, stopping periodically for gas, they were continually followed by the local police, and occasionally stopped for questioning. In a fit of frustration, they sent a telegram to the president of Algeria but, of course, received no reply.

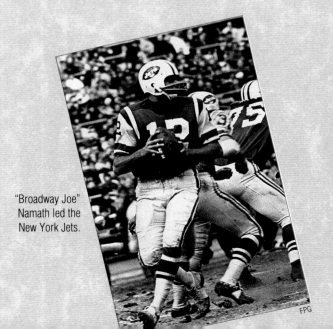

"Broadway Joe" Namath led the New York Jets.

FPG

On February 27, disaster struck when Dick Ewing took a bad spill after being passed by a VW. Thinking he had broken an ankle, they loaded his bike on a passing truck and continued south to Arak. Unable to get proper medical help when they arrived, Dick was convinced to continue with the truck to a city called Tamanrasset, where a fluoroscope showed he had suffered torn ligaments, rather than a broken bone. Nonetheless, his riding days were over for a while.

Frank and Russ enlisted a 22-year-old Dutchman, named Rob, to continue with the third Rapido, while Dick continued by other means. For safety and convenience, the trio hooked up with a group of Germans who were traveling in a converted personnel carrier. Riding twelve hours a day over washboard roads for the next several days, left all three men butt sore and weary as they caravaned southward, but their little Harley-Davidsons performed well.

By March 15, they began to notice changes in the surrounding scenery. The bleak barrenness of the desert was gradually giving way to shrubs and greenery. At last, they realized that they had conquered the desert. They had crossed the mighty Sahara and were ready to continue on to the coast.

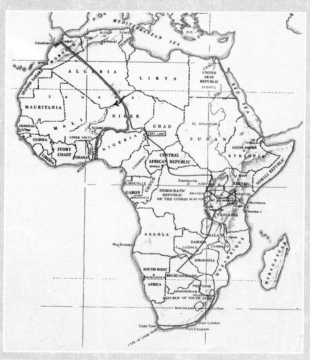

After 2,000 miles of blowing sand, primitive roads, cold nights and sunny days, the group had done what many thought was impossible. With little more than planning and a handful of Harley-Davidson Rapidos, they had conquered the mighty Sahara.

By 1969, Harley-Davidson had a well-rounded line of lightweight motorcycles and a proven and popular pair of heavyweights in the Sportster and Electra Glide. The golf car business was very strong and growing stronger. The decade had seen Harley-Davidson dominate nearly every area of motorcycle competition, and the words Daytona and Harley-Davidson had become nearly synonymous. Despite the many victories and records at the legendary Florida race, Cal Rayborn's 1969 win marked the last trip to the winner's circle at the Daytona 200 miler for Harley-Davidson. Having been around since early in the decade and no longer content with the lower end of the market, the Japanese motorcycle manufacturers entered the big bike arena with their multi-cylinder models and became a force to be reckoned with.

As the Sixties wound to a close, Harley-Davidson prepared to enter another era in its long history. Having gone public in 1965, the company's stock was well spread among both the officers and the public. Late in the decade, facing a hostile takeover from a company intent on making broad and sweeping changes, Harley-Davidson instead merged with an East Coast firm with a heavy commitment to leisure products. In 1969, Harley-Davidson became a part of American Machine and Foundry (AMF), a conglomerate of small- to medium-sized companies chaired by a one-time Harley rider, Rodney C. Gott. After six and a half decades of forging ahead on its own, Harley-Davidson now had to answer to a higher corporate authority.

Rodney Gott, chairman of AMF, tries out a 1970 Sportster on a 1969 visit to Milwaukee. Gott learned how to ride back in the early Thirties on a Harley-Davidson VL.

Left: Cal Rayborn dives under the checkered flag at the 1969 Daytona 200-mile road race for his second win in as many years. Below: Robert Redford and Paul Newman as "Butch Cassidy and the Sundance Kid." Left center: A 1967 Utilicar.

215

THE 1970'S

Under the AMF Banner

THE 1970'S

Entering the Seventies, Harley-Davidson motorcycles and golf cars continued to be in great demand despite the growing number of foreign-made competitive products flooding the marketplace. While it was no longer the fastest motorcycle on two wheels, the Sportster still retained its image as the ultimate macho machine and was highly sought after by enthusiasts. Because the demand so greatly exceeded the supply, it was not uncommon for a rider to wait months for delivery of a new Sportster, or fly a thousand miles to purchase one available on the showroom floor of a remote Harley-Davidson dealership.

The 1970 Sportster featured an updated, more modern look which included a boat-tail fiberglass seat/fender combination, totally covering a cutoff rear fender which jutted out the back like a torpedo. To Sportster purists, it was too radical a departure from the motorcycle's classic look, and the Sportster seat aftermarket flourished among riders anxious to change them.

New for that year were two hot competition machines. The Baja was introduced as a 100cc high performance, off-road model. With its aggressive tires and long-legged stance, it proved ideal for moto-cross, enduros and desert racing and quickly ran up a string of victories in Southern California's District 37 desert racing.

The other hot performer was a full-blown racer, designed to compete on the Class C professional racing circuit. Powered by a destroked Sportster engine, the XR 750 debuted on America's racetracks as a powerful successor to the time-honored KR. Because its powerplant was essentially a street engine with cast-iron cylinders and certain performance modifications, the XR was really a stopgap race bike, designed to be campaigned while development proceeded on a more advanced version. Despite the engine's many inherent limitations, it still proved itself a worthy competitor. In its most impressive win of what proved to be a short career for the "iron XR," the machine was campaigned by the late, great Harley-Davidson team racer, Cal Rayborn, at a series of six 1970 Anglo-American match races in England. In a performance that stunned the European road racers and spoke more of the rider than the motorcycle, Rayborn rode the XR to three firsts and three seconds in the six races.

The 1970 XR-750.

HARLEY-DAVIDSON

The U.S. invasion of Cambodia caused widespread antiwar demonstrations.

PEACE

Racing Director Dick O'Brien, left, and Jules Horky of the AMA inspect a massed array of XRs prior to the start of the 1970 racing season.

221

In October of 1970, the Sportster was a headliner once more in motorcycle publications, as Harley-Davidson journeyed to the Bonneville salt flats for an assault on the motorcycle land speed record. As in past record-setting attempts, the company again called on its premier racer to pilot its Harley-Davidson down the course. This time, it was Cal Rayborn. Laying almost flat on his back with a souped-up Sportster engine right behind his head, Rayborn steered an orange, cigar-shaped streamliner resembling a jet fighter's wing tank down the course, setting a two-way record of 265.492 miles per hour. It was the fastest speed any motorcycle-powered vehicle had ever attained.

The year closed with even more news as Harley-Davidson entered a totally different arena of leisure vehicles. After years of testing and evaluating other machines on the market, in late 1970 the company unveiled its brand new snowmobile, a 398cc beauty made available that season on a limited basis. Harley-Davidson felt that many snowmobile manufacturers would soon fall by the wayside and customers would want a product backed by a solid, established dealer network. Snowmobiles went into full production the next year and were highly praised for their quality, comfort and reliability, if not for their sizzling performance.

In October of 1970, Harley-Davidson went to the salt flats of Bonneville near Wendover, Utah, to prove that a single Harley-Davidson engine could break an absolute motorcycle land speed record held previously by twin-engine machines.

The vehicle they chose to make the record run was a computer-designed monocoque streamliner which measured nineteen feet long and a scant 25 inches high. The streamliner was so low that its driver, veteran road racer Cal Rayborn, had to lay almost flat on his back and look out either of two side windows to steer the machine down the course.

With 1930s Harley-Davidson racing great Joe Petrali present as the official United States Auto Club timer, Rayborn blasted down the ten-mile course to clock a speed of 266.785 miles per hour for the measured mile. His return run of 264.200 was good enough for an average of 265.492 and another page in the record books for Harley-Davidson.

Since the merger between Harley-Davidson and AMF, the influence of the corporate parent received little notice by riders and dealers as the company proceeded more or less with business as usual. The fact that Harley-Davidson was no longer master of its own destiny became evident soon after the addition of the AMF corporate logo to all 1971 motorcycle gas tanks. From that time on, the company was to be known as AMF Harley-Davidson, a decree that rankled enthusiasts everywhere.

That summer, AMF flexed its corporate muscles even more by naming a new president and elevating William H. Davidson to chairman. For the first time in sixty-eight years, someone other than a Davidson sat in the president's chair. At the same time, John Davidson was promoted from vice president of sales to executive vice president. Earlier that year, William J. Harley, engineering vice president, passed away. His brother, John, remained as the last Harley to hold a position of responsibility in Harley-Davidson Motor Company until his death five years later.

There was a bright spot in 1971—or perhaps a solar flare-up would be more appropriate—as Harley-Davidson unveiled a new heavyweight motorcycle destined to change the face of American motorcycling forever. Customizing and personalizing Harley-Davidsons had long been a right and privilege of owners, who tailored their motorcycles to their own tastes. This growing trend reached its zenith by the Seventies, and Harley-Davidson felt it was time to take an active part.

Clint Eastwood's movie role as Harry Callahan began with "Dirty Harry."

The 1971 Harley-Davidson Outperformers.

Joe Smith, riding a dragbike powered by a single Harley-Davidson motor, was the first to break the nine-second barrier in motorcycle drag racing in 1971. Using a double-engine machine in 1974, he set a new record of 8.20 seconds for the quarter mile.

...orn leads Briton Ray Pickrell through a curve at ...Park in England during the 1971 Anglo-American ...ces.

1970

News of U.S. invasion of Cambodia results in campus violence and demonstrations.

George C. Scott wins Oscar for role as Patton, but refuses it.

1971

The 26th Amendment to the Constitution, lowering voting age to 18, is approved.

Charles Manson found guilty of 1969 slaying of Sharon Tate and six others.

U.S. and South Vietnamese military enter Laos.

1972

Alabama Gov. George Wallace shot and seriously wounded by Arthur H. Bremer.

Five men arrested for break-in at Democratic headquarters in Watergate office complex.

1973

OPEC oil embargo causes long lines at gas stations and shuts down factories.

Charged with tax evasion, Vice President Agnew resigns; succeeded by Gerald Ford.

Last U.S. troops leave Vietnam March 29.

1974

President Nixon resigns under threat of impeachment; Gerald Ford becomes president.

Fresh from the design studio of Willie G. Davidson came the boldly massive FX 1200 Super Glide. The FX got its name and custom looks by mating the frame and running gear of the FL series to the lighter, sportier front end of the XL series. The FX was derived by using the first letter of FL and first letter of XL. Like the earlier Sportster, the Super Glide also sported a fiberglass seat/fender, although in a more detailed form. Rounding out the custom look was a red, white and blue color scheme the factory called "Sparkling America." While the fiberglass seat/fender never gained widespread popularity, the "Sparkling America" versions became instant collectors' items.

In the middle of the product line, a new on-road/off-road version of the 350cc Sprint made its appearance in the rugged SX 350. The street version with its low exhaust disappeared, at least for 1971, but was to reappear in mid-1972.

In addition to its new models and racing successes, Harley-Davidson was also gaining publicity from unusual quarters. Early in the decade, the company began working with a super showman whose career was just beginning to rise. In what proved to be an interesting and rewarding relationship, Harley-Davidson began supplying motorcycles and support to a charismatic daredevil by the name of Evel Knievel.

While jumping over long lines of cars parked side by side was his main stock in trade, Knievel attracted considerable attention to himself and Harley-Davidson through his flamboyant lifestyle and by his abortive attempt to pilot a rocket-powered "skycycle" over the Snake River Canyon. While many serious motorcyclists scoffed at Evel Knievel's antics, he gained a great deal of favorable publicity for Harley-Davidson through personal appearances and two feature-length films dramatizing his adventures.

Donald Sutherland and Jane Fonda in "Klute."

The Sprint SX 350.

Clockwise,
from upper left:
the 1971 Super Glide
in "Sparkling America"
red, white and blue;
Robert Blake in
"Electra Glide in Blue";
Olympic star Mark
Spitz; a composite
photograph illustrating
Evel Knievel's
technique as he
hurtles his XR 750
over nine trucks.

In 1972, the Sportster was the hot news again as it grew in size to 1000cc or 61 cubic inches. The Sportster also received a baby brother called the Shortster in the form of a sturdy little 65cc minibike. Also, the Sportster-based XR 750 was replaced by a more advanced, more powerful version with a new aluminum alloy engine. So strong was the new XR that it propelled team racer Mark Brelsford into the title of Grand National Champion for 1972, Harley-Davidson's first Number One plate since Mert Lawwill's achievement in 1969 on the KR.

Celebrating the fiftieth anniversary of Harley-Davidson's 74 cubic inch engine, the majestic FLH Electra Glide was fitted with a mighty 10 inch front disc brake, making it the first production motorcycle to have hydraulic front and rear brakes. Little wonder it was often referred to as "King of the Highway."

Liza Minneli in "Caberet."

The 19
Shortst

The Electra Glide, blue and white.

The Beatles changed the face of popular music.

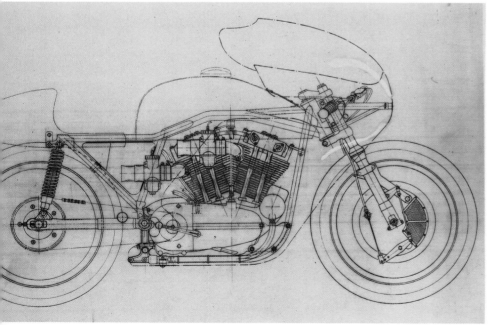

A blueprint drawing of the 1972 alloy engine XR 750 road racer.

Harley-Davidson has had a long history of speed records at the Bonneville salt flats. In 1972, Warner Riley set a new two-way speed record of 206.544 miles per hour on a nitro-fueled Sportster.

"The Godfather" starred Marlon Brando.

229

Big changes were brewing in the world of Harley-Davidson in 1973. Actual assembly of motorcycles and golf cars was moved from Milwaukee to a modern 400,000-square-foot, single-story AMF plant in York, Pennsylvania. Harley-Davidson's headquarters, racing division, and parts and accessories operation remained at Milwaukee's Juneau Avenue plant, while its Capitol Drive plant was used chiefly to produce engines, transmissions and component parts to support the York assembly line.

William H. Davidson, who had served as chairman for two years after twenty-nine years as company president, retired in 1973. Later that year his son, John, was promoted to the position of president.

Almost the entire line underwent changes for 1973, the most extensive improvements being in the line of Italian lightweights. All the model names were dropped in favor of letter and number designations, which was more in line with the rest of the industry. In addition, numerous features like oil injection were incorporated in an effort to put the motorcycles more on a par with others in their class. New tanks, frames, fenders and graphics were all part of this upgrading process.

The minibike got a bigger, better engine and transmission and was reborn as the X-90. Replacing the Rapido was the TX-125, and a smaller version of it became the Z-90. The Sprints received electric starters in addition to their many other improvements and became known simply as the SX-350 and the SS-350.

The old Sprint gas tank, a streamlined teardrop, was added to the Super Glide for a longer, leaner look and more of a custom appearance. The fiberglass seat was history. By 1973, all of the heavyweights had received a front disc brake.

Harley-Davidson continued to expand its line of riding apparel.

The addition of the York plant gave Harley-Davidson sorely needed room for expanded production.

Discover the shortest distance between two points.

The new Harley-Davidson TX-125.

An on-road, off-road, 5-speed, oil injected goodtime machine.

With a look that moves people to envy and delight.

A double downtube frame makes the riding so sweet, that before you know it, you're where you want to be.

Sun-drenched, tingly and feeling like new money.

The Harley-Davidson TX-125.

Restyled. Eager.

The nicest way you'll ever go from one place to another.

AMF Harley-Davidson,
Milwaukee, Wisconsin 53201
Member Motorcycle Industry Council

Harley-Davidson TX-125.
The Great American Freedom Machine.

Below: Robert Redford starred with Paul Newman in "The Sting" and with Barbra Streisand in "The Way We Were."
Bottom: Harley-Davidson snowmobiles and golf cars continued to be in demand.

In Europe, the Ameracchi Harley-Davidson plant began to campaign an awesome 250cc, twin-cylinder road racer in Europe called the RR-250. In the hands of a skilled road racer like Italy's Renzo Pasolini, it quickly became a force to contend with. Later, Walter Villa rode the RR-250 to three consecutive World 250 championship titles in 1974-76, a feat never previously accomplished. The RR-250 debuted in the U.S. in 1974 when team racer Gary Scott won the 250cc road race at Loudon, New Hampshire, marking the first time Harley-Davidson had won an American 250cc road race in four years.

After the extensive improvements to the product line in 1973, few changes occurred the following year. The most significant event was the addition of an electric starter model to the Super Glide line, the FXE. Now riders who favored the laid-back, low-down look of the Super Glide were able to choose between a button starter or kick starter. Also, a brand new 2-stroke 175 was unveiled, which was head and shoulders above the other Harley-Davidson lightweights for style and performance.

A year later, Harley-Davidson introduced a larger version of the 175 in the form of a 250, both of which received the SX designation for their on-road/off-road abilities. The Sprint, long past its prime in the motorcycle world, was dropped from the line. By 1975, after three relatively snowless winters, Harley's snowmobile also faded quietly from the scene.

Richard Nixon met his Watergate in 1973.

AMF
Harley-Davidson
SX-175

Above: Willie G. Davidson, left, and William H presented a restored racing motorcycle to Ton for display in the Indianapolis Motor Speedwa in 1974. The racer was originally campaigned Petrali, six-time national motorcycle champio Left: Fay Dunaway and Jack Nicholson in "Chinatown."

Pleasant dreams.

're big enough to do all those neat things you've been dreaming about
a Harley-Davidson X-90.
nd it's a real motorcycle. With a man-size engine and 4-speed transmis-
. Plus all the other freedom and fun features that are on bigger cycles. Rear
ks, full electrics, all-new brakes, even a spark arrestor muffler.
e can help make your dreams more pleasant by making them real.

he Great American Freedom Machine.

Harley-Davidson
AMF Harley-Davidson
Milwaukee, Wisconsin 53201
Member Motorcycle Industry Council

1974 Motorcycle Enthusiast and General Magazines

Actor Sam Elliott
playing the title role
in the TV movie
"Evel Knievel."

1975 Harley-Davidson
materials promoted The
ican Freedom Machines
and rider's accessories.

America's bicentennial year, 1976, was a cause of great celebration throughout the country. Everyone was swept up in the fervor of a two-hundredth birthday party, and Harley-Davidson was no exception. As America's sole remaining motorcycle manufacturer, it was logical and fitting that the company do something special to commemorate the event.

For years, Harley-Davidson had been making the circuit of consumer motorcycle shows, displaying its products to an enthusiastic public. The biggest show, which traditionally kicked off the start of the motorcycle season, was held annually at Daytona Beach in conjunction with the week of races in March. Hordes of riders flocked south for sun, fun and racing. All major motorcycle manufacturers and many from the aftermarket regularly showed their products at a large show in a hotel on the beach.

To celebrate its American heritage, Harley-Davidson pulled its booth out of the regular motorcycle show and put together its own exhibit several miles down the beach, in the ballroom of a luxury hotel. With motorcycles from its extensive collection of antiques plus existing new products, Harley-Davidson created a stunning display entitled "A Salute to American Motorcycling." Thousands of motorcyclists and enthusiasts endured long lines to view Harley-Davidson's show, the likes of which Daytona Beach had never seen.

Originally intended to be a bicentennial event only, Harley-Davidson's extravaganza proved so successful that the decision was made to hold it every year and to make it bigger and better. The events surrounding the show gradually multiplied, as Harley-Davidson worked to get more riders involved in the sport by making more activities available to them in Daytona. As activities increased in the following years, there were poker runs, field meets, ride-in shows, a special section for Harley-Davidson riders at the speedway and much more.

Above, the 1976 Liberty Edition Superglide and, at right, the Liberty Edition FLH.

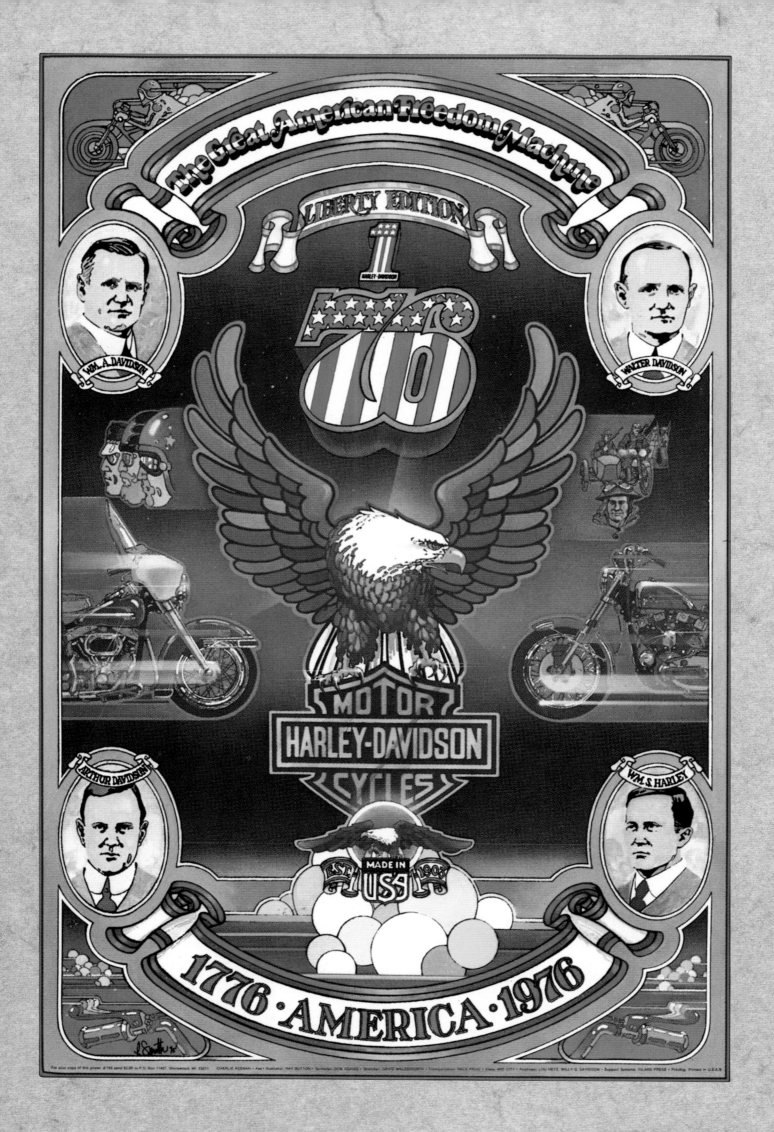

The hit of the 1977 show was a beautifully-detailed Willie G. Davidson creation called the FXS Low Rider. Featuring mag wheels, lettered tires, drag style handlebars, plus special paint and engine treatments, it epitomized everyman's ideal of what a custom motorcycle should be. The Low Rider was an instantaneous success and launched a whole new generation of motorcycles, the factory customs.

Later that year, a second Willie G. factory custom, the XLCR Cafe Racer, made its appearance. Based on a Sportster engine, the XLCR was a black-on-black beauty that capitalized on the prevailing cafe racer popularity in vogue at the time. Unlike the Low Rider, which went on to unprecedented popularity, the XLCR proved to be too much of a departure from traditional Harley-Davidson styling to ever gain widespread acceptance and was only produced through the 1978 model year. However, a lasting legacy of the Cafe Racer was the extensive auditing and road testing to ensure a top quality product, which eventually filtered into the other motorcycles coming out of the York operation.

With a history as long and varied as Harley-Davidson's, the company felt it should be shared with its many devotees, and opened a museum at the York plant in Pennsylvania. After viewing a selection of landmark motorcycles from the company's past, viewers would be free to tour the production facilities. With a least one motorcycle available to draw upon from every production year, the museum is changed on a regular basis, so repeat visitors are treated to a kaleidoscope of Harley-Davidson history. Tens of thousands tour the museum and plant annually.

"Laverne and Shirley" was a successful spinoff from TV's "Happy Days."

...the man who wears
...e Harley-Davidson Brand

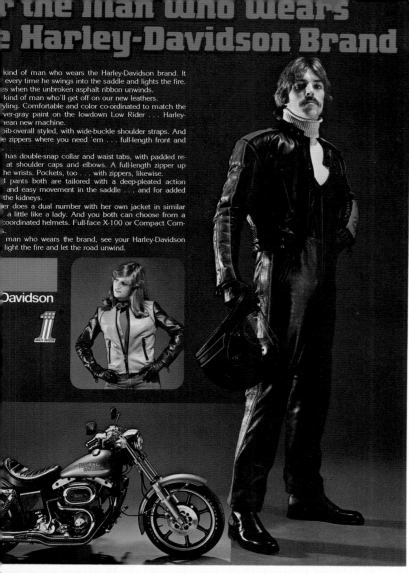

...kind of man who wears the Harley-Davidson brand. It
...every time he swings into the saddle and lights the fire.
...es when the unbroken asphalt ribbon unwinds.
...kind of man who'll get off on our new leathers.
...yling. Comfortable and color co-ordinated to match the
...ver-gray paint on the lowdown Low Rider . . . Harley-
...lean new machine.
...bib-overall styled, with wide-buckle shoulder straps. And
...e zippers where you need 'em . . . full-length front and

...has double-snap collar and waist tabs, with padded re-
...at shoulder caps and elbows. A full-length zipper up
...he wrists. Pockets, too . . . with zippers, likewise.
...d pants both are tailored with a deep-pleated action
...and easy movement in the saddle . . . and for added
...the kidneys.
...er does a dual number with her own jacket in similar
...a little like a lady. And you both can choose from a
...coordinated helmets. Full-face X-100 or Compact Com-
...s.
...man who wears the brand, see your Harley-Davidson
...light the fire and let the road unwind.

Left: A 1977 ad for Harley-Davidson leathers. Below: A promotional brochure touted the Low Rider as "one mean machine."

AMF
Harley-Davidson
Low Rider

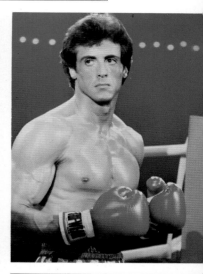

Above: Sylvester Stallone's star rose in "Rocky," while "Happy Days" used Milwaukee as a sitcom setting. Left: The Harley-Davidson Cafe Racer.

As happens nearly every decade, a star rose from the galaxy of motorcycle racers to shine as the outstanding performer in motorcycle competition during the second half of the Seventies. A youngster from Michigan first burst on the scene as a privateer in 1975, campaigning a Harley-Davidson XR-750 on the nation's dirt tracks. Because of his successes, he quickly caught the eye of Harley-Davidson's longtime Director of Racing, Dick O'Brien, and Jay Springsteen was signed for the 1976 factory team.

Riding in a spectacular style that pleased crowds and subdued competitors, Springsteen—or Springer, as his fans called him—fulfilled O'Brien's confidence in him by winning the title of Grand National Champion his first year on the team. At 19, Springsteen became the youngest man ever to wear the Number One plate. He repeated as Champion in 1977, and again in 1978.

Below: Michael Jackson originally caught the public's fancy as a member of The Jackson Five.

Right: The 1977 Daytona show featured a salute to Harley-Davidson racing. Bottom left: Walter Villa rode the potent RR-250 to three successive World 250 titles.

AMF
Harley-Davidson

FLH Accessories

Top left: John Davidson cuts the ribbon, opening Harley-Davidson's 1977 Daytona Show. On his right is World 250 Champion Walter Villa and on his left is AMA Grand National Champion Jay Springsteen. Left center: Springsteen in action. Right center: John Travolta in "Saturday Night Fever."

Late in 1977, the company began making plans for the kind of event that only Harley-Davidson can pull off successfully. The next year was to be Harley-Davidson's seventy-fifth anniversary and John Davidson, who was chairman, and Vaughn Beals, who had just become president, agreed that a massive ride of Harley-Davidson executives would be just the thing to draw attention to this very special occasion.

Sixteen executives, ranging from managers to the chairman, departed from points on the perimeter of the United States and followed seven different routes across the nation, with a final rendezvous at the Louisville motorcycle races in early June. Riding in teams of two or three riders, the men collectively traveled over 37,000 miles, visiting over 160 Harley-Davidson dealers along the way. At almost every stop, the riders were greeted by throngs of well-wishers, and were often interviewed by local media. The fact that the people who ran the company were all riders—and that they would take two weeks out of their busy schedules to get out on the road and meet their customers—impressed everyone who came into contact with them.

Above: Burt Reynolds was a big box office star in the mid-seventies. Right: Led by (front row from left) John Davidson, Vaughn Beals and Willie G. Davidson, sixteen Harley-Davidson executives toured the country in celebration of the company's seventy-fifth anniversary.

Harley-Davidson
V-Twin Motorcycles

AMF

WE DON'T WANT OTHER PEOPLE'S PARTS IN OUR MOTORCYCLES.
(A Less Than Tolerant Viewpoint From Harley-Davidson.)

This should be a polite message that attempts to persuade you to use only genuine Harley-Davidson parts.

We don't feel all that polite about the subject, however.

Our engineers and designers, quite frankly, lack tolerance. They seem to take great joy in constantly reminding us that

Harley-Davidson motorcycles are expected to be classics.

Naturally, with that kind of pressure from within, we've become somewhat exacting and inflexible.

For example, the piston to cylinder wall fit on a Harley-Davidson FX-1200 motorcycle is between .001 and .002 of an inch. That's 1/3 the thickness of a human hair!

So you can see why we come unglued when instead of seeing your authorized Harley-Davidson dealer and using only genuine Harley-Davidson replacement parts, you put in somebody else's heads, valves, pistons, cables, and even oil and oil filters.

Worse yet, when you don't use our parts, you don't use the one guy out there who we trust to be just as tenacious as we are—your Harley-Davidson dealer.

To you it's no big deal. To our guys, you're violating a basic law of physics.

The Whole Equals the Sum of its Parts.

AMF Harley-Davidson

A CHOICE BETWEEN COMFORT OR STYLE IS NO CHOICE AT ALL.
[A Less Than Tolerant Viewpoint from Harley-Davidson]

of your image, and ours, we cordially suggest a way you can avoid all that.

A clothing store for motorcyclists.

Simply visit an expert with such a wide variety of styles he could stock a clothing store—your Harley-Davidson dealer.

The first thing he'll tell you is that no style looks good on a shivering rider. Then he'll show you some features to look for.

Like the specially sewn-in wind flap that's on our Pioneer leathers and Cycle Champ jackets. A wind flap that's not just covering the front of the zipper, but rather, is on the inside, behind the zipper where the wind can't get at it.

He'll show you the special sleeve closures on many of our jackets, to keep the wind from whistling up your arms. And specially-designed, pleated "action backs" to give you freedom of movement when you bend forward on the cycle.

Common sense.

He'll show you the common sense thinking behind our snap-down collars. And demonstrate how they're designed to keep you from being flapped to death at 40 MPH.

And he'll show you how to determine the proper length riding jacket so that it's long enough to protect you from wind whistling up under it, yet short enough not to bunch up beneath you.

You see it all the time. Some poor joker takes one look at some fancy leathers modeled by a California actor leaning on a rented motorcycle and before you know it, he's out on the highway in them. Touring Milwaukee in late October, freezing his ____ off.

Or he turns practical. And winds up in an outfit that looks like something from a late night, Science Fiction, TV show.

Nobody wins.

Naturally, we feel a great deal of sympathy when this happens. For us, The Human Icicle and Space Oddity don't exactly make great ads for motorcycling. So, in the interest

You'll be able to choose intelligently from more jackets, vests, boots, gloves and riding apparel than you'll see from any other motorcycle manufacturer.

And you'll hit the highway confident that Harley-Davidson would never leave you out in the cold.

It takes a warm body to tame cold steel.

AMF Harley-Davidson

ANYBODY CAN DRESS UP A HARLEY-DAVIDSON. NOT EVERYBODY CAN DO IT RIGHT.
[A Less Than Tolerant Viewpoint.]

Too many riders treat the purchase of a set of pipes or a sissy bar as though they were buying a star for the top of their Christmas tree. So long as it stays on, everything's fine.

Well, everything isn't so fine.

To most of you this won't be news, but you don't hang pipes on a Harley-Davidson motorcycle. You fit them. Perfectly. So they become part *of* the machine.

The Sportster shown here illustrates our point. It's dressed with a chrome-finished sissy bar, padded backrest, flat black cast wheels, independent staggered dual exhaust pipes, chrome oil cooler and chrome point cover. And it's 100 per cent Harley-Davidson. Because every part on it is a perfectly tooled-to-fit genuine Harley-Davidson accessory.

What's more, every Harley-Davidson accessory—from coolers to highway pegs to touring seats—is available at any Harley-Davidson dealer. So when you dress your Harley-Davidson motorcycle, you can dress it right.

Look at it this way. You've already committed yourself to riding one of the finest motorcycles the world has ever known. A cycle built to such exact tolerances that the piston to cylinder wall fit on an FX 1200, for example, is between .001 and .002 *of an inch*—1/3 the thickness of a human hair!

That's what you paid for. That's what you got.

This is no time to start making compromises.

Part of a motorcycle. Not parts on a motorcycle.

AMF Harley-Davidson

For a free accessories catalogue see your Harley-Davidson dealer or write Harley-Davidson direct at 3700 W. Juneau, Milwaukee, Wisc. 53201, desk J-1.

This long-established practice of mingling with the people who use the product has since grown to become one of Harley-Davidson's most important and consistent policies. Following the Seventy-Fifth Anniversary ride, Harley-Davidson executives and employees have participated in several similar marathon rides, plus hundreds of local, regional, national and international motorcycling events.

Further commemorating its three quarters of a century mark, Harley-Davidson produced special anniversary XL and FL models in black with striking gold trim. In addition, the Electra Glide had its engine increased in size to eighty cubic inches, or 1340cc.

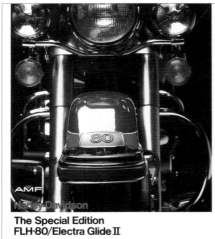

The Special Edition
FLH-80/Electra Glide II

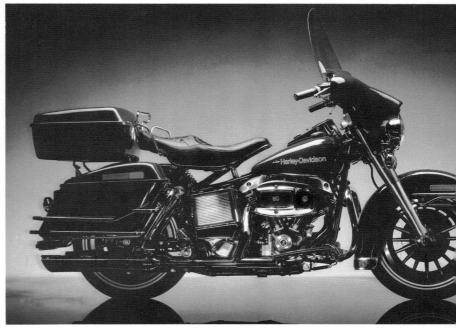

Top: The 75th Anniversary Sportster.
Right: The Special Edition
Electra Glide II.

242

With the exception of the Sportster, the products changed little in 1979. The XL received an updated, state of the art frame and a two-into-one exhaust. Also, because the Low Rider proved so successful, a similar Sportster-based version called the XLS Roadster was produced. The most notable change throughout the product line was the addition of large "ham can" air cleaners, which were needed to meet federally mandated noise limits. Federal regulations regarding noise and emissions were to play an increasingly prominent role in Harley-Davidson's product development in the coming years.

Left: The 1978 Electra Glide. Below: TV hits ranged from Donnie and Marie to "Charlie's Angels." Bottom left: The 75th Anniversary Electra Glide.

By 1979, after thirty years of making lightweights, Harley-Davidson had stopped producing the smaller machines, choosing instead to concentrate all its efforts on the V-twin heavyweight models. As the decade rolled to a close, Harley-Davidson experienced its most successful sales year ever. Thanks to a large influx of capital from AMF for needed machinery and the addition of the York assembly plant, Harley-Davidson was able to produce a record number of motorcycles in 1979. Despite all of AMF's efforts at making the company a more powerful and effective manufacturing force, many riders and enthusiasts came to blame the parent company for a number of Harley-Davidson's shortcomings, real or imagined. The truth of the matter is that AMF provided Harley-Davidson with the necessary funds to modernize and a facility to increase production, at a time when both the market and the competition were growing.

As the company prepared to enter the Eighties, customer dissatisfaction with AMF continued to fester. It was their fascination with the product, combined with mammoth public relations efforts of people like Vaughn Beals and Willie G., that sustained customer loyalty and kept them interested in Harley-Davidson.

The 1979 Electra Glide "Classic" with Sidecar

The unequalled prestige of riding a 1979 Electra Glide "Classic" can only be enhanced by showing off the enviable utmost in touring fun: The 1979 Electra Glide "Classic" with Sidecar.

Designed by Willie G. Davidson for availability as a complete vehicle unit, the 1979 limited edition Electra Glide "Classic" with Sidecar is Willie G.'s "piece de resistance" — for the die-hard tourist who *thought* he had everything. The two-tone tan and creme color scheme and hand-applied brown pinstriping which perfectly match the "Classic" are just the beginning. Willie G.'s eye for making the unusual dramatic insisted upon equipping the Sidecar with the same black cast mag wheel that you see on the "Classic".

You'll find other little details similarly rewarding, like the Sidecar drum brake, matching brown vinyl Sidecar bench seat and color coordinated snap-on tonneau cover.

Did Willie G. do it up right? We think it's a knock-out!

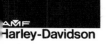

FPG

President Jimmy Carter was completing a turbulent term.

Bo Derek was a perfect '10."

245

AMF
Harley-Davidson
MX-250

THE 1980'S

The Eagle Soars Alone

THE 1980'S

The Eighties burst upon the scene in a flurry of excitement for Harley-Davidson that was to continue through the entire decade. More events of major significance occurred at Harley-Davidson during those years than in any previous decade, as the company produced an array of the most exciting, trend-setting motorcycles the sport has ever seen, and they engaged in a variety of events that set the industry and the nation buzzing.

The 1980 model year brought several exciting introductions. The 80 cubic inch FLT Tour Glide was born, with five-speed transmission, oil-bath-enclosed rear chain and a vibration-isolated engine. Together with a totally redesigned frame and steering geometry for "sport bike handling," the FLT was destined to become the inheritor of the FLH's "King of the Highway" crown. Also introduced was the 80-inch Wide Glide factory custom and the Sturgis. What made the latter so unique was that the 80-inch engine transmitted its power to the road through a twin belt drive. Thus the belts, which are lighter and simpler than a shaft, smoother than a chain and required no lubrication, made a comeback after a several-decade absence—with the latest in modern technology applied, of course.

The company also held an increasing number of consumer promotions, like the annual motorcycle show at Daytona during Bike Week and sponsorship of the "Bikers' Fight Against Muscular Dystrophy."

The popularity of "Star Wars" continued with sequels.

The 1980 FLT Tour Glide.

Top: The 1980 Sturgis marked the return of the drive belt, but with the technology of the Eighties. Left: The flamed Wide Glide personified the factory custom motorcycle.

At the 1981 Daytona activities, the air was full of big news concerning the company's future. It had begun on February 26, 1981, when a group of senior Harley-Davidson executives signed a letter of intent with AMF to purchase Harley-Davidson Motor Company from AMF. The purchasing group was headed up by Vaughn Beals, an AMF executive in charge of Harley-Davidson operations, and included Charles Thompson, company president; William G. Davidson; and others in the company.

During a press conference at Daytona Beach on March 3, 1981, Beals talked about the positive aspects of the AMF and Harley-Davidson association, "From 1969 through 1980, AMF's substantial capital investment in the motorcycle and golf car businesses permitted Harley-Davidson revenues to grow from $49 million to approximately $300 million . . ."

Beals went on to say, "AMF helped the Motor Company through a critical stage of growth . . . the most tangible evidence of their success is the company's ability to now stand on its own once again and to look to the future with pride and expectation."

The return to private ownership was completed June 16, 1981 as the shareholder group of the new Harley-Davidson company celebrated the event with a York-to-Milwaukee ride, proclaiming "The Eagle Soars Alone."

Signing documents to mark the return of Harley-Davidson to stand-alone status in June 1981, were (from left): Ralph Swenson, Charles K. Thompson, and (seated) AMF President Ray Tritten and Vaughn Beals.

The first non-AMF motorcycle to roll off the York assembly line receives a gold dipstick from Vaughn Beals as company officers look on. From left: Ralph Swenson, Charles Thompson and Willie G. Davidson.

Christopher Reeves as "Superman."

RUN TO THE SUN.

1 Harley-Davidson Wide Glide, Low Rider, Roadster and Sportster. Valdosta, Georgia to Daytona Beach, Florida.

It happens every year. The classic union of Harley-Davidson® motorcycles and the men who ride them down to Bike Week in Daytona Beach. But the run means more than a machine. You have the unique feel of our legendary 1000 cc and 1340 cc engines, the heartbeat of every Harley-Davidson. No other motorcycle built can match it.

You have our tradition of custom styling. The look that *means* American. You see it in all our gas tanks, from the original teardrop Peanut to Fat Bob. You feel it with our pullback buckhorn handlebars, low stepped seats with sissy bars and the unique Harley riding position. And chrome is where it belongs: on the hardware and the staggered shorty duals.

We do more with custom paint, too. There's matching painted tanks and fenders. Hand-applied pinstriping. Unique tank graphics and dramatic engine finishes. Yet every 1981 Harley-Davidson has a distinctive character completely its own.

The Wide Glide.™ From extended front forks and custom bobbed rear fender to the flamed bob-and-a-half tank, it's the first factory built custom.

The Low Rider.® It's where custom styling begins. Extended front forks, 9-spoke cast wheels and a riding position just 27″ from the ground.

The Roadster.™ With flashing new 2-tone silver metallic paint with black pinstriping and a lot of Low Rider style.

Then, to this custom trio add our stylish '81 Sportster.® Latest edition of the classic American street machine. The one so many riders choose to join the Harley-Davidson tradition.

Your own Run to the Sun starts the moment you get on a Harley. Now you're part of a 78 year tradition that announces your commitment to motorcycling. That's a Harley-Davidson. It's more than a machine.

We support the Motorcycle Safety Foundation and the A.M.A. and recommend you ride with lights and helmet. Specifications subject to change without notice.

AMF Harley-Davidson
Support the Bikers Fight Against Muscular Dystrophy.

Above:
Painted illustrations
supplemented photography to
promote Harley-Davidsons in the
early Eighties.
Left: Pop idols Tom Selleck as
"Magnum" and super model
Christie Brinkley.

253

The buy-back was accompanied by an even firmer resolve to build motorcycles in the best American tradition of quality and durability. An internal program called "I Make The Eagle Fly" was instituted in all areas of the company and in dealerships, with a commitment to build, sell and service the products with a new level of quality. Two models introduced for 1982—the FXR Super Glide II with its rubber-isolated, five-speed power train, and a new welded and stamped-frame Sportster—quickly became prime examples of the company's commitment to a future of exciting products.

After nearly 80 years as the leader of America's motorcycles, Harley-Davidson was embarking on a course that was very much a reflection of the company's pioneering spirit and founding standards of excellence.

This pioneering spirit would be essential to the survival of the new privately-held Harley-Davidson. In 1982, the demand for motorcycles in the 651+cc market (Harley-Davidson's niche in the motorcycle industry) dropped by

Top: Bruce Springsteen. Bottom: Tony Dorsett, Dallas Cowboys vs. Minnesota Vikings, ran the longest run from scrimmage, 99 yards.

Below right: The introduction of the 1982 FXR heralded the beginning of a new era of performance and handling for Harley-Davidson motorcycles.

Soar wit

Motorcycle Week
Mar 4-8, Daytona Hilton

over 33,000 units compared to 1981 figures. Harley-Davidson laid off employees to bring production and inventories in line with demand, while Japan continued to export in record numbers.

In September of 1982, Harley-Davidson petitioned the International Trade Commission (ITC) for tariff relief from Japanese manufacturers who were building up inventories of unsold motorcycles. On April 1, 1983, upon ITC recommendation, President Reagan imposed additional tariffs on all imported Japanese motorcycles 700cc or larger. The additional tariff was to be effective for a five-year period ending in April 1988, at annually declining rates of 45, 35, 20, 15 and 10 percent.

In 1982, the company produced a special 25th Anniversary Sportster to celebrate the proud motorcycle's heritage as the first of the superbikes.

e Eagles.

255

Harley-Davidson had made it clear from the beginning that special tariffs were not aimed at preventing free market competition. According to Vaughn L. Beals, Jr., Harley-Davidson chairman and chief executive officer, "We simply wanted the U.S. government to restore order to a motorcycle market under siege by Japanese manufacturers who increased production in the face of sharp market decline."

One of the major factors in the ITC's decision to recommend tariffs was the fact that Harley-Davidson had started a major revitalization campaign in the late 1970s. The campaign was aimed at improving efficiency and product quality through programs like Just-In-Time manufacturing, Employee Involvement and Statistical Process Control.

A different campaign was aimed at getting Harley-Davidson owners more involved in the sport of motorcycling. The Harley Owners Group (H.O.G.), the only factory-sponsored motorcycle club in the world, was formed in 1983. H.O.G. played a significant role in the company's revitalization as it refocused attention to customer satisfaction after the sale. H.O.G.'s special benefits and motorcycle rallies helped boost membership to over 90,000 in six years.

The company also took steps to resolve another problem. For years, some people from time to time had been using the Harley-Davidson name and logos on various products without company permission. In some instances, the name was used on items of questionable taste or in conjunction with profanity or vulgarity. To remove these products from the marketplace, Harley-Davidson mounted a vigorous trademark-enforcement campaign, prosecuting trademark infringers. Soon after, it embarked on a broad program of licensing its name and trademarks. An array of items ranging from neckties to jewelry to wall hangings soon began appearing, not only in motorcycle shops but also in department and specialy stores. These broad merchandising efforts, combined with the company's enforcement efforts, gradually cleaned up the bootleg product market and served to boost the company's image in the eyes of the general public.

Sylvester Stallone as *Rambo,* and Arnold Schwarzenegger as *Conan.*

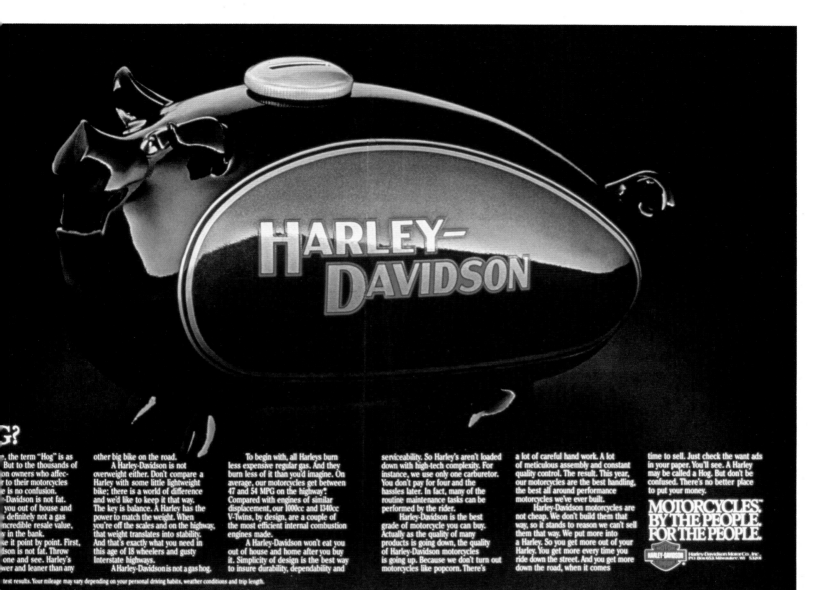

The FXRT
Sport Glide.

During this time period, Harley-Davidson was also working on further improvements to the product. In 1983, Harley-Davidson introduced a critically acclaimed "anti-dive" air-assisted suspension system on a sport-touring model called the FXRT, as well as the first computer-controlled ignition. Although the new designs did a lot to improve the motorcycles, the big V-Twin shovelhead engine didn't live up to the current levels of consumer expectations for function and durability.

In 1984, Harley-Davidson introduced the 1340cc V^2 Evolution engine on five models. The product of seven years of development, the Evolution engine produced more power at every engine speed and was also lighter, cooler and cleaner running, and extremely oil-tight. It was designed for high reliability and durability with a minimum of scheduled maintenance.

Revolutionary new motorcycles like the FXST Softail, an industry trendsetter in styling, and the XR1000, with an engine based on the XR 750 racing power plant, were also introduced in 1984 and did a great deal to help increase sales.

For the first time in years, Harley-Davidson motorcycles were given good grades in motorcycle magazine reviews. Belt-drive, five-speed transmissions, and rubber-isolated engines improved the product line. To get the word out to the public, the company created an industry "first" when it started a "Super Ride" demo program at dealerships nationwide. A fleet of demo bikes was also put into service at all major motorcycle rallies, to let riders everywhere experience the new Harley-Davidson quality.

Harley-Davidson also won the California Highway Patrol contract in 1984. This was the first time in ten years that a Harley-Davidson motorcycle was able to meet the rigid standards of the CHP—a tribute to Harley-Davidson's improved quality and performance. The contract awards were repeated in 1985, 1987, 1988 and 1989 increasing the number of Harley-Davidsons in the CHP fleet.

The sight of a highway patrol officer mounted on a Harley-Davidson is becoming more common in California.

Top left, actor Sam Elliott riding a Harley in a scene from the movie *Mask*.
Top Right Cher and Sam Elliott in *Mask*.

Left: The 80 cubic inch Evolution motor and unparalleled styling helped make the 1984 FXST Softail one of the most popular motorcycles.

Harley-Davidson beer, produced in limited quantities, quickly became a collectible.

A view of the powerful 1340cc Evolution V-twin engine.

With an engine based on the potent XR-750 power plant, the XR-1000 was the most powerful street machine Harley-Davidson ever produced.

259

Harley-Davidson's 1985 motorcycles received a special AIW/IAM union label. The label was a tribute to the two international unions that represent the Harley-Davidson work force: the Allied Industrial Workers of America and the International Association of Machinists and Aerospace Workers. AIW Local 209 President Jerry Knackert said, "The union label is a reassurance to consumers that the people responsible for the product have confidence enough to put their seal of approval on it."

Harley-Davidson also created three special "Liberty Edition" models in 1985, with a total of 1,750 Liberty Edition motorcycles in all. In a salute to the Statue of Liberty and the loyal riders of American-made Harley-Davidsons, the company donated $100, for each Liberty Edition purchased, to the Statue of Liberty/Ellis Island Foundation, Inc., for restoration of the statue. Harley-Davidson also organized a cross-country "Ride for Liberty."

Vaughn Beals traveled on a northern route from the west coast to the east and Willie G. Davidson took a southern route. They rendezvoused in Washington, D.C., and led thousands of riders to Liberty State Park, New Jersey. At the concluding ceremony there, Vaughn Beals presented a check for $250,000 to the Statue of Liberty/Ellis Island Foundation.

The big product news for 1985 was the introduction of Harley-Davidson's 1986 V^2 Evolution Sportster 883. The 883cc aluminum V-Twin engine gave Harley-Davidson its first entry in a decade in the smaller-than-1000cc market and carried a suggested retail price of $3,995—eight hundred dollars less than the 1985 XLH 1000. The Evolution XLH 883 Sportster gave Harley-Davidson a full line of Evolution-engined motorcycles.

Below: Bill Cosby and Eddie Murphy.

Yet, with all the hoopla over the new Sportster and Liberty Editions, Harley-Davidson didn't forget about its own heritage. A new addition to the FL family emerged in the Heritage Softail, a motorcycle with the timeless look of the 1950s backed by the technology of the 1980s. The Heritage front end sported a wide front fender and a front suspension that looked like the first telescopic fork on the 1949 Hydra-Glide. The rear end of the Heritage Softail had the no-suspension, hard-tail look of the 1950s and a contemporary soft ride, due to the concealed gas-charged, horizontally-mounted rear shocks.

UNION MADE

AIW — ALLIED INDUSTRIAL WORKERS OF AMERICA · AFL-CIO

INTERNATIONAL ASSOCIATION OF MACHINISTS AND AEROSPACE WORKERS · IAM

Marking the end of an era, the last Shovelhead Sportster engine rolls off the assembly line followed by the first Evolution Sportster engine. Opposite page: A column of riders heads for the capitol of the U.S. on the final leg of the Liberty Ride.

Word of Harley-Davidson's improved quality had spread far beyond the motorcycle industry. In April of 1986, Harley-Davidson Chairman and Chief Executive Officer Vaughn L. Beals, Jr. accepted the prestigious Corporate Quality Award from the three Colorado sections of the American Society of Quality Controls (ASQC). The ASQC is a nationwide organization of more than 50,000 professional members dedicated to the improvement of quality and productivity in American industry.

Also in 1985, the buy-back team learned that the leading member of the four financing banks wanted to back out of the deal. The company needed to round up cash in a hurry. To the rescue was Harley-Davidson Chief Financial Officer Rich Teerlink. Teerlink successfully negotiated a loan-refinancing package with a new lead lender in late December. By placing the company on a firmer financial footing, Teerlink was then able to guide the company to public ownership, in June 1986, by offering two million shares of common stock and a concurrent offering of $70 million principal amounts of subordinated notes due 1996.

This public offering helped reduce outstanding debt and also enabled Harley-Davidson to acquire Holiday Rambler Corporation, the world's largest privately-held producer of recreational vehicles and a major supplier of specialized commercial vehicles. Headquartered in Wakarusa, Indiana, Holiday Rambler Corporation was a perfect complement to Harley-Davidson. Teerlink said, "We found Holiday Rambler to be a natural fit because it is in a closely-related industry and because of the many similarities it has to Harley-Davidson. Like Harley-Davidson, Holiday Rambler is a manufacturing-intensive, leading producer of premium quality recreational vehicles."

From its inception in 1953, Holiday Rambler Corporation developed a strong brand name recognition, a reputation for high-quality products, and a broad base of loyal dealers and customers. The acquisition helped Harley-Davidson to broaden its earnings base.

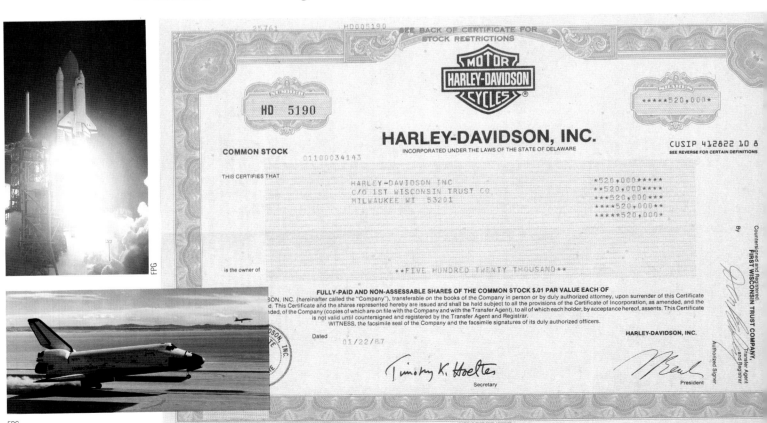

Tom Cruise became a super star with his role in "Risky Business."

Two heavyweight contenders joined forces as Harley-Davidson acquired the Holiday Rambler Corporation.

"Dynasty" became a top-rated nighttime TV soap opera.

"Miami Vice" becomes a TV hit, as Robert Redford hits a homer in "The Natural."

HRC
HOLIDAY RAMBLER CORPORATION

I n 1987, Harley-Davidson initiated a bold, new marketing strategy that guaranteed a resale value of $3,995 on the Evolution Sportster XLH-883 motorcycle. Riders who traded in their 883 within two years for an FL or FX model Harley-Davidson would be allowed $3,995 for the trade-in, a program that was unprecedented in any industry.

Four new motorcycles were introduced in the 1987 model line. The FLHS Electra Glide Sport, FLSTC Heritage Softail Classic, the FXLR Low Rider Custom and the 30th Anniversary 1100cc Sportster. The 30th Anniversary Evolution Sportster marked the first time the XL engine received the chrome and black engine treatment found on many of its FL and FX relatives. Available in limited quantities, the 30th anniversary Sportster featured a special orange and black paint scheme with 30th anniversary graphics on the gas tank and front fender.

The FLST Classic featured a black and chrome power train and custom two-tone paint, similar to the colors that were original specification on Harleys during the 1950s. The Special also featured some touring amenities: windshield and passing lamps, leather saddlebags, and a two-piece seat and backrest, all complete with studs and conchos. Wire wheels and floorboards were also standard equipment.

The FLHS Electra Glide Sport, a sportier version of Harley's premium touring machine, featured lighter, more nimble handling in the style of traditional American touring bikes of the '50s. And the FXLR celebrated the 10th anniversary of the Low Rider. It featured a unique handlebar and gas tank complete with a 10th anniversary leather center strap.

The XLH Sportster 883.

Far right: "Three Men and A Baby" and "Good Morning Vietnam."

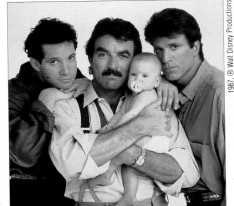

But the new bikes were not the biggest news for Harley-Davidson in 1987. On March 17, 1987, Harley-Davidson petitioned the International Trade Commission for early termination of the five-year tariffs on heavyweight motorcycles. The move was unprecedented! No other American company had asked for removal of import protection, and it was hailed by the press as one of the best public relations moves in history.

"We have informed the ITC that we no longer need tariff relief to compete with the Japanese," said Vaughn L. Beals, Jr. "We're taking this action now because we believe we're sending a strong message out to the international industrial community: U.S. workers, given a respite from predatory import practices, can become competitive in world markets."

To celebrate Harley-Davidson's successful turnaround, Mr. Beals invited President Ronald Reagan to visit Harley-Davidson's final assembly plant in York, Pennsylvania. On May 6, 1987, a presidential helicopter landed at the test track behind the York plant. Accompanied by presidential aides and security people, representatives from Harley-Davidson led President Reagan on a tour of the final assembly facility. After touring the assembly line, President Reagan started the engine of a newly built 30th Anniversary Sportster. He then met with a group of employees in a round-table forum, prior to delivering a speech hailing the company's comeback.

"We looked at you carefully," said Reagan. "We asked, 'Is Harley-Davidson really serious about getting into shape?' And the answer came back, a resounding 'Yes.' Harley was hard at work with new products and finding better ways to make better bikes. And Harley's shape-up was not relying just on the top management. Everyone from the board room to the factory was involved. No matter how we looked at it, we could see that everyone at Harley-Davidson was serious about getting into fighting shape," said Reagan.

"Who Framed Roger Rabbit?"

1988, ® Walt Disney Productions

Dolly Parton.

FXLR Low Rider Custom and FXST Softail.

As Chairman Vaughn Beals looks on, Ronald Reagan addresses a group of Harley-Davidson employees at the York plant during his 1987 visit.

Apparently the people at the New York Stock Exchange (NYSE) felt the same way about Harley-Davidson's accomplishments. On July 1, 1987, Harley-Davidson, Inc. was approved for listing on the NYSE. Harley-Davidson, Inc. had been listed on the American Stock Exchange since its initial public offering in July 1986.

According to Vaughn Beals, the move "provided Harley-Davidson with improved market liquidity and visibility and will bolster our stature as a broadly-diversified, international company."

Above: Prince, Madonna and Michael Jackson. Right: The perfect way to celebrate the listing on the New York Stock Exchange was to parade through the streets of New York on the machines that made Milwaukee famous.

On October 10, 1987, acquired the design and worldwide manufacturing rights for its model MT500 military motorcycle from Armstrong Equipment of North Humberside, England. "This purchase is part of Harley-Davidson's plan to continue looking at new opportunities to expand its earnings base," said Richard F. Teerlink, president and chief operating officer of the Motorcycle Division of Harley-Davidson. The MT500 is a single-cylinder, 500cc four-stroke, off-road motorcycle.

Chairman Vaughn Beals and President Rich Teerlink monitor the ticker on the day Harley-Davidson was listed on the American Stock Exchange.

Armstrong's general purpose military motorcycle is designed to be strong, for use in off-road conditions. A range of engines can be fitted into the welded steel, box-section frame. It features heavy-duty suspension, sealed-wheel bearings, and dust- and water-resistant brakes.

The 1988 product line featured the biggest Sportster ever. The Sportster 1200, with its 74 cubic inch engine and 40mm constant-velocity carburetor, put out 12 percent more horsepower and 10 percent more torque than the 1987 1100cc Sportster. The 1200 Sportster also featured a 39mm front fork and revised rear suspension.

The FXRS Low Rider was also revamped for 1988. Its twin-cap Fat Bob gas tank sported a built-in fuel gauge and brought back fond memories of the 1977 Low Rider. The new 39mm fork replaced the former 35mm unit on all FXR and XL models.

Also new for 1988 were the special 85th Anniversary motorcycles. Four models sported special 85th Anniversary graphics in celebration of the company's 85th birthday. One bike created especially for the 85th Anniversary was the FXSTS Springer Softail. The "Springer" front end was the subject of more computer-aided design and finite elements computer analysis than any other component in Harley-Davidson's history.

Harley-Davidson also organized a special 85th Anniversary celebration and tied-in a cross-country ride—all to benefit the Muscular Dystrophy Association. Riders departed from ten points around the United States and headed for festivities in the motorcycling mecca of Milwaukee.

"Hulk" Hogan.

Pee Wee Herman.

The FXSTS Springer Softail featured a Springer front end that sported a look of the '40s, backed by engineering of the '90s.

The event was attended by over 35,000 motorcycle enthusiasts and helped raise nearly $600,000 for Muscular Dystrophy. It typified Harley-Davidson's close-to-the-customer philosophy and changed some people's image of what a Harley-Davidson rider is really like. The Milwaukee Ride for MDA was one of the biggest motorcycling events of the century and did a great deal to fuel the fight against muscular dystrophy.

Over 35,000 motorcyclists flocked to Harley-Davidson's celebration on the shores of Lake Michigan following the 85th Anniversary Milwaukee Ride.

The 1988 version of the FXRS Low Rider.

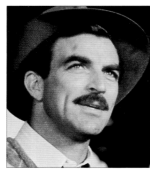

Above: Tom Cruise in "Top Gun"; Tom Selleck as "Lassiter"; William Hurt in "Body Heat"; Mel Gibson is "Mad Max"; Harrison Ford as "Indiana Jones."

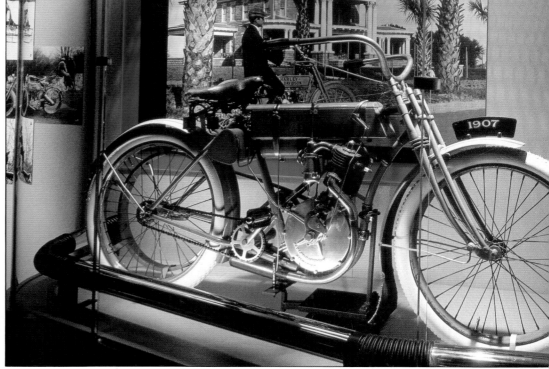

In 1988, Harley-Davidson took its heritage on the road in the form of a traveling museum, housed in a huge semitrailer truck painted with the company's award-winning graphics. The photos above and on the opposite page offer a brief "tour" inside.

As the events of summer in 1988 began cooling down, the race for the presidency of the United States started heating up. Vice President George Bush, the Republican candidate, and Democratic candidate Michael Dukakis both mentioned Harley-Davidson as success stories in their campaign speeches.

In a different kind of election in August of 1988, the board of directors of Harley-Davidson, Inc., elected Richard F. Teerlink to the new post of president and chief operating officer of Harley-Davidson, Inc., and James H. Paterson to the position of president and chief operating officer of the Motorcycle Division.

Meanwhile, Harley-Davidson was aiming for a successful 1989 model line with the introduction of some new motorcycles. A line of touring machines called Ultra Classics with luxurious standard equipment was introduced. The Tour Glide and Electra Glide Ultra Classics featured cruise control, fairing lowers with a built-in glove compartment, an 80-watt four-speaker stereo system with volume and tuning control for the passenger, built-in CB, and special silver and black paint.

The special 85th Anniversary Springer Softail was carried over for 1989 and offered in a variety of colors. The FL touring models received a newly de-signed gas tank, 32 amp alternator and also featured self-cancelling turn signals controlled by a microprocessor.

As Harley-Davidson headed for the 1990s, the emphasis on technological improvements was balanced by the emphasis on the rich heritage of the past. America's only surviving motorcycle manufacturer hasn't lost sight of what it has taken to get this far and plans to keep improving into the 21st century.

The Eighties was the decade of Harley-Davidson as the company prospered and grew, and ultimately became not only an American success story but the very image of success itself. By keeping in close touch with its devoted and dedicated customers—and never wandering far from its heritage of building basic and stylish motorcycles—Harley-Davidson prepared to enter the Nineties as the most successful manufacturer of motorcycles marketed in the United States and perhaps the world.

Right: Few heads of large corporations would spend as much time on the road on company products as Vaughn Beals and his wife, Eleanore.

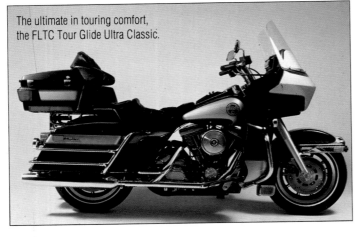

The ultimate in touring comfort, the FLTC Tour Glide Ultra Classic.

The selection of fashions & collectibles created exclusively for Harley-Davidson continues to expand.

FPG

FPG

Presidential candidates Republican George Bush and Democrat Michael Dukakis.

Harley-Davidson's traveling ambassadors of goodwill and probably the most recognized couple in the sport, Nancy and Willie G. Davidson.

The FLSTC Heritage Softail Classic is one of the most visually striking motorcycles in the Harley-Davidson lineup.

273

THE 1990'S

Building for the future.

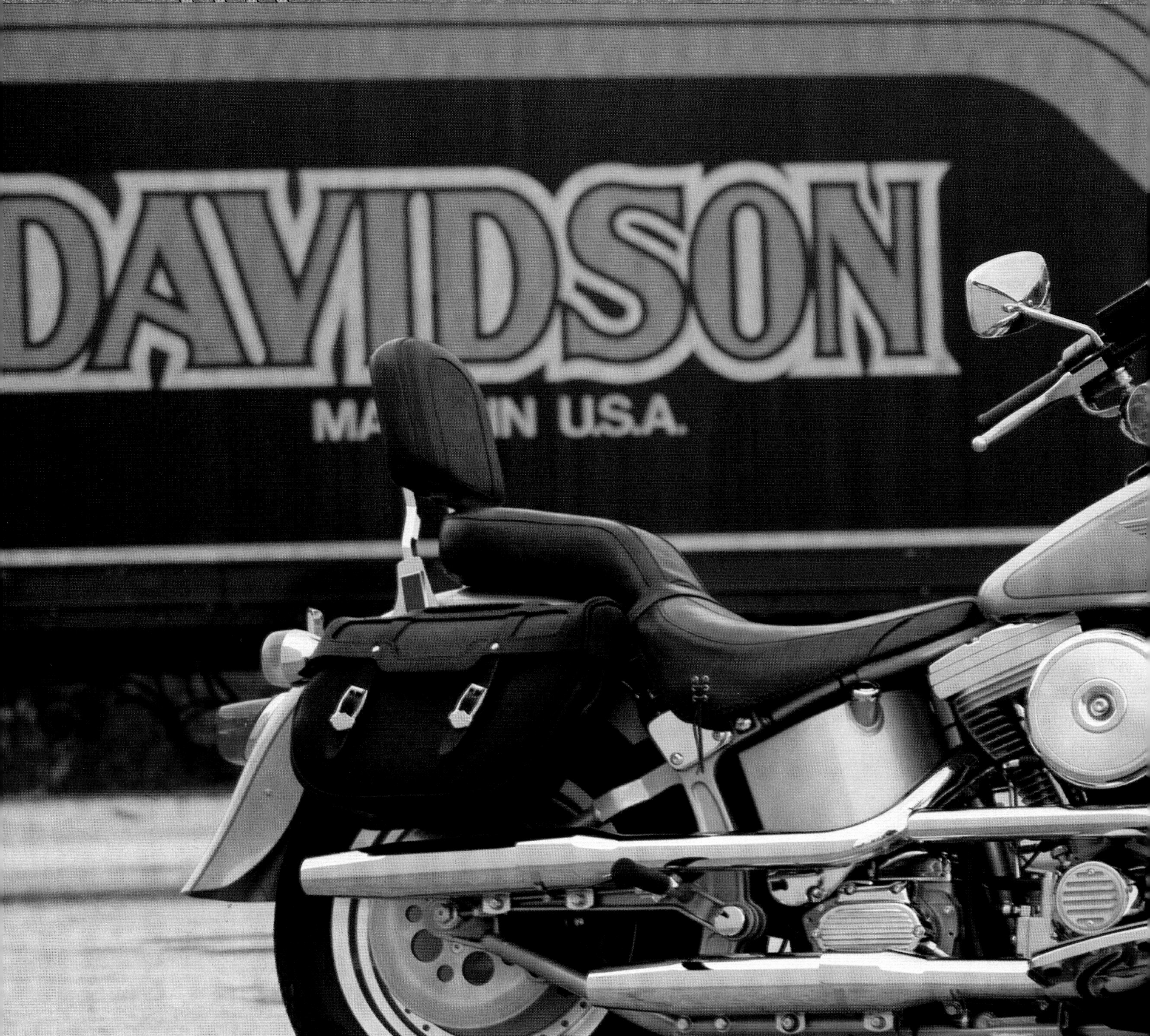
DAVIDSON

THE 1990'S

"Hey, Fat Boy."

On this somewhat humorous note, Harley-Davidson ushered in its 1990 model year with what many perceived to be Willie G. Davidson's most customized factory custom motorcycle to date, the FLSTF Fat Boy. Basically an updated, sleeker version of the Heritage Softail, the 1990 Fat Boy was the kind of motorcycle, and motorcycle name, that only Harley-Davidson could introduce without making itself look ridiculous to its riders and the other manufacturers.

Keenly aware of what appeals to the Harley rider, Willie G. was careful to retain the general profile of the nostalgic Heritage in the Fat Boy but give it,

Some bikes just sit there. Some just sit there better than others. But one truly sticks out. The Fat Boy.™

No doubt some people are asking themselves: Who would devote the time, effort and money to develop a new motorcycle, and then give it a handle like that? Of course. Only Harley-Davidson.® Who else could get away with it?

This is more than factory custom styling. This is a two-wheeled testament to American industrial art. Big time. It starts with 80 cubic inches of V² Evolution® engine. Sweeping back from there is a new shotgun-style dual exhaust system. Front and rear, you've got solid disc wheels. The bold, mechanical, silver-on-silver color scheme ties it all together. And hot yellow splashes on the rocker box spacers, new derby and timer covers, center console and

tank graphic keep everyth
Beyond that, the Fa
custom details. Like a new
A textured leather seat ins
trim strip and seat valance
genuine FLH-issue handle
It's definitely extra

at the same time, some of the styling traits of today. The Fat Boy rode on a pair of cast disc wheels topped by gently flared front and rear fenders. The entire motorcycle, including the frame and oil tank, was monochromatic in fine metallic silver with subtle yellow accents on the engine and Fat Bob tanks. Combined with shotgun-style exhausts and a pigskin seat with hand-laced leather detailing, all these elements resulted in a look unlike any other in the world of contemporary motorcycling.

Richard Grieco of TV's "Booker" (top) and actor Mickey Rourke (bottom) rode Harleys both on and off the set. (Middle:) Sultry Michelle Pfeiffer in "The Fabulous Baker Boys."

When Did It Start For You?

Like a spark, at a single point in a lot of people's lives, something happened that changed things. The urge to have a Harley-Davidson® took hold. From that point on, and especially after seeing the world from the seat of their very own Harley,® each one of these people became very different. They found something that the average population will never discover. Maybe you were made to be a Harley owner. Maybe you were born to be one. Ever thought about it? Maybe it's time you started.

Things Are Different On A Harley

controversial. After all, the Fat Boy is one very heavy-duty hunk of style. This Harley® doesn't invite comment, it demands it. Can you handle it? Hey, don't just sit there.

tank
ast,

bit

Things Are Different On A Harley

A longtime participant in the many activities surrounding speed week in Daytona Beach, Florida every March, Harley-Davidson had been hosting its own show and a myriad of rider-related events at several different area hotels for fifteen years. So greatly had its involvement grown there, it became evident that a larger facility was needed. Fortunately, the city's new Ocean Center, just a hundred yards or so north of the hub of area action on Main Street, opened up and Harley-Davidson was able to set up its operations there. With ride-in shows, exhibits, MDA fund-raising activities, a traveling museum, a retail store and a number of Harley Owners Group (HOG) functions, it soon became clear that the Ocean Center was the place to be for motorcycle speed week visitors.

The 1990 version of the annual Sunday morning motorcycle parade from the beach to a reserved Harley-Davidson section at the speedway took on a special significance for motorcyclists that year. Billed by the company as the world's largest motorcycle parade, and open to all brands of motorcycles, the event was dedicated to billionaire publisher Malcolm Forbes. An avid motorcyclist known as much for his love of the sport as he was for his worldwide odysseys, Forbes passed away unexpectedly earlier in the year. His presence at numerous motorcycling events over the years, usually on one of his many Harleys, did much to improve the image of and generate new interest in motorcycling.

Many notables made final exits as we entered the Nineties: billionaire publisher Malcolm Forbes; the legendary Greta Garbo; film *femmes fatales* Ava Gardner & Barbara Stanwyck.

Early in the year, it was evident that a growing demand for Harley-Davidson products necessitated a more concentrated effort on the part of the company to meet the needs of the world market. Realizing it was only scratching the surface in terms of global potential, Harley-Davidson shifted its international offices from Connecticut to its headquarters in Milwaukee. This move allowed the utilization of corporate resources and the capacity to triple the staff. It also opened up a European parts and accessories warehouse near Frankfurt, Germany, stocked with many of the fastest-moving products.

From sixteen percent of total production in 1987, exports of Harley-Davidson motorcycles grew steadily to over thirty percent by 1991, even as total production continued to increase significantly. Top export markets included Canada, West Germany, Japan and Australia with established channels of distribution in virtually every other industrialized nation in the world. Because of the Company's success in the overseas market, Wisconsin Governor Tommy G. Thompson remarked, "Harley-Davidson is a great example of a respected American manufacturer bouncing back from adversity. It's great to see another fine Wisconsin company take the offensive in our global economy."

So successful had Harley-Davidson become by that time that the board of directors approved a two-for-one stock split effective the first of June. In exactly four years, Harley-Davidson stock had soared from the original issue price of eleven dollars a share to around fifty-six dollars. The split served once again to bring the cost down to a more generally affordable level and allow more investors to join the Harley-Davidson family.

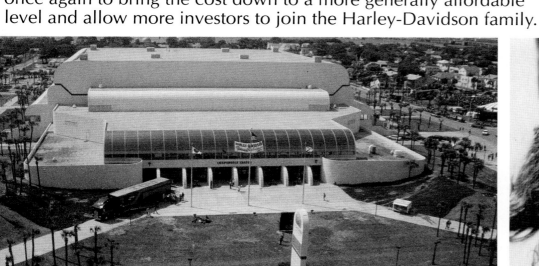

Box office bonanzas varied from sequels to love stories: Bruce Willis in "Die Hard 2;" Mel Gibson in "Lethal Weapon 2;" Richard Gere & Julia Roberts in "Pretty Woman;" Demi Moore & Patrick Swayze in "Ghost."

Motorcycle safety, a longtime concern of the company, took on added emphasis as Harley-Davidson embarked on a campaign to reward Harley Owners Group members for participating in rider education activities. Since 1986, HOG has been reimbursing members up to $25 in tuition costs for successfully completing a certified Motorcycle Safety Foundation Course. Under the expanded program, HOG also recognized chapters for encouraging member participation in MSF courses, appointed additional personnel to assist in rider education at the chapter level, and offered seminars and skill tests at HOG rallies nationwide.

Harley-Davidson felt so strongly that even experienced riders could learn additional skills by taking an MSF rider education course that the successful completion of one became a mandatory requirement for all employees riding company-owned motorcycles.

Every summer Harley-Davidson hosts a national convention to introduce new programs and products to its dealer network. In July of 1990, the dealers gathered in Washington, D. C. to preview the new motorcycles with a number of product improvements including better, longer-lasting tires and self-cancelling turn signals on all models, and a voice-activated intercom on the Ultra touring models, an industry first.

Of greater significance to the dealers were two other announcements. The first was the addition of a belt drive and a five-speed transmission to all Sportster models. These were changes often asked for by riders and dealers alike.

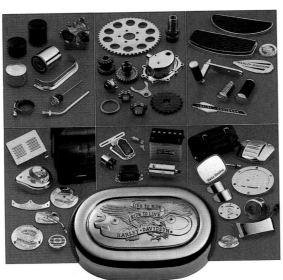

"Home Alone" was the biggest hit of Christmas 1990.

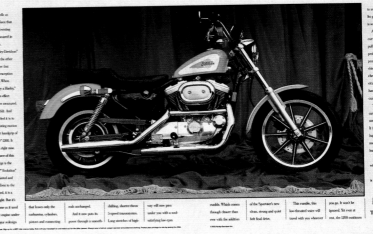

The second, and more exciting, announcement was the unveiling of a brand new rendering of an older, very popular model. All new for 1991 was a totally redesigned motorcycle called the FXDB Dyna Glide Sturgis. While at first glance the Sturgis closely resembled its 1980 namesake, the 1991 version boasted major technological differences over its predecessor from a decade earlier.

The first Harley-Davidson motorcycle devised from the ground up using computer-aided design, the tough-looking black-on-black beauty featured a totally new frame, a two-point rubber engine-isolation mounting system, an oil tank mounted under the transmission, a more accessible rear belt, redesigned locks using high-security round keys and more.

The new Sturgis combined the look of the ever-popular rigid mounts of the Seventies and early Eighties with the handling and smooth ride of the Harleys of the Nineties. The dealers loved the new bike, and it was hoped the riders would, too.

Below, Nineties-style sex appeal exemplified by recording star Paula Abdul; pop music's Janet Jackson; Ellen Barkin in "Sea of Love;" Kim Basinger in "Batman;" Sherilyn Fenn in TV's "Twin Peaks;" music video queen Madonna.

Germans celebrate the end of the Berlin Wall and Cold War separation.

Just two weeks later, in early August, was the fiftieth anniversary celebration of the annual rally in Sturgis, South Dakota, an event that had grown to rival Daytona both in attendance and in importance to motorcyclists. Approximately 300,000 motorcyclists, mostly Harley enthusiasts, from all over the world converged on the area to celebrate the event by touring the area's historic landmarks and beautiful canyons and parks, and generally just socializing with friends and fellow riders.

As in Daytona, Harley-Davidson was actively involved in the area, first with its annual HOG rally in Rapid City, South Dakota and later by inviting all riders to join in many of the same attractions and MDA fund-raising events as those held in Florida. Special attractions included a traveling version of the Vietnam Veterans Memorial (also known as the "Moving Wall"), a flying of the late Malcolm Forbes' huge Heritage Softail hot air balloon, a concert by big-name performers and guest appearances by media celebrities who posed for pictures for donations to MDA.

The 1991 Sturgis was the hit of the show, so much so that one specially detailed by Willie G. Davidson was auctioned off for MDA bringing in over $34,000. An ultra-limited edition collectors' knife commemorating the anniversary brought in over $3,800. In total, through the generosity of the motorcycle enthusiasts there, Harley-Davidson raised over $100,000 in the Sturgis area for the fight against muscular dystrophy.

As a special tribute to the Vietnam veterans during the 50th anniversary of the Black Hills Motorcycle classic, Harley-Davidson sponsored an exhibition of the traveling version of the Vietnam Veterans Memorial, also known as the "Moving Wall," on the grounds of the Rushmore Plaza Civic Center.

The ever-popular ride-in show at the Rushmore Plaza Civic Center in Rapid City during the Sturgis fiftieth anniversary celebration.

Peter Fonda offered his services at the fiftieth anniversaries of Sturgis and Daytona to help raise money in the bikers' fight against muscular dystrophy.

John Goodman rode a Harley in the TV series "Roseanne."

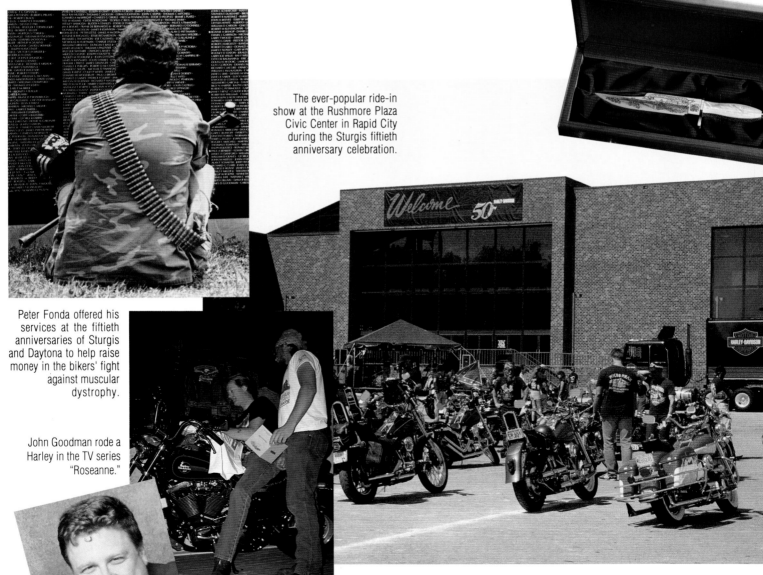

The Sturgis rally was the most successful one ever held by the company, largely due to the efforts of two individuals with a special interest in Harley-Davidson. Bill Davidson and his sister Karen, two of Willie G.'s children, played key roles in the Sturgis event and helped to make it the tremendous success it was. They represent the fourth generation of Davidsons to serve the company.

Bill, the fourth consecutive William Davidson to work at Harley-Davidson, joined the company in 1984, overseeing the national demo ride program. After gaining experience in advertising and promotion in addition to managing the company's consumer events, Bill was named to head the 135,000 member Harley Owners Group in mid-1991 and to direct the operations of the worldwide factory-sponsored rider organization.

Karen joined the company more recently, drawing on her college degree and work experience in fashion design to coordinate Harley-Davidson's extensive MotorClothes line of fashionable clothing for on or off the motorcycle. She also became deeply involved in promoting the clothing line at shows and rallies through exhibits and choreographed fashion shows.

Just as the massive Sturgis anniversary celebration got underway, the attention of the world was diverted to the Persian Gulf as the massive military forces of Iraq poured across the border into Kuwait to overwhelm and totally subdue its smaller neighbor. As the nation and the world rallied behind President George Bush, the U.S. and its allies rushed troops and supplies to the region in an attempt to stem further Iraqi aggression into nearby Saudi Arabia.

This holding action, dubbed Desert Shield, ignited the fervor of the U.S. citizenry in an outpouring of support for military action unheard of for decades. As it became apparent that Iraq would not withdraw, and more and more American reservists were being activated, Harley-Davidson stepped forth in its traditional support of military service personnel and announced one of the most generous military leave policies in the country for employees who were called up. A short time later, the U.S. and its allies unleashed Desert Storm, a full-blown, high-tech military operation that brought the invader to its knees in a matter of weeks and started bringing the troops home a short time later.

Bill Davidson, interviewed during Harley-Davidson's celebration of the fiftieth anniversary of the Sturgis rally, was largely responsible for the company's involvement in rallies and special events before being named to head the Harley Owners Group.

Karen Davidson combined her background in clothing design with her lifelong involvement in motorcycling to help guide the direction of the MotorClothes line of apparel for motorcycle enthusiasts.

General "Stormin' Norman" Schwarzkopf led allied forces to quick and decisive victory in Operation Desert Storm.

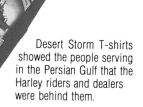

Desert Storm T-shirts showed the people serving in the Persian Gulf that the Harley riders and dealers were behind them.

eanwhile, on the home front, Harley-Davidson was enjoying resounding success on the race tracks as Scott Parker battled his Harley-Davidson teammate Chris Carr down to the last dirt track event of the season to capture his third consecutive 750cc AMA Grand National Championship title. Parker and Carr dominated the circuit all season winning, between the two of them, eleven of the fifteen races on the schedule.

Can you say "Parker and Carr" three times fast?

Congratulations to Scott Parker for winning his third AMA Grand National Championship, and to Chris Carr, who also scored his third consecutive 600cc National Championship. And finally, thanks to tuners Bill Werner and Kenny Tolbert for helping us win the manufacturer's trophy for the third straight year. That's "Harley-Davidson", Harley-Davidson, Harley-Davidson."

Chris Carr was to exhibit his own championship style as he captured his third consecutive 600cc championship title in the first three years since the series debuted in 1988. Proving the old adage that things always happen in threes, Harley-Davidson won its third consecutive AMA manufacturer's title making it three for three for three in 1990.

The fall of the year saw two significant advances in the areas of marketing and manufacturing. Because of the growing broad-based appeal of the MotorClothes line of garments to both riders and non-riders alike, the decision was made to open a consumer-oriented clothing store separate from any Harley-Davidson dealership. The site chosen was Bannister Mall in Kansas City where a pilot MotorClothes outlet was created "for motor enthusiasts who want to share and participate in the Harley-Davidson tradition of freedom and individuality."

The new store featured Harley-Davidson collectibles, jewelry, accessories, and men's and women's fashions. If successful in the long term, the test outlet in Bannister Mall may be the predecessor to a chain of retail outlets nationwide designed to cater primarily to the general public.

On the manufacturing front, the addition of a fifth gear to the transmission in the 1991 Sportster models was causing problems on the engine line in Harley-Davidson's Capitol Drive plant by slowing down production of all engines. Employees at the plant were asked to assist in finding a solution. The result was the creation of a dedicated assembly line solely for 883 and 1200cc Sportster engines which not only relieved the strain on the original line but also resulted in improved quality.

In "Dances With Wolves," Kevin Costner starred and won the Oscar for best director. Alec Baldwin played a sociopath in "Miami Blue."

As the first year of the new decade drew to a close, it was quite clear that the past twelve months had been very good to Harley-Davidson. Significant product improvements had been made both in existing models and in additions to the model line. The international business was taking off at a record pace. The company's stock had performed marvelously on the big board; consumer and investor interest in the company and its products remained extremely high. By year's end, Harley-Davidson had earned a whopping 62.3 percent of market share in the 850cc and larger category. While the overall motorcycle market showed little, if any growth, Harley-Davidson just kept getting stronger and healthier as demand for Harleys outweighed supply for the fourth consecutive year, despite significant increases in production.

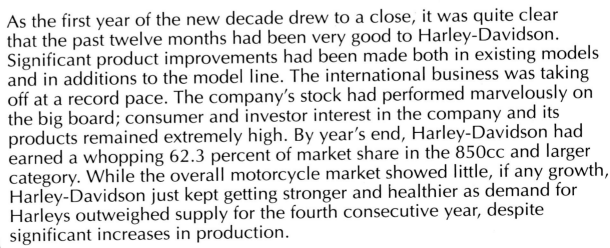

BANNISTER MALL:

Strictly an outlet for Harley-Davidson apparel and fashion accessories, the MotorClothes store in Kansas City marked the company's first attempt to establish a retail outlet that did not sell motorcycles. Owned and managed by the local Harley-Davidson dealer, the test store featured a unique interior designed to mimic the boutique streets of New York with a different "storefront" for each product category.

DON'T BUTCHER YOUR HOG WITH IMITATION PARTS.

When you're looking for parts, look at the label first. If it doesn't say Genuine Harley-Davidson, forget it. Because that's the only way you'll be sure that the quality of the parts in the box is the same as original equipment. And anything less can bring your Hog to a halt in a hurry. So insist on Genuine Harley-Davidson parts, at your authorized Harley-Davidson dealer. Everything else is just an imitation.

Genuine Parts
Maintain The Harley Difference.
©1991 Harley-Davidson, Inc.

1990

Iraq invades Kuwait; UN authorizes military action unless Iraq forces are withdrawn by January 15.

USSR President Gorbachev wins 1990 Nobel Peace Prize.

1991

After peace efforts fail, allied forces launch Operation Desert Storm against Iraq.

Allies crush Iraqi forces and complete liberation of Kuwait February 17.

In March, Iraq accepts all allied terms to end Persian Gulf War.

Harley-Davidson® MotorClothes™ . . . *Feel The Difference*

Visit your local Harley-Davidson dealer for a Fall 1990 MotorClothes Catalog, or send $2 to Harley-Davidson MotorClothes, P.O. Box 92918, Milwaukee, WI 53201.

Enter 1991 and Harley-Davidson was on the road again, heading to the fiftieth anniversary of a major motorcycling event, this time in Daytona Beach. Returning once more to the spacious Ocean Center, the company made its presence known with a large display of new motorcycles, stylish clothing, and factory-accessorized and customized motorcycles, plus the usual galaxy of related events and activities for the throngs of riders.

Fox TV Network established itself in late night talk show competition with host Arsenio Hall.

Just as the Sturgis model was unveiled to commemorate the fiftieth celebration of that event, the 1992 Dyna Daytona was unveiled to hail the half-century mark for the Florida rally. Also based on the new Dyna Glide chassis, the Daytona was equipped with dual disc front brakes, a two-tone color scheme, black and chrome engine, and the company's first true pearl paint. It became available that August along with the rest of the 1992 lineup.

Two traditions were carried on in Daytona that year. The first was the crowning of the new Ms. Harley-Davidson, Krisann Whitley of Loveland, Texas. Selected from a national field of entrants, Krisann was chosen as much for riding ability and motorcycling experience as her ability to meet and relate to riders everywhere. The fifth to carry the title of Ms. Harley-Davidson, Krisann, like her predecessors, spends the majority of her time attending dealer-sponsored events all over the country, generating goodwill and interest in Harley-Davidson and the sport of motorcycling.

James Marshall is a Harley enthusiast in TV's "Twin Peaks."

The celebration of the fiftieth anniversary of [saw all the usual attrac[but in greater abundanc[There were beautiful bi[miles of stunning beach[more beautiful bikes, ab[beautiful weather, more[welcome sunshine, crov[bikers, and the ever-pr[Nancy and Willie G. Da[

At 44, Nolan Ryan showed no signs of age in pitching his seventh no-hitter.

Courtesy of Score Trading

Harley-Da[new 23 millio[paint facil[York, P[

The second tradition carried on was raising money for MDA. Through field events, admission to the show, poker runs and an auction of Harley memorabilia, including the buckle Peter Fonda wore in "Easy Rider," over $154,000 was raised for that worthy cause. Some $8.6 million had been raised in the first ten years of the company's sponsorship.

While all appeared rosy in the world of Harley-Davidson, there were dark clouds rising. A brief strike in February, coupled with some production problems in manufacturing, caused a worldwide shortage of product at the height of the selling season. One of the major contributors to the problem was the paint shop in the York, Pennsylvania plant.

Above, Bart Simpson in the animated TV series, "The Simpsons." Below, the fifth Ms. Harley-Davidson, 23-year-old Krisann Whitley, and the Dyna Daytona.

Despite the scheduled opening of a new, robotic $23 million paint facility late in the year and an exclusive Sportster line to facilitate the assembly of the different models, demand continued to rise beyond the company's ability to produce.

Nonetheless, with its proven track record for solving its problems while maintaining quality, Harley-Davidson was able to sustain both rider and investor confidence. In the showrooms, riders eagerly snapped up new motorcycles as they were delivered, and in the market, Harley stock continued to trade at a brisk pace. By late spring, Harley-Davidson stock was worth nearly seven times its 1986 issue price.

Maintaining Harley-Davidson's growth through the recessionary period of the early Nineties would be a difficult but not impossible task. The company was doing many things to encourage rider and dealer loyalty and confidence by planning solidly for the future. The key to continued success lay with long-term thinking rather than short-term profits.

A few years earlier Harley-Davidson embarked on a worldwide store design program that modernized dealers' stores by introducing them to up-to-date marketing and display techniques. Largely gone were the stereotypical biker shops of the past. In their place were clean, modern, well-lighted and thoughtfully laid out stores where comfort, cordiality and convenience were stressed. Not only were traditional Harley riders impressed by the new look, but people who had never dreamed of visiting a dealership to purchase a jacket or T-shirt had now found a new place to shop with the family.

Harley Owners Group continued to hold rallies and events to cement the loyalty of the riders and to give them a good reason to come together and share their favorite sport. By mid-1991, there were over 650 HOG chapters worldwide and the first-ever European HOG rally was held in England in June of that year.

Licensing of Harley-Davidson's trademarks and logos also went worldwide in the early Nineties. Less than ten years old, the trademark licensing program was begun so the company could not only exercise control over the types of products bearing the marks of Harley-Davidson but also to clean up the image of the company by removing products of questionable taste. Through careful granting of licenses, combined with a vigorous policy of prosecuting infringers, Harley-Davidson made its image more socially presentable and, at the same time, brought a broad spectrum of Harley-identified products to the marketplace for both riders and non-riders alike.

As Harley-Davidson looked ahead to its ninetieth birthday in 1993, plans were well developed by the summer of 1991 for a huge year-long celebration of that important landmark. Among the projects underway was a homecoming event to rival that of the eighty-fifth anniversary in 1988 and a beautiful new museum and visitors' center in the Milwaukee area.

And the century mark is not that far away!

Kevin Costner in the latest remake of "Robin Hood.."

Arnold Schwarzenegger rode his FLSTF Fat Boy™ to another multi-million dollar success in "Terminator II."

-Davidson dealerships that ┆ the designer store treatment ┆o a total face-lift that includes ┆porary slatwalls and gridwalls, ┆display towers, waterfall racks ┆-thing, state-of-the-art floor ┆ling improvements, and more ┆e lighting and fixtures. The ┆edesign program takes into ┆t the dealership's existing ┆ons and opportunities, and ┆to maximize the facility's ┆ities. It even goes so far as to ┆sh lines of sight for specific ┆ areas and create customer ┆ patterns.

┆ 1991, over a third of all the ┆-Davidson dealers in the world ┆edicated to the program with ┆ecoming involved on an ┆g basis. So great has been ┆cess of the redesign program, ┆ dealers who take advantage ┆at some of the earliest dealers ┆cipate have asked to have ┆ores remodeled and updated ┆ the most current plans.

At the close of the 1991 racing season, factory racer Scott Parker rewrote the record books by edging out teammate Chris Carr in the points battle to earn his fourth consecutive AMA Grand National title, matching the record of former Harley racer Carroll Resweber. He also became the winningest racer on record with 43 victories, thirty of them on mile dirt tracks.

"Backdraft" star, Kurt Russell, astride his Harley.

No Trespassing.

We have a problem, and maybe you can help. Knowingly or otherwise, some people have been trespassing on our rights by using the Harley® name or our logo without permission, or using the bar and shield symbol for their own purposes. These trespasses, quite simply, are illegal. Naturally, we're always glad to see authorized Harley-Davidson® dealers and licensees use our logos to sell Harley motorcycles, parts and accessories. But there are trademark laws to protect the rights of ownership. When our logos are used in any manner that violates those laws, we must defend ourselves or risk losing our rights to our own trademarks. Prosecution is often our only defense, and we do prosecute. But it's expensive — for us and the people we take to court — and we'd rather avoid that.

So remember, it's illegal to misuse the bar and shield shape shown above, even by inserting other words. If you're buying products with our trademarks from anyone who's not an authorized Harley-Davidson dealer, insist on seeing one of the Official Licensed Product logos or MotorClothes logo shown below. Otherwise, be careful of the product: It may be counterfeit.

Defending our trademarks is in the best interests of us both, so if you see any Harley-Davidson trademarks used in a way that appears illegal — or have questions about the use of our logo — please let us know immediately. Write to Manager, Trademark Enforcement, Harley-Davidson, Inc., P.O. Box 653, Milwaukee, WI 53201.

Your best bet is to patronize those Harley-Davidson dealers and vendors who have helped us protect the Harley-Davidson name throughout the years. We thank them, and also thank all of you loyal Harley riders for your understanding and support.

When was the last time you met a stranger and knew he was a brother?

THE SPORTSTERS

Thirty-five years old and younger than ever, the Sportster for 1992 is as popular as it's ever been in its long history. Available in four models, from a bare-bones 883 for the entry-level rider to the top-of-the-line 1200, the Sportsters offer all the heritage and mystique of owning a Harley for a lot less money than most would expect. The price may be a bargain, but there is no compromising the quality, look, feel and sound that is typically Harley-Davidson.

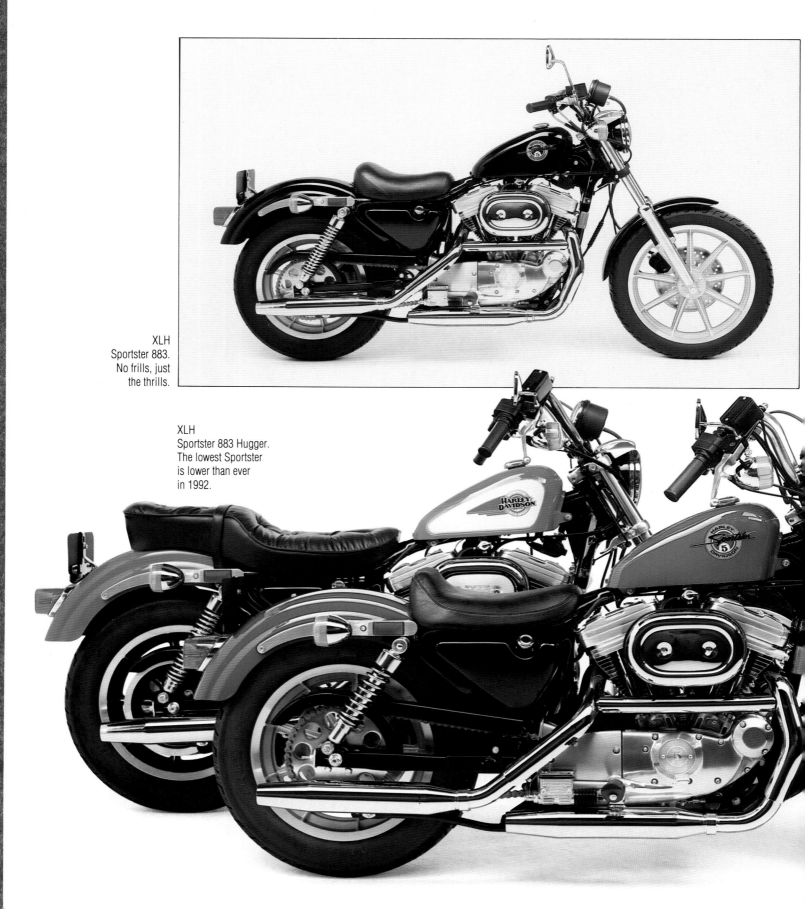

XLH
Sportster 883.
No frills, just
the thrills.

XLH
Sportster 883 Hugger.
The lowest Sportster
is lower than ever
in 1992.

XLH
Sportster 1200.
The most powerful
Sportster ever with
looks to match.

XLH
Sportster 883 Deluxe.
Buckhorn handlebars
and a new seat in 1992.

Custom paint and
Harley-Davidson
accessories can create
a whole new personality
for the Sportster.

THE DYNA GLIDES

To commemorate the fiftieth anniversary of the Sturgis rally, Harley-Davidson unveiled a brand new version of an old favorite, the 1991 Sturgis, which combined the look of the Eighties with the technology of the Nineties. The Sturgis, along with the 1992 additions to the Dyna Glide line, all feature a computer-aided designed frame with the engine and transmission isolated by a redesigned, two-point mounting system. While the Dyna Glides look and feel like the earlier rigid mounts, they handle and ride like the widely acclaimed FXRs.

FXDB-Daytona.
The first production
Harley to carry true
pearl paint.

FXDC
Dyna Glide Custom.
The silver and black
is reminiscent of the
'79 Low Rider.

THE SOFTAILS

For the uninformed, the hardtail frame was the one used on Harley-Davidson motorcycles before the advent of rear suspension in the Fifties. For those who want a more modern ride, the Softail frame is the high-tech equivalent for the Nineties. Inspired by the timeless hardtail look, the four Softail models all sport a pair of concealed horizontal shocks under the frame to provide a softer ride while maintaining the nostalgic appearance of no rear suspension. While each is distinctively styled, all also carry the wraparound oil tank that is characteristic of the line. With looks like these, it's not hard to figure out why the Softails are so wildly popular.

FLSTF
Fat Boy.
With disc wheels, flared fender and shotgun pipes, it's a modern classic.

FXSTC
Softail Custom.
Long, low and lean, it's the ultimate motorcycle custom.

FLSTC
Heritage Softail Classic.
The classic look of the Fifties with the ride of the Nineties.

With custom paint and tastefully added Harley accessories, this Softail Springer takes on a whole new look.

THE FXR LINE

Just as the Super Glide of twenty years ago spawned a whole class of diversified street cruisers, its 1992 namesake provides the essentials for a line of street machines that goes from basic bike to comfortable tourer with stops in between at classy custom and the convenience of dual purpose. Each of the six models in the line are powered by the mighty Evolution 1340 engine mated to a five-speed tranny, both rubber-isolated from a computer-designed frame. From there, each model charts its own course in style, equipment and function. In the FXR line, there is a motorcycle for every purpose.

FXRT
Sport Glide.
Wind tunnel tested
and rider approved.

FXRS
Low Rider Convertible.
From street bike to
highway cruiser in
just minutes.

FXLR
Low Rider Custom.
The jewel of the line
sports a 21-inch
front wheel.

FXRS
Low Rider Sport Edition.
Makes getting there
more than half the fun.

An accessorized
Low Rider-Sport Edition.

FXR
Super Glide.
The foundation for
the entire FXR line.

FXRS
Low Rider.
A name and a style
synonymous with
Harley-Davidson.

THE MIGHTY FL'S

In 1980, a new star arose in the world of motorcycling to take over the crown as King of the Highway from the time-honored FLH. With a totally new frame, engine mounting system and revolutionary steering geometry, the FLT soon proved that it could eat interstates for breakfast, city streets for lunch and back roads for dinner and still beg for more. Never before had there been a Harley that could digest the miles so smoothly and effortlessly. From a basic, no-frills sport tourer to fully loaded, got-it-all dressers, the FL line for 1992 has a model for every over-the-roader.

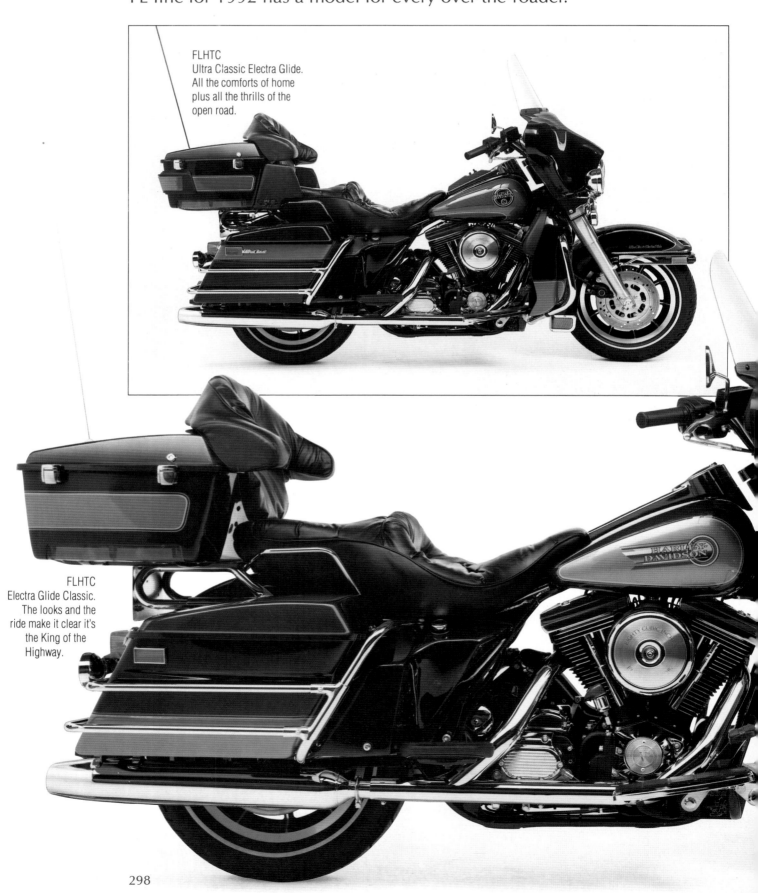

FLHTC
Ultra Classic Electra Glide.
All the comforts of home
plus all the thrills of the
open road.

FLHTC
Electra Glide Classic.
The looks and the
ride make it clear it's
the King of the
Highway.

FLTC
Ultra Classic Tour Glide.
The latest edition of the
bike that started it all
is loaded for the
long haul.

FLHS
Electra Glide Sport.
The simplest, most direct
approach to big bike
comfort.

Touring riders make liberal
use of Harley-Davidson
accessories to create the
road machine of their dreams.

Photo Acknowledgements

FPG International, Photo Collection:
Chapter One,
    Page 24, Photo 4; Page 28, Photo 1; Page 34, Photos 1,2,5; Page 35, Photos 2,6,7; Page 37, Photo 2; Page 41, Photo 2.
Chapter Two,
    Page 49, Photos 4,5; Page 51, Photos 3,4; Page 52, Photo 1; Page 53, Photos 2,3; Page 55, Photo 2; Page 58, Photo 2;
    Page 59, Photo 4;
    Page 62, Photos 1,2; Page 64, Photos 1,2; Page 66, Photo 4; Page 68, Photo 1.
Chapter Three, Page 84, Photo 1; Page 91, Photo 5; Page 96, Photo 5; Page 102, Photos 1,4; Page 105, Photo 1; Page 106, Photo 4.
Chapter Four, Page 127, Photo2; Page 129, Photos 3,4,9; Page 131, Photos 6,7,8,9,10,12.
Chapter Five,
    Page 137, Photo 1; Page 138, Photo 1; Page 139, Photos 2,4; Page 145, Photos 1,2; Page 146, Photos 2,4; Page 147,
    Photo 1; Page 150, Photo 3; Page 156, Photos 1,3; Page 157, Photos 4,5,6.
Chapter Six,
    Page 170, Photos 2,3; Page 174, Photo 1; Page 181, Photo 5.
Chapter Seven,
    Page 198, Photo1; Page 200, Photo 1; Page 202, Photo 1; Page 203, Photos 2,3,4; Page 210, Photo 2; Page 212, Photo 4;
    Page 215, Photos 1,5,6.
Chapter Eight,
    Page 221, Photo 2; Page 225, Photo 5; Page 227, Photo 3; Page 232, Photo 1; Page 245, Photo 2.
Chapter Nine,
    Page 262, Photos 1,3; Page 273, Photos 2,3.

"The Sheik Of Araby" sheet music, from the James W. Craig Collection.
Chapter 3, Page 99.

Photos and Movie Memorabilia from the Dale E. Kuntz Collection:
Chapter Three, Page 105, Photo 3.
Chapter Four, Page 127, Photo 3; Page 128, Photo 1; Page 130, Photo 2; Page 131, Photos 2, 11.
Chapter Five, Page 140, Photo 3; Page 141, Photo 5; Page 145, Photo 4; Page 147, Photo 4; Page 152, Photos 2,3.
Chapter Seven, Page 215, Photo 3.

Photos and Memorabilia from the Frank Seiy Collection:
Chapter Three, Page 86, Photo 1; Page 99, Photos 5,7,10; Page 102, Photo 6; Page 106, Photo 4.
Chapter Four, Page 113, Photo 4, Page 116, Photo 1; Page 117, Photo 3; Page 119, Photos 2,4,5,7,9; Page 120, Photo 6; Page 121,
    Photos 2,4; Page 122, Photo 5; Page 126, Photo 1; Page 128, Photos 6,7,8.
Chapter Five, Page 136, Photo 1; Page 144, Photo 1; Page 148, Photo 1; Page 149, Photo 2; Page 151, Photos 1,2; Page 153, Photo
    3; Page 158, Photo 2, Page 159, Photos 2,4,5; Page 162, Photo 1; Page 163, Photo 4.
Chapter Six, Page 168, Photo 1; Page 172, Photo 3; Page 173, Photos 3,4; Page 175, Photos 4,5; Page 176, Photo 1; Page 178, Photo
    1; Page 180, Photos 1,3; Page 181, Photo 1; Page 183, Photo 5; Page 184, Photo 1; Page 186, Photo 1; Page 187, Photo 4.
Chapter Seven, Page 193, Photo 3; Page 195, Photo 4; Page 196, Photos 2,4; Page 201, Photos 7,10; Page 204, Photos 2,3; Page
    205, Photo 5; Page 206, Photo 3; Page 207, Photos 2,5,6; Page 209, Photos 6,8.
Chapter Eight, Page 224, Photo 1; Page 226, Photo 2; Page 228, Photo 1; Page 229, Photo 4; Page 231, Photo 3; Page 232, Photo 4;
    Page 233, Photo 3; Page 237, Photos 4,5; Page 238, Photo 1; Page 239, Photos 4,5,6,7; Page 240, Photo 3; Page 243,
    Photos 3,5; Page 245, Photo 5.
Chapter Nine, Page 250, Photo 1; Page 252, Photo 4; Page 253, Photos 3,4; Page 254, Photo 1; Page 256, Photos 1,3; Page 259,
    Photos 1,2; Page 260, Photos 1,4; Page 263, Photos 2,4,5; Page 264, Photos 3,4; Page 265, Photos 1,2; Page 266, Photos
    1,3,4; Page 268, Photos 1,3; Page 270, Photos 1,3,5,6,7.
Chapter Ten, Page 278, Photo 1, 2, 3; Page 280, Photo 3, 4, 6; Page 281, Photo 2, 3, 5, 7; Page 282, Photo 3; Page 283, Photo 3, 4, 5,
    6, 7, 8; Page 284, Photo 5; Page 286, Photo 2, 3: Page 288, Photo 1, 4; Page 289, Photo 1; Page 291, Photo 1, 2, 4.

Stamps and Buttons from the Elizabeth B. Greeley Collection:
Chapter Five, Page 138, Photos 1,4,7,8; Page 139, Photo 2; Page 145, Photo 2; Page 146, Photo 1; Page 150, Photos 3,4; Page 155,
    Photo 5, Page 156, Photo 1; Page 157, Photo 4.
Chapter Eight, Page 226, Photo 1;
Chapter Nine, Page 252, Photo 2.

Nolan Ryan, Score baseball card from the Lisa Heideman Collection.
Chapter Ten, page 288.

Wide World Photos, Inc.
Chapter Ten, Page 283, Photo 1; Page 285, Photo 3, 5.

Antique Victrola, from the Bernadine and Lawerence Ybema Collection:
Chapter One, Page 35.

and all Harley-Davidson related photos from the Harley-Davidson Photo Archives.